SEX AND THE INTERNET

SEX AND THE INTERNET:

A Guidebook for Clinicians

Edited by
Al Cooper

Brunner-Routledge
New York • London

Published in 2002 by
Brunner-Routledge
29 West 35th Street
New York, NY 10001

Published in Great Britain by
Brunner-Routledge
27 Church Road
Hove, East Sussex BN3 2FA

Brunner-Routledge is an imprint of the Taylor & Francis Group.

Printed in the United States of America on acid-free paper.

10 9 8 7 6 5 4 3 2

Library of Congress Cataloging-in-Publication Data
Cooper, Al.
    Sex and the Internet : a guidebook for clinicians / by Al Cooper.
        p. cm.
    Includes bibliographical references and index.
    ISBN 1–58391–355–6 (pbk.)
    1. Sex addiction. 2. Computer sex. 3. Sex counseling. I. Title.

    RC560.S43 C664 2002
    616.85'83—dc21

                                            2002018287

CONTENTS

113211

FOREWORD

The Internet is here to stay, and in the future it will most probably be much more widely used for psychological and clinical education than it is at the present time. The Internet is already used to disseminate a considerable amount of mental health information, to provide psychotherapy, and as an adjunct to more traditional forms of psychotherapy. I predict that this trend will steadily increase in the coming years. At the psychological clinic of the Albert Ellis Institute in New York, we have started using the Internet for personal sessions of rational emotive behavior therapy (REBT) with both American and international clients. We have found this type of usage to be so effective that we will soon expand it considerably.

Sex, relationships, and family involvement on the Internet has greatly widened in recent years, and will most probably continue to do so. This kind of participation has its problems and dangers, as shown in some of the chapters in this book. But it also has distinct advantages for communication that are not readily available through other media. Both private and public presentations in these areas provide fascinating alternatives to other means of communicating.

In *Sex and the Internet: A Guidebook for Clinicians*, Al Cooper and his collaborators present a wealth of relevant material about the Internet's facilitation of sex, relationships, and family matters. The various chapters describe the Internet's present coverage in these areas, as well as its future possibilities. They include a surprising amount of enlightening material that has not previously been available in book form. Readers will gain unusual knowledge of the Internet itself and how it can beneficially be adapted to dealing with significant sexual and relationship issues. Read it and enjoy!

—Albert Ellis, Ph.D.

PREFACE

One of the most fundamental conclusions from Alfred Kinsey's research of more than 50 years ago was that human sexuality is extraordinarily variable in its expression. Basic biological mechanisms interact with a variety of sociocultural factors to shape a bewildering array of patterns of sexual response. This interaction between biology and culture is poorly understood, but the capacity to associate sexual response with diverse stimuli, based on the principles of learning, is fundamental, and sociocultural influences can both encourage and discourage, intentionally or unintentionally, what stimuli are involved.

When we consider the society that Kinsey studied, we can see how easily sexual expression was distorted by socially driven guilt and anxiety and by the social promotion of sexual stereotypes, fostering problematic power relationships between men and women and ostracizing those with unconventional sexual values. The negative consequences, to both the individual and society, were plain to see. But have we been moving toward a better socially determined pattern of sexuality since Kinsey's time? That is also questionable. The past 50 years have seen social change at a rate and extent unprecedented in history. A number of changes that are clearly to be welcomed have combined with other changes of less certain advantage to impact sexuality at the end of the 20th century, and we enter the 21st century far from certain where we are heading.

One fundamental part of this changing picture has been called the "triumph of the individual over society" (Hobsbawm, 1997). People have increasingly been giving their own individual welfare and personal development top priority in their lives. Primary allegiance to the family is becoming a thing of the past. While traditional marriage has been taking a beating, at least as a long-term commitment, we have seen the impact of the women's movement on the structuring and negotiating of what have been called "pure" relationships. The *pure* here has nothing to do with virtue, but rather the idea that it is a relationship for its own sake, not as part of an institution such as marriage, and not for outward, material, or official reasons. Such a relationship may be heterosexual or homosexual. It lasts as long as both partners are satisfied with the personal bonus it provides. It is therefore, by nature, of uncertain duration and often short-lived. It reflects each individual's commitment to his or her own personal growth and well-being as well as a negotiated, and hence more equitable, way of relating to one another. Within such relationships we can see how sex can contribute to intimacy, serving to bond the relationship if it works well, weakening it if it does not.

But for some, particularly men, the sexuality of this type of pure relationship is emotionally demanding, more so than in more traditional relationships of the past. Increasingly, especially for those who have relatively high needs for sexual outlet, sex is, at least partially, being separated off from the relationship. Most commonly this involves masturbation. Schmidt (1998) described a young man who came to his clinic because he didn't feel like having sex with his girlfriend but was an enthusiastic masturbator. The man summed it up as follows: "If I masturbate I can start when I like, come when I like and stop when I like; I needn't bother with foreplay, or romantic lighting, or tender nothings murmured in her ear; I don't have to guess what she might like; or discuss afterwards how it was; I can go to sleep when I feel like it" (p. 232)—a somewhat depressing account for the romantics among us. But apparently this is an increasing trend, at least in part. Masturbation is the simplest and least problematic way of separating sex from relationships. There are, of course, others, and always have been. Prostitution and various ways of "cheating" on one's partner have a long history, but in recent years there has been an explosion of other alternatives, such as telephone sex and now the Internet.

The Internet presents us with the latest and, in many respects most powerful form of new technology to impact on sexuality. In the nineteenth century one of the earliest uses of the new daguerreotype technology was to capture sexually explicit images. We have many examples of early photography of this kind in the Kinsey Institute. Whereas initially such images were available to relatively few people, the accessibility of erotic images produced by these emerging technologies has gradually widened. We now have many examples of early stag films and their subsequent developments, and we have many sexually explicit videos. Videos brought much wider accessibility. Over the relatively short history of the erotic video, we see some striking changes. Whereas in the 1970s many such videos told erotic stories, those of the last decade of the 20th century were often zoomed in to genital sexuality with minimum delay. Our impression is that the earlier videos were used more by couples, for whom the erotic contact would impact the sexual relationship. By contrast, later videos seem more designed for the individual viewer, presumably male, who is pursuing the uncomplicated, uninvolved release of masturbatory sexual pleasure. As if to compensate for this change, we have seen the development of erotic videos designed for women, by women, where the erotic story regains importance. The technology and the accessibility were probably not responsible for the "triumph of the individual," but they undoubtedly fostered it.

With the arrival of the Internet, we take a huge leap into a comparable but much, much more complex arena, where at best we can only speculate about possible consequences. The "individual" has enormously expanded possibilities. This can work in various ways. First, he or she can find an endless array of images. The ability to select those that are particularly stimulating may serve to reinforce a particular preference, which then has the potential for becoming a "late onset fetish." The user may even find that the emerging fetish has its own Web site, indicating that there are others who share it. This "identification with subculture" may further reinforce the fetish pattern. The unending availability of new or different images may in some way reinforce a "rapid habituation" pattern so that before long, old or repeated images rapidly lose their effect. We were recently confronted with this possibility at the Kinsey Institute in our ongoing psycho-physiological studies. We started to encounter a high proportion of "flat responders," who simply didn't find any of our images stimulating. Neither Erick Janssen nor I, both of whom had been involved in such psycho-physiological studies over quite a few years, had ever encountered such a high rate of nonresponse. This led us to revise the protocol so that subjects could choose from a menu of possibilities. This is working, and may well reflect what is happening when people use the Internet for erotic stimulation.

But the individual can experiment with relationships as well. Chat rooms are adding a fundamentally new dimension to our experience of relationships. We can be stimulated by the interactive process, remaining sublimely unaware of the physical and other realities of the people involved. We can even confront the realities and meet up with them in "real space" offline. Though we can see how some individuals may actually learn to improve their social skills online, others may slip from online to offline into highly risky sexual situations.

Given the formidable potential for learning varied sexual response patterns, it is difficult to avoid feeling bewildered by the range of possibilities that the Internet makes available. In most respects we are considering "double-edged swords." For example, the same possibilities that lead to someone discovering the erotic potential of autoerotic asphyxia, to take an extreme example, may also lead people, engaging in this practice, to communicate with others about it. In this particular case, I am alarmed at the prospect of this highly dangerous sexual behavior spreading, but at the same time I'm encouraged by the possibility that for the first time we might be able to increase our understanding of it by actually communicating with its proponents, which was not hitherto possible because they are usually dead before we find out about it.

The benefits of "special information," much of which is consumer rather than provider driven, are already very apparent. People with minority interests can make contact with each other and share the information that is important for their futures.

And should we assume that the Internet will continue to be uncontrollable? While we tend to be suspicious of social control, it is difficult to escape the conclusion that for any society, control of sex is necessary to some extent. There is, of course, good and bad control. Attempts are currently underway to gain control, both legal and political, over what is happening sexually on the Internet. Let us hope that such control, if gained, will be to our general advantage and will not repeat the old cycles of liberation and suppression that pervade the history of sexuality.

As the foregoing indicates, we are just starting to grapple with many crucial issues, so this book comes at an important time.

—John Bancroft, M.D.
Kinsey Institute

☐ References

Hobsbawm, E. (1997). *Age of extremes: The short twentieth century 1914–1991*. London: Little, Brown.
Schmidt, G. (1998). Sexuality and late modernity. *Annual Review Sex Research, 9*, 224–241.

ACKNOWLEDGMENTS

Editing a book is a monumental undertaking. As with both sex and being online, it is better to do it with others than by yourself. This book is the result of both direct and indirect contributions from many different people whom I want to acknowledge and thank.

Of course, there would be no book without the hard work of the various dedicated and talented authors who wrote the 14 chapters and introductory material, as well as Tim Julet, Jill Osowa, and George Zimmar from Brunner-Routledge who encouraged me to undertake this endeavor and then guided me through the process. In addition, valuable input and fine tuning was provided by my friend and colleague, Coralie Scherer, and the other 14 voluntary reviewers who read their respective chapters.

Behind the scenes were my colleagues at the San Jose Marital and Sexuality Centre and at the Counseling and Psychological Services, Cowell Health Services of Stanford University. These people are the ones who gave me daily support through my 9 to 5 life, while I crammed work on the book into evenings and weekends. My primary supports were also there for me in direct and indirect ways—Fred, Lynne, Greg, Andy, and Ulrike. They listened to my complaining and encouraged me during the times I felt overwhelmed and fearful that the book would never be done. More importantly, they helped me to intermittently escape the computer so that I might have another dimension to my life beyond work.

Finally, at the risk of sounding somewhat strange, I want to specifically acknowledge the many imaginative visionaries and technical grunts whose minds and efforts have brought us the Internet itself. Without this new medium for human communication there would be no topic for this book. In addition, without the Internet I would not have been able to practically manage the numerous tasks involved with this project: exchanging drafts, coordinating and updating authors, finding reviewers and providing them with chapter drafts, and seeking guidance for the unexpected developments inherent in the process. How did people handle the complexities of editing a book before the Internet, even 10 years ago? What will life be like in the next iteration of the Internet 10 years from now? Hmm, now that will be a book.

Al Cooper
Eric Griffin-Shelley

Introduction. The Internet: The Next Sexual Revolution

A new sexual revolution has commenced with the staggering growth of computers and technology and the exponential expansion of the Internet. While some individuals recognize the profound social changes swirling around the Internet, most are just beginning to grasp both the promise and peril that it brings regarding a host of issues concerning human relationships.

The focus of this book is sexuality and the Internet. In it, we explore the major issues that clinicians, mental health professionals, and society's leaders need to know about the impact of Internet sexuality on their work with clients, families, and society at large. The contributors—researchers and clinicians—review the most current empirical data and provide accurate and in-depth information and analysis designed to update general understanding as well as clinical practice. Internet sexuality already reflects the conflicts around sexual issues that are pervasive throughout our culture, for example, the tension between freedom of expression and the protection of children. By becoming informed and engaged, clinicians can treat problems and answer questions arising from Internet sexual activity. Armed with knowledge, mental health practitioners can be proactive in shaping the future of the new sexual revolution.

☐ Understanding Sexuality

Love and sex are essential to human life, and therefore integral to clinical work. Generally, people are more open about their romantic lives than about the details of their sexual lives. Consequently, our understanding of human sexuality has been more limited than our knowledge of interpersonal relationships. The available objective information about sex and love pales in comparison with scientific knowledge in other areas of health. Sexuality remains rather hidden and, for some, stigmatized and shame-filled. As a consequence, research on human sexuality is inadequately funded. In contrast, AIDS, cancer, mental illness, and chemical dependency all suffer from similar negative perceptions, but over the past three decades, each of these areas has received gradually increasing public and governmental recognition and support. Science rockets ahead in the understanding of the human genome and how to extend life past the century mark, yet we lag far behind in our science and understanding of human sexuality, particularly the nonbiological aspects (Donahey & Miller, 2001).

☐ Sexual Revolution

A new sexual revolution has begun with the explosion of electronic technology, computers, and especially the recent, rapid expansion of the Internet, also known as the World Wide Web, "the Net" or "the Web." As we move into the information age, it is clear that the world is irretrievably changing. Jerome et al. (2000) asserted that "rapid and far-reaching technological advances are revolutionizing the ways in which people relate, communicate, and live their daily lives." They went on to say that "increased access to information and individuals will fundamentally alter the way people see the world, establish communities, and work within these structures" (p. 407). Most people acknowledge that these profound changes are occurring, but the social implications and effects on members of the global community are poorly understood, at best. One thing that is known is that sex has been a major factor in the development of, activity on, and interest in the Internet (Cooper, 1997; Cooper, Boies, Maheu, & Greenfield, 1999).

☐ Staggering Growth

Most people are only marginally aware of how the Internet is changing every facet of our lives, probably more dramatically in the next 20 years than in any previous period in history (Cooper et al., 1999). A recent composite profile reveals that about 167 million people in the United States use the World Wide Web. Of those, the average visitor logs on three times, visits an average of five sites, and spends a little over three hours per week online (Nielsen NetRatings, 2001). In October 2000, the U.S. Department of Commerce published the fourth report in a series entitled, *Falling Through the Net: Toward Digital Inclusion.* They indicated that "more that half of all households (51.0%) have computers, up from 42.1% in December, 1998" (Department of Commerce, 2000). In addition "there were 116.5 million Americans online at some location in August 2000, 31.9 million more than there were only 20 months earlier" (DOC, 2000). The information and opportunities available on the Internet are exploding, with over 1 billion unique pages available in January, 2000 (Inktomi, 2000).

The rate of growth for new Internet service is estimated to be a meteoric 25% every 3 months. New developments in the merging of once separate telephone, television, and computer technologies, a phenomenon known as *convergence*, are being introduced daily. Work, school, and even social activities are becoming increasingly dependent upon, and centered around, computers (Cooper, 1997). Ten years ago most people could not even imagine the concept of online chatting or shopping. How quickly people adapt to and take for granted that which was science fiction just moments before!

☐ Definitions

In order to better describe and study this phenomenon, we need a common lexicon. Thus, for the purposes of this text, *online sexual activity* (OSA) is defined as use of the Internet for any activity (including text, audio, graphic files) that involves sexuality for purposes of recreation, entertainment, exploration, support, education, commerce, efforts to attain and secure sexual or romantic partners, and so on.

Cybersex is a subcategory of OSA and can be defined as using the medium of the Internet to engage in sexually gratifying activities, such as looking at pictures, participating in sexual chat, exchanging explicit sexual images or emails, *"cybering"* (i.e., sharing fantasies over the Internet that involve being sexual together while one or both people masturbate), and so on.

Online sexual problems (OSPs) include the full range of difficulties that people can have due to engaging in OSA. Such difficulties include negative financial, legal, occupational, relationship, and personal repercussions from OSA. The "problem" may range from a single incident to a pattern of excessive involvement. The consequences may involve feelings of guilt, loss of a job or relationship, sexually transmitted diseases (STDs), etc.

Finally, *online sexual compulsivity* (OSC) is a subtype of OSP and refers to excessive OSA behaviors that interfere with the work, social, and/or recreational dimensions of the person's life. In addition, there are other indications of the "loss of control" of their ability to regulate the activity and/or minimize adverse consequences (Cooper, 1998b).

☐ The Internet and Sexuality

Since its inception, the Internet has been inextricably associated with sexuality in a synergistic dance, each fueling and ultimately contributing to the transformation of the other. That people are fascinated with sexuality and sexual relationships is clearly manifested on the Internet. An estimated 20% of Internet users engage in some form of OSA (Cooper, Delmonico, & Burg, 2000). Sexual pursuits may account for almost 70% of all dollars spent online (Sprenger, 1999). One report indicated that 18 million people in the United States accessed pornography sites in the year 2000, a figure that is three times higher than for 1999 (Carr, 2000). Yet, even as the Web continues its exponential expansion, little is known about how this new medium is affecting sexuality in the United States and around the world. It might be helpful to begin this discussion by providing a little more information on the more general impact of the Net.

☐ The Internet: Connecting or Dividing?

Will the Internet ultimately unite people or divide them by who is "online" and who is not? Will the gaps between generations, income levels, cultures, or countries become even wider? There are already disparities between children and teenagers who have "grown up with" computers and the many adults who lack even basic familiarity with the online world. Will this add to the generation gap or will technology render innovative ways for our younger and older people to "connect"? Similarly, the affluent, not surprisingly, have easier access to the Internet than do the poor (Jerome et al., 2000). However, the U.S. Department of Commerce (2000) recently reported that "groups that have traditionally been digital 'have nots' are now making dramatic gains." Perhaps Internet accessibility will some day help to decrease social and economic divisions.

Geographic distribution of online users is uneven. Currently the United States has the greatest number of people online, with Japan (31.9 million), Germany (27.1 million), the United Kingdom (23.4 million), Italy (18.1 million), Canada (13.2 million), and Australia (9.2 million) following in succession (Nielson NetRatings, 2001). The Nua Web site reports 407 million online users worldwide, with 167 million in the United States and Canada, 113 million in Europe, 104 million in Asia and the Pacific, 16 million in Latin America, 3 million in Africa, and 2 million in the Middle East (Nua, 2001). Although the Nua and NetRatings methods of tallying differ, both sets of figures indicate that the online world is primarily English speaking and that large portions of the world are still unconnected. Yet, even without direct access, the effects of the Internet are being felt around the world and providing opportunities for those who know how to make use of them.

Meeting and communicating with people is no longer limited by propinquity or even time of day (Cooper & Sportolari, 1997). The interpersonal cues so often relied on in face to face interactions are generally not available online. Cybercommunication is still overwhelmingly text-based, so that variables such as age, gender, physical appearance, race, or disability, which are typically subject to visual and auditory verification, are less important online. On one hand, ambiguity is increased, but on the other, the Internet can be a means to reducing interpersonal barriers, overcoming common stereotypes and prejudices, disseminating information, as well as increasing variety in relationships, both sexual and nonsexual.

☐ The Internet Is Powered by the "Triple A Engine"

Computers speed things up. With regard to sexuality, this shift in speed evokes intense emotional reactions. For instance, flirtation and innuendo, long the staples of leisurely seduction, can rapidly escalate into frank sexual discussions and proposals on the Internet. The changes in speed and intensity of sexual encounters online are without precedent. Cooper (1997) stated that the three central components that combine to turbocharge, that is, accelerate and intensify, OSA include access, affordability, and anonymity. These three components are referred to collectively as the "Triple A Engine."

Access

The Internet is available, convenient, and easily accessed by increasing numbers of people worldwide. They log on from their homes, schools, and places of work or leisure. Accessibility has contributed to sex becoming one of the most commonly searched topics on the Internet (All Knight

Systems, 1999; Cooper, 1998a; Freeman-Longo & Blanchard, 1998) and to its widespread use for sexual pursuits (Goldberg, 1998). People can find a Web site to satisfy any sexual need or desire they may have without the need to delay gratification. Consumerism is further facilitated by the ready availability of products, services, and people (Fisher & Barak, 2000). The Internet is a virtual store open 24 hours a day, 7 days a week for social and business transactions.

Affordability

Affordability is based on the economic principle of supply and demand. The seemingly infinite number of sites and products means that the supply is plentiful, and this increased competition, when combined with a lower overhead than a "bricks and mortar" business, leads to lower prices for consumers. This is particularly true for those sexual items and experiences that are less easily available in real time, such as sado/masochistic (S/M) dating services or a sexual enhancement workshop for lesbians. With improvements in search engines, the Internet serves as a central clearinghouse that keeps time and costs in check. Consumers who know their way around the Net can easily find free sexuality-related items and services (Hapgood, 1996). Additionally, the declining costs of server space and increased revenue from banner and link advertising helps keep user fees low.

Anonymity

The belief, whether true or not, that one's identity is concealed online can have a powerful effect on sexual expression. Branwyn (1993) observed that use of the Internet increases the sense of freedom, willingness to experiment, and pace of self-disclosure, as well as enhancing a person's ability to talk openly about their sexual questions, concerns, and fantasies. For example, those who might be hesitant to purchase sexually explicit materials, products, or aids in a face to face encounter may be more comfortable doing so when protected by the anonymity they feel online.

☐ The Internet and Telehealth: A Tool for Health Promotion

As a communication tool, the Internet offers a means of promoting physical and mental health, especially sexual health, through innovative methods. For example, it is becoming a common practice for health professionals to use video-conferencing as a means to provide patients in rural clinics with access to specialists in other geographic locations (Jerome et al., 2000). Online mental health services currently maintain educational Web sites that include diagnostic questionnaires, interactive bulletin boards, support groups and chat rooms. Hospitals, insurance companies, and other healthcare organizations are developing ways to communicate with and offer services to their customer base via the Internet.

As people increasingly turn to the Internet for health information and support, it is important that they bear in mind that technology can be misused. Some Web sites are filled with inaccurate information and biased points of view. Incompetent and unscrupulous people motivated by greed and self-interest exist online as well as off. As both the benefits and risks of the cyberworld are more fully understood, people will be better able to navigate it safely.

Offerings of online counseling and psychotherapies are proliferating, yet remain controversial. Internet-mediated psychotherapy cannot be adequately dealt with in this book because of the complexities surrounding it at present. Most likely, the ethical, legal, and technical concerns will be worked out in the next few years, and in future texts one can expect this area to have a chapter of its own.

☐ Commercial, Positive, and Negative Aspects of Internet Sexuality

Cooper (1998a) noted that the use of the Internet for sexual purposes can be classified in three broad categories: commercial aspects, positive connections, and negative patterns.

Commercial Aspects

Sexuality has long been a significant financial engine driving the growth of the Internet (Hapgood, 1996). The profits generated by sexual commerce have funded major online technological advances that have been quickly adopted by mainstream businesses. Analyst Mark Hardie of Forrester Research is quoted as saying,

> What I see when I look at this industry [online adult sites]—putting aside any moral judgments about reprehensible content—is an amazing example of an industry that has banded together to protect its business, push revenue across the industry, and innovate cutting-edge technologies. (Branwyn, 1999)

Sex sites routinely make money, a still unusual status among businesses in the contemporary world of e-commerce. Given that less than 1% of visitors to adult sites actually spend money on them (Branwyn, 1999), these businesses need to attract and retain large numbers of visitors in order to make a profit. The number of individual visitors at such sites grew more than 27% from December 1999 to February 2001, to nearly 28 million from 22 million (Schwartz, 2001). The Internet has become a very common pathway to explore and engage in sexual activity, particularly for persons and cultures for whom sex and sexuality is a source of shame and embarrassment (Cooper, McLoughlin, & Campbell, 2000). In addition to products, the Internet has also become another medium for marketing romance and sex, from dating services and personal ads to the popular sexual chat rooms. There are a multitude of ways to "meet interesting people" online. Those with an enterprising spirit have found ways to collect fees from those who participate in these activities, Internet-savvy sex workers find search engines and Web sites to be excellent venues for advertising their services (Cooper et al., 1999).

Positive Potential

In a world fraught with sexual problems, pitfalls, and prejudices, the Internet offers many ways to positively impact sexuality and sexual connections between people. One trend is the proliferation of virtual communities around common sexual interests, whether they be pro-choice or pro-life advocates, "leather aficionados," or those with shared sexual life concerns, such as rape survivors, herpes sufferers, or paraplegics. The sense of community and belonging derived from such contacts can have important and salubrious psychological effects on individuals and contribute to the changing political and social perceptions of these groups. Isolated and disenfranchised individuals, such as gay and lesbian youth, ethnic minorities, or persons with disabilities, can come together online and find social support that may not otherwise be available to them. Professionals are recognizing that these virtual communities impact peoples' lives significantly and are increasing their efforts to study and understand them (Burke, 2000; Palandri & Green, 2000).

Another important development is the rapid increase in the number of specific Web sites that educate people about such sexual matters as sexual dysfunction, sexual enhancement techniques, safer sex practices, reproduction, abstinence, and sexually transmitted disease. The lack of factual information is a major contributor to the enormous amount of fear and anxiety many feel about sexuality (Williams, 1994). In response, a wide range of sites has been developed to provide sexual education in the form of Web sites with frequently asked questions lists (FAQs), advice columns, and discussion groups, and e-mail distribution lists for cutting edge news and information.

In particular, the Internet may offer an alternative way to provide sexual education and interventions for our young people. If used effectively, it may be able to positively influence their perceptions about sexual matters via fresh, hip, accurate, and informative Web sites that combine entertainment, education, and meaningful discussions of sexual values in ways that attract and hold their interest. Similarly, professionals are finding that the Internet can help them stay informed and abreast of relevant developments in their respective fields. Sexual education materials are increasingly available through major sexuality organizations, such as the American Association of Sex Educators, Counselors and Therapist's Web site (www.aasect.org) or that of the National Council on Sex Addiction and Compulsivity (www.ncsac.org). These organizations have their own Web sites available to the public as well as to their members. Additional Internet-based methods of informing and educating professionals include improved online continuing education courses; e-mail lists, which encourage the exchange of views on current and controversial issues; and bulletin boards (BBs), which promote posting recent research findings, questions, and comments among members.

Negative Effects and Risks

The Internet is not without its risks. In addition to expanding knowledge and providing support, the Internet can negatively impact people's lives and their sexuality. Clinicians are reporting a dramatic increase in the number of patients with issues related to their OSA. For many of these clients, the Internet has become an outlet for unresolved sexual difficulties and unfocused sexual energy, including the acting out or repetition of traumatic experiences (Schwartz & Southern, 2000). Some individuals who go online for their social and sexual needs forsake, avoid, or neglect real-world relationships (Kraut et al., 1998; Greenfield, 1999). Others find enough solace in their online lives that they lose the motivation to address dissatisfactions in their offline lives and, therefore, neither address nor resolve them. OSA is particularly tempting for those who already experience problems with sexual compulsivity, as well as those who are psychologically predisposed or vulnerable to act out compulsively (Leiblum, 1997). It is easy to see how many might choose to hide from their real-world problems through increased or exclusive online interaction.

☐ Contributors and Chapter Summaries

The contributors to this volume provide in-depth examinations of various trends that individual clinicians may have difficulty keeping up with by themselves. The authors represent a diversity and richness of perspectives and viewpoints, much like the Web itself. They include a collection of North American and international experts in various areas of sexuality from prestigious universities, private foundations, clinics, and world-renowned hospitals. They represent diverse disciplines, including public health, medicine, law, psychology, and psychiatry. Each has been selected because of his or her knowledge of some unique dimension of Internet sexuality, and we believe their contributions combine to provide a comprehensive foundation for anyone interested in the area of online sexuality.

The book begins with a foreword and preface by two of the pioneers in the field of sexuality, Albert Ellis and John Bancroft of the Kinsey Institute. They talk about the profound impact the Internet is having on the area of sexuality and help to provide some historical context.

Part 1: Populations of Concern

The five chapters of Part I deal with populations of concern and how they are being influenced by online sexuality. Sandra Leiblum and Nicola Döering begin by examining the growing presence of women on the Internet. Then Michael Ross and Michael Kauth explore the role of the Internet for men who have sex with men. Following that, Mitchell Tepper and Annette Owens examine how the Internet impacts persons with disabilities, chronic illnesses, and normal lifecycle changes (e.g., puberty, pregnancy, menopause, and aging). The section ends with an important discussion by Robert Longo, Steven Brown, and Deborah Orcutt, who look at the impact of online sexuality on our children and adolescents.

Part II: Cybersex Problems: Therapeutic Considerations

The next part begins with an exploration of the complex issues of virtual sexuality in the workplace by Al Cooper, Irene McLoughlin, Pauline Reich and Jay Kent-Ferraro. This is followed by David Greenfield and Maressa Orzack offering an overview of assessment issues pertaining to OSPs. Following that chapter, David L. Delmonico, Elizabeth Griffin, and Patrick J. Carnes discuss treatment strategies for OSPs. Next, Jennifer Schneider focuses specifically on the concerns of partners and family members of those with OSPs and examines these issues in the context of cyberspace.

Finally, Nathan Galbreath, Fred Berlin, and Denise Sawyer describe some of the most severe types of OSPs and the increasing popularity of the Internet as a venue for those with a variety of paraphilic interests.

Part III: Other Areas of Special Interest

Starting this final part, Al Cooper, Coralie Scherer, and David Marcus suggest practical ways for clinicians to use the Internet as an adjunct to more traditional therapeutic interventions used to improve sexual relationships. Next, Michael Plaut and Karen Donahey examine how the anarchy of the early Internet is being transformed into a kinder, gentler place where "netiquette" is enforced by Internet service providers' (ISPs) policies, ethical guidelines, and laws and regulations. Eric Ochs, Kenneth Mah, and Yitzchak Binik then outline the opportunities for important new research on human sexuality offered by the Internet.

The book concludes with a chapter by Azy Barak and William Fisher, who offer their thoughts about the future of Internet sexuality. Their projections about future trends will enable clinicians to be on the forefront of these developments.

☐ Limitations

While this volume attempts to be comprehensive, the field is newly emerging and evolving, and thus, there remain areas that are not adequately represented and still need further professional investigation. For instance, though lesbian involvement with the Net is mentioned in several chapters, a more in-depth exploration of the topic, as well as more empirical data, is needed. In addition, most current research bases its models of Internet sexuality primarily on the presumption that it takes the same form everywhere that it takes in the United States. This may or may not be true, and OSA in this country may be similar to, or vastly different from, its manifestations in other parts of the world (or even in different ethnic or cultural subgroups within the United States). At present, there are many more questions than answers.

☐ Professionals, Prevention, and Policies: A Call for Action

Rather than react to events as they unfold, professionals have the option to forge ahead, using their knowledge and training to proactively develop the content, use, and evolution of OSAs. Informed professionals can facilitate the appropriate use of the Internet for sexual health while attempting to minimize potential problems and adverse effects.

There is an immediate need for more attention to the impact on sexuality of this rapidly developing technology. Mental health professionals need to go online and study online behaviors in schools, homes, businesses, libraries, and cafes. They can partner with other interested individuals and organizations, such as school administrators, educators, parents, employers, law enforcement agencies, and representatives of local, state, and national governments, to develop strategies to deal with Internet sexuality concerns.

To this end, it is recommended that the following policies and interventions be considered:

1. Develop programs to educate the public about the potential for positive effects that the Internet can have on sexuality and public health, such as
   - the development of healthy sexual self-esteem and behaviors;
   - the correction of misinformation about sexuality and relationships;
   - the development of sex-positive virtual communities for minority and disenfranchised populations;
   - the offering of first-line interventions for persons struggling with issues they are not yet ready to acknowledge offline, such as sexual orientation, survival of sexual abuse or assault, "embarrassing" and anomalous sexual and somatic concerns, or affairs or domestic violence.

   Implementation of these goals via the Internet has the potential to lead to an increase in medical and emotional help-seeking behaviors with concomitant decreases in STDs, unwanted pregnancies, depression, suicide, or divorce.
2. Post warnings and criteria about potential negative effects of going online for sexual pursuits, for example, "spending more than 10 hours per week or using OSA to relieve stress is likely to be problematic" (Cooper, Griffin-Shelley, Delmonico, & Mathy, 2001). These could be placed in appropriate places by ISPs and providers of online adult entertainment, along with hyperlinks and invitations to visit other Web sites, such as the American Psychological Association, the American Association of Sex Educators, Counselors, and Therapists, or the National Council of Sexual Addiction and Compulsivity, where OSAs, treatments, and related issues would be addressed in more detail.
3. Develop and implement programs to educate the public about those who are "at risk" for developing OSPs and OSC. It would be useful to provide "markers" for individuals to assess whether their particular

behaviors might leave them vulnerable to more serious problems or not (Cooper et al., 2001).

At the same time as these larger changes are happening, mental health professionals can become directly involved in acquiring and disseminating accurate, ethically rendered, accessible information that is specifically tailored to targeted sexual communities, such as in the following ways.

1. Becoming familiar with the Internet, visiting sexuality-related Web sites, and incorporating Web-based interventions in their practices.
2. Creating Web sites (or pages within a Web site) expressly designed for a single sexuality issue. Such sites would include FAQs, screening questionnaires, self-help tests, or interactive behavioral treatment and educational modules, including accurate and ethical online movies and animations, that address the specific sexual concern.
3. Becoming expert moderators for scheduled interactive online chats or monitors of sexuality-focused BBs.
4. Developing sites for other mental health professionals, independently or through professional organizations, which encourage collegial support, consultation, and continuing education. Such sites would include targeted news items and announcements, links to resources, e-mail lists, BBs, or other forums for the exchange of ideas, new research, and resources.
5. Expanding our understanding of Internet sexuality through empirical research. By writing articles and book chapters, presenting at conferences, soliciting funding for research, and developing viable theories about these issues, professionals will become increasingly aware of the effects of OSA and develop effective and innovative interventions.

By being involved in these cutting edge activities, mental health professionals can have a presence on the Internet and other forms of telehealth and shape this emerging and central influence on sexuality in the 21st century. However, concerned professionals will only have a voice in these developments if they are informed, active, and contributing. Reading this book will help you to be more informed. As for becoming active and contributing, that part is up to you!

☐ References

All Knight Systems. (1999). *A ranking of what people are searching for on the web.* www.searchterms.com
Branwyn. G. (1993). Compu-sex: Erotica for cybernauts. *South Atlantic Quarterly, 92*(4), 779–791.
Branwyn, G. (1999). *How the porn sites do it: "Adult e-commerce" is still one of the few profitable*

online enterprises. Can others learn anything from its tricks of the trade? http://
www.thestandard.com/article/display/0,1151,3779,00.html

Brooks, M. (1999). The porn pioneers. *The Guardian* [online], 2–3. http://www.guardian.
co.uk/Archive/Article/0,4273,3907225,00.html

Burke, S. K. (2000). In search of lesbian community in an electronic world. *CyberPsychology
and Behavior, 3,* 591–604.

Carr, L. (2000). *Sizing up virtual vice: Porn and gambling are making more money than ever.*
http://www.thestandard.com/article/display/0,1151,17549,00.html

Cooper, A. (1997). The Internet and sexuality: Into the new millennium. *Journal of Sex
Education and Therapy, 22,* 5–6.

Cooper, A. (1998a.) Sexuality and the Internet: Surfing its way into the new millenium.
CyberPsychology and Behavior, 1(2), 24–28.

Cooper, A. (1998b). Sexually compulsive behavior. *Contemporary Sexuality, 32,* 1–3.

Cooper, A., Boies, S., Maheu, M., & Greenfield, D. (1999). Sexuality and the Internet: The
next sexual revolution. In F. Muscarella & L. Szuchman (Eds.), *The psychological science
of sexuality: A research based approach* (pp. 519–545). New York: Wiley.

Cooper, A., Delmonico, D., & Burg, R. (2000). Cybersex users and abusers: New findings
and implications. *Sexual Addiction and Compulsivity: Journal of Treatment and Prevention,
1–2,* 5–30.

Cooper, A., Griffin-Shelley, E., Delmonico, D. L., & Mathy, R. M. (2001). Online sexual
problems: Assessment and predictive variables. *Sexual Addiction and Compulsivity: The
Journal of Treatment and Prevention, 7,* 59–74.

Cooper, A., McLoughlin, I. P., & Campbell, K. M. (2000). Sexuality in cyberspace: Update
for the 21st century. *CyberPsychology and Behavior, 3*(4), 521–536.

Cooper, A., & Sportolari, L. (1997). Romance and cyberspace: Understanding online attraction, *Journal of Sex Education and Therapy, 22*(1), 1–12.

Department of Commerce. (2000, October). Americans in the information age: Falling
through the net series: Toward digital inclusion. http://www.ntia.doc.gov/ntiahome/
digitaldivide/execsumfttn00.htm

Donahey, K. M., & Miller, S. D. (2001). Applying a common factors perspective to sex
therapy. *Journal of Sex Education and Therapy, 25,* 221–230.

Fisher, W. A., & Barak, A. (2000). Online sex shops: Phenomenological, psychological, and
ideological perspectives on internet sexuality. *CyberPsychology and Behavior, 3,* 575–590.

Freeman-Longo, R. E., & Blanchard, G. T. (1998). *Sexual abuse in America: Epidemic of the
21st century.* Brandon, VT: Safer Society Press.

Goldberg. A. (1998). *Monthly users report on MSNBC for April, 1998.* Washington, DC: Relevant Knowledge.

Greenfield, D. N. (1999). *Virtual addiction: Help for netheads, cyberfreaks, and those who love
them.* Oakland, CA: New Harbinger.

Hapgood, F. (1996). Sex sells, Inc. *Technology, 4,* 45–51.

Inktomi. (2000). *Web surpasses one billion documents.* http://www.inktomi.com/new/press/
2000/billion.html.

Jerome, L. W., DeLeon, P. H., James, L. C., Folen, R., Earles, J., & Gedney, J. J. (2000). The
coming of age of telecommunication in psychological research and practice. *American
Psychologist, 55*(4), 407–421.

Kraut, R., Lundmark, V., Patterson, M., Kiesler, S., Mukopadhyay, T., & Scherlis, W. (1998).
Internet paradox: A social technology that reduces social involvement and psychological well-being? *American Psychologist, 53*(9), 1017–1031.

Leiblum, S. R. (1997). Sex and the net: Clinical implications. *Journal of Sex Education and
Therapy, 22,* 21–28.

Nielsen NetRatings. (2001). http://www.nielsen-netratings.com/hot_of_the_net_i.htm

Nua. (2001). http://www.nua.ie/surveys/how_many_online/index.html

Palandri, M., & Green, L. (2000). Image management in a bondage, discipline, sadomasochistic subculture: A cyber-ethnographic study. *CyberPsychology and Behavior, 3*, 631–642.

Schneider, J. P. (2000). A qualitative study of cybersex participants: Gender differences, recovery issues, and implications for therapists. *Sexual Addiction and Compulsivity: Journal of Treatment and Prevention, 7*, 249–278.

Schwartz, J. (2001, April 9). New economy: The steamy side of the Internet, pervasive and resilient to recession, is the underpinning of a new online cash venture. *New York Times*, p. 4.

Schwartz, M. F., & Southern, S. (2000). Compulsive cybersex: The new tea room. *Sexual Addiction and Compulsivity: Journal of Treatment and Prevention, 1–2*, 127–144.

Williams, M. A. (1994). The Chicago study at a glance. *Contemporary Sexuality, 28*, 2.

Young, K. S. (1997). *Internet addiction: What makes computer-mediated communication habit forming?* Paper presented at the 105th annual convention of the American Psychological Association, Chicago.

I

POPULATIONS
OF CONCERN

Sandra Leiblum
Nicola Döring

2

CHAPTER

Internet Sexuality: Known Risks and Fresh Chances for Women

In the last decade of the 20th century the Internet was still regarded by many as a male domain. Sex on the Net was viewed as an erotic paradise for heterosexual men, replete with easy access to pornography or prostitutes. On the other hand, cyberspace was believed to offer few enticing sexual options or opportunities for women. The situation has changed dramatically, though, and now, at the start of the 21st century, almost half of Internet users are women. They use the various Internet services for a variety of purposes, including sexual stimulation and information. The female Internet user of today is confronted on the one hand with unwanted sexual solicitation, but also a chance to use online services individually and collectively to enhance, extend, and experience sex in either virtual or real-life space, with or without men.

"Cyberspace" is not an illusory world detached from "real life," but rather a segment of reality that women can turn to with everyday sexual concerns and desires. Women who surf the Internet are as varied and heterogeneous as women everywhere. There is no specific "feminine" approach to Internet sexuality, so any generalization about women, sex, and the Internet is likely to be an oversimplification. In fact, it will become apparent that women use the Internet in diverse, and sometimes contradictory, combinations of sexually related online and offline activities. For instance, some women who are conservative and inhibited in real-life may engage in active pursuit of sadomasochistic images and discussions online.

Clinicians should be aware of the wide spectrum of sexually related Internet experiences available to women in order to be able to identify problematic patterns of use and to offer appropriate treatments. Clinicians should also be knowledgeable about how to educate their female clients about the possible ways in which the Internet may be used to extend and support their sexuality and sexual knowledge. The Internet is neither positive nor negative insofar as it affects women. Rather, what is significant is the way it is used in different situations and real-life contexts.

Traditionally, women and girls have had a marginalized role in technology discourses as well as in sexual discourses generally. Men have tended to occupy a central role as either spokespeople or protagonists, while women appear underrepresented or are seen in sex-stereotypical ways. Nevertheless, the intersection of technology and sex in online sex has changed all that. Who would have predicted that women would be overrepresented among cybersex addicts (Cooper, Delmonico, & Burg, 2000)? And who would have thought that in times of cyberporn hysteria, some feminists would publish autobiographical self-reports (Benedikt, 1995; Odzer, 1997; Ullman, 1996), practical advice (Levine, 1998; Semans & Winks, 1999), and academic analyses (e.g. Blair, 1998; Döring, 2000; Leiblum, 1997; McRae, 1996), which combine sexually related Net activities and recreational cybersex with liberation and empowerment? A sophisticated analysis of sexually related Internet activities is necessary to appreciate how the Internet plays an increasingly significant role in women's private and professional daily lives. Many assumptions about female sexuality will be challenged when we examine the reality of Internet usage among women.

☐ An Analytical Framework for Understanding Women, Sex, and the Internet

Internet sexuality is a collective concept for many different Net activities; the term requires further differentiation as well as consequent contextualization.

The following dimensions should be considered when we evaluate the positive or negative implications of Internet sexuality for women since peculiarities in connection with online sex are not solely determined for women and girls by their biological sex but are influenced by their unique gender role and their levels of sexual and technological sophistication. These characteristics are themselves affected by the woman's socioeconomic background (age, race, class, occupation, ethnicity, religion, etc.).

Comparisons between women and men in terms of sexually related Net usage without a theoretical background reproduces the questionable dichotomous gender model and neglects systematic differences that exist between various subpopulations of women. How subpopulations of women differ from one another and how they may resemble male subpopulations cannot be addressed here. Rather, the following dimensions should be acknowledged when discussing Internet sexuality from a gender perspective.

Gender Role

Whether women rate a particular sexually related Net offering as "woman friendly" or reject it as "sexist" is not determined by their biological gender per se, but is influenced by their interpretation of their own gender role. For example, a Web site fashioned in pastel tones, with romantic drawings and love poems but without any sexual explicitness will be received differently by women with a more feminine gender role orientation than by women with indifferent, masculine, androgynous, or transgender orientation.

Sexual Identity

An online community that features women staging S/M play with each other will have different valences for women depending on their sexual identity and orientation. Lesbian or bisexual women who are comfortable with S/M desires may identify strongly with this community, while conservative, heterosexual women may find it offensive. Similarly, the degree to which women are erotophilic or erotophobic will influence their reaction to such stimuli (Fisher, Byrne, White, & Kelley, 1988). Prior sexual socialization and current sexual lifestyle are also important considerations.

Internet Competence

Despite the much-publicized ready availability of sexual material on the Internet, neither meaningful sexual discourse nor satisfying sexual action is available "at the click of a mouse." Rather, women must search for, select, and evaluate adequate offerings or create their own and become familiar with the technical and social conditions of Internet use. Among women with little or no Internet experience, for example, the "anonymity of the Internet" is often perceived as a threat. On the other hand, women with Internet experience know that Net communication is not at all anonymous per se, but just offers the possibility of anonymity. This is helpful when dealing with delicate issues such as sexuality. Women who are competent users of the Internet are not at the mercy of objectionable Web sites but can decide when and whether they want to appear anonymously, pseudonymously, or under their own name, and conversely when they want to prevent or enable others to address them under the protection of anonymity.

Psychological Health

The Internet permits individuals to explore their gender and sexual identity in safe ways. It is possible to use the Internet as a means of "trying on" different sexual identities as a first step in altering their behavior offline (McKenna & Bargh, 1998). On the other hand, using the Internet to the exclusion of real-life experience can reinforce preexisting social and sexual fears.

Gwinnell (1998, p. 158) described the case of a young woman who suffered from agoraphobia but who pretended to her online lover over a period of months to be having an active, outgoing life with many social contacts. The online couple planned a marriage, but in the end the woman was never able to meet her cyberlover face-to-face, resulting in the termination of the relationship. Obviously, women (and men) with psychological handicaps can use the Internet to hide behind rather than to face their social or sexual fears and conflicts.

Features of the Context of Usage

Even when she metaphorically "enters cyberspace," the woman sitting at the computer remains a prisoner of her current reality. Does she have enough time and money at her disposal to be able to turn to sexually related Net activities? What about other social constraints and controls that may exist in her living or working situation?

Social Control of Net Use

Societal asymmetries of power between the sexes often extend to private relationships. Heterosexual women, in particular, may be confronted with a continuum of sexual aggression on the Internet (Kelly, 1996). Sometimes, women are subject to pressure from a partner or a third party to use the Internet in specific ways. There have been instances of forced participation by women in Internet-related sexual activities (e.g., trading of women for cyberprostitution). It is not uncommon for a male partner to attempt to induce that their female partner explore the Internet with them for sexual titillation or involvement that may or may not be congenial to the woman but that she feels powerless to refuse.

Social Integration of Net Use

Women experience different degrees of comfort in talking about or even divulging their use of the Internet for sexual purposes. Some women feel that they must hide their sexual cyberexperiences from others, while other women enjoy talking about theses experiences with partners, friends, and therapists. Possible dangers associated with cyberlove and cybersexuality, such as an escapist drifting off into imaginary or idealistic worlds, may not just lie in the "nature" of their computer-mediated relationships but rather in the fact that these relationships are not subject to objective discussion and consideration of the possible (or likely!) risks or rewards. For example, a woman might avoid telling her Net-abstinent girlfriend or counselor about her latest online love if she believes the person will not be sympathetic or will be unable to comprehend how significant and meaningful she finds the virtual relationship.

Special Features of the Internet

Most of the sexual discourses and exchanges that take place on the Internet are purely text-based. Given that written means of communication have been around for centuries, it may be asked, What makes the Internet special? Two models provide a summary of the unique qualities of the Internet, especially in the sexual arena.

Triple-A Engine

Cooper (1998) suggested that there are three primary factors that "turbocharge" online sexuality and make it such an attractive venue for sexual pursuits. He called these the "triple-A engine," and they include *accessibility* (i.e., millions of sites available 24 hours a day, 7 days a week), *affordability* (i.e., competition on the Web keeps all prices low and there are a host of ways to get "free" sex), and *anonymity* (i.e., people perceive their communications to be anonymous). The triple-A engine principally refers to the use of available Web offerings.

Triple-C Engine

We have additionally postulated the "triple-C engine," which emphasizes the Internet's status as an interactive medium in which all participants are not only recipients, but also potential senders. The Net provides the opportunity of widespread *communication* of messages via self-maintained Web pages and postings in online forums. People living far away from each other can engage in computer-mediated *collaboration*. They can offer support to each other via the Net, and they can initiate real-life activities or actions. Finally, Net-based exchange can fulfill diverse social functions and can result in the construction of virtual *communities* (Rheingold, 2000).

Types of Use

These A and C features are not in themselves either positive or negative. The way in which the user accesses the Internet is also an important feature to evaluate when considering the impact of the Internet on female sexuality. The following types of usage patterns may be classified:

- rare versus frequent,
- passive-receptive versus active-productive,
- social versus nonsocial,
- commercial versus noncommercial,
- talking about sexuality versus sexual interaction.

Although representative data are lacking, it may be assumed that the majority of women users are not very affected by the plethora of sex on the Net because most women do not access the Net very frequently. For instance, one common pattern of use is to look for free sexual health Web pages but little else. This might be characterized as a usage pattern of rare, passive-receptive, nonsocial, noncommercial use. Other women might engage in the sporadic exchanging of erotic e-mails with real-life acquaintances or lovers (rare, active-productive, social, noncommercial, sexually interactive). These two usage patterns, which seem rather typical of women, would be unlikely to either endanger or enrich the sexuality of the user. At the collective-societal level, revolutionary radical changes for women would not be expected. It is likely, however, that the women who consult us clinically with concern about their own behavior are more intensely involved with Internet sexuality and with its attendant opportunities and risks.

Partners' Internet Sexuality

If one assumes that most women live in heterosexual relationships and that men spend more professional and private time online than women, then it is likely that the sexually-related activities of one's partner will pose more of a problem for women than for men. Triple-A and triple-C factors offer the sexually curious and motivated husband or partner many possibilities to enliven his sexual life and to keep these activities relatively secret for long periods of time.

The consequences for their female partners can be quite negative. Often, there is a deterioration in the primary relationship: The cybersexually involved partner may become more withdrawn and sexually avoidant and display less interest in his wife and children. Estrangement and couple conflicts emerge even before the cybersexual activities are discovered. When the wife or lover discovers what she perceives as "infidelity," she typically feels betrayed, hurt, and humiliated.

In a recent case seen in treatment, a husband exchanged romantic e-mails with his much younger unmarried graduate assistant. Although they never "consummated" their relationship sexually, they did correspond frequently and intimately. When his wife of 30 years discovered her husband's correspondence, she was devastated. She felt so betrayed that she insisted on an immediate physical separation and entered therapy to discuss whether or not to reveal her husband's cyberaffair to their grown children and thereby further punish him. It was only after many sessions of conjoint therapy that she was persuaded to adopt a more reasoned way of dealing with this situation and to view it as an indication that perhaps there was something basically amiss in their relationship for which she needed to take some responsibility.

In fact, the couple had become increasingly remote over the years and their relationship had evolved to one of convenience rather than intimacy. They had been leading separate lives. The cyberaffair provided the much-needed stimulus for initiating couple's therapy.

In other instances, women may agree to engage in sexual practices they are not really comfortable with or to view pornography which both stimulates and disgusts them in order to distract their husband from the feared competition with online sexual partners.

Sometimes women resort to "snooping" or "detective" behavior in order to determine why their husband or partner has become remote or sexually disinterested. Computer-savvy women often learn how to trace their partner's Internet activities, and in some cases may even try to entice him by logging into the same chat rooms themselves (Schneider, 2000, p. 52).

Clinically, the crises that online sexual involvement can precipitate sometimes lead to important modifications in the primary relationship. Longstanding marital or sexual problems may be uncovered by an Internet-mediated crisis. Sometimes, discovering that one's partner is engaging in compulsive online sexual behavior leads to effective clinical intervention and improved relationship functioning. Other times, it leads to a climate of suspiciousness and clandestine surveillance.

A recent case highlights both the negative and subsequent positive consequences of a husband's online and offline sexual behavior.

The middle-aged husband had retired 4 years earlier after a successful and stressful career in business. His abundance of spare time coupled with a growing dissatisfaction with his wife's weight gain, clumsiness, and sensual ineptitude, led to an increasing reliance on the Internet for sexual stimulation. He progressed from pornography to chatrooms and from chatrooms to an online affair. Eventually, he entered into a real-life sexual liaison with his Internet correspondent.

His wife noticed that he hastily changed the screen on the computer whenever she entered his study, but had no real proof of his affair until his Internet lover called to inform her of her husband's infidelity. This led to a marital crisis and then to psychological consultation.

Although the wife was greatly distressed by the discovery of this relationship, she came to accept the fact that she had contributed to it by both failing to appreciate how important an active sexual life was to her husband and how she had let her appearance go over the 25 years of their marriage. She took his affair as a "wake-up call" to diet, exercise, and pay more positive attention to her husband.

Although the preceding examples have been ones in which it was the husband who had become seduced and waylaid by cybersexual opportunities, increasingly women, too, are succumbing to the attractions of on-line sexual chat rooms and cybersexual relationships (see chapter 9 of this volume, by Schneider, and chapter 6 of this volume by Cooper, McLoughlin, Reich, & Kent-Ferraro). For instance, women who have felt sexually ignored or rejected by their real-life partner may go online and discover that they become sought-after sexual playmates and the recipient of gratifying comments and compliments. Some women develop an online persona that results in far more affirmation and attention than they experience in real life. Some of these women find themselves spending increasing amounts of time in online chatrooms and face the same likelihood as men of developing an excessive reliance on cybersex for personal gratification.

Cybersexual Addiction

Some men do become cybersex "addicts" and need treatment in order to cease or gain control of their compulsive sexuality (Schneider, 2000; Schneider chapter 9 of this book). Adverse consequences of cybersex addiction include depression, social isolation, marital problems, inadvertent exposure of children to online pornography, and decreased job performance or job loss (Schneider, 2000). Guidelines for evaluating the possibility of cybersex addiction have been published, as well as treatment interventions (see Greenfield & Orzack and Delmonico, Griffin & Carnes in chapter 7 this book).

Therapists need to take cybersex addiction seriously since it can have a cascade of negative consequences for the user, his partner, and his children. Apart from the psychosocial implications, the cybersexual addiction of a partner may confront women with legal and financial problems. For example, some men run up huge financial debts in their quest to look at or purchase pornography (pornography that may or may not be illegal, such as pornography involving children) or to seek sexual services that require payment.

Willpower and exhortation to stop is often insufficient, and treatment should include careful assessment of both the risks and extent of the cybersex behavior.

If the compulsive Internet user is not willing to enter treatment, his or her partner can receive support from self-help groups. Often, they seek the assistance of therapists. Relevant information can also be found online, for example, on the homepage of the National Service Organization of COSA: Co-Sex Addicts Anonymous (http://www.shore.net/~cosa).

Cyberinfidelity

When the partner's sexually related use of the net does not focus on searching for, collecting, and receiving stimulating texts and pictures or enlisting sexual services (e.g., online peepshows, commercial telephone sex), but rather on erotic and sexual contact with other individuals, the issue of cyberinfidelity is raised (see Maheu, 2000).

Most couples embrace the ideal of a monogamous relationship and view sexually related activities with someone other than themselves as a breach of faith, even if a real-life meeting has not (yet) taken place. There are, of course, different degrees of sexual exploration on the Internet. Some women are tolerant of the viewing of pornography or stories but draw the line at actual face-to-face meetings, while other women view any sexual stimulation online that precludes them as a breach of trust.

However, cyberinfidelity is sometimes in the eye of the beholder. For instance, some women feel justified in engaging in online sexual forays as a reaction to their partner's past behavior or as a way of remaining in a relationship that has become physically barren because of either their partner's disinterest or incapacity.

One female patient, for instance, said, "I knew my married sex life was over when my husband had prostate surgery and refused to go for treatment for his erection problems." She wanted to remain with her husband, but could not tolerate a life without any physical intimacy. She felt little compunction in going online to seek casual lovers and has been successful (so far) in keeping these relationships discreet and infrequent while maintaining what she feels is a meaningful commitment to her husband and children.

By far the most common reaction of women (and men) to the discovery of a partner's cybersexual affair is a feeling of betrayal, hurt, and anger. However, if a partner is willing to acknowledge his extrarelationship sexual activities, psychotherapy can often help resolve the crisis (see Young, Griffin-Shelley, Cooper, O'Mara, & Buchanan, 2000).

From a feminist point of view, special attention should be devoted to ensuring that any rapprochement between partners does not result in a woman's subordination or self-denial. That is, women may need affirmation from a therapist that their feelings of betrayal are legitimate, since the partner who is engaging in extramarital sexual activity will tend to minimize indiscretions. On the other hand, the immediate assumption that the "cheating" husband is only interested in finding a younger, more beautiful, and more willing playmate may be erroneous. In some instances, men use the Net in order to explore homosexual desires (see Ross & Kauth, chapter 3 of this book) or to have the opportunity to assume a sexually passive or submissive role (Leiblum, 1997, pp. 24; for the meaning of Internet sexuality in connection with paraphilias see chapter 10 of this book).

Relational Problems: Partners' Internet Sexuality as Cause, Symptom, Catalyst, or Cure?

Relational problems in connection with sexual compulsivity and unfaithfulness are not unique to heterosexual couples. Lesbian relationships are similarly affected by such conflicts. The Internet should not be viewed as the *cause* of cybersexual crises, however. Rather, crises involving cybersex signal the need for more comprehensive clinical assessment. A partner's online sexual activities may be a *symptom* rather than a *cause*. It may signal preexisting problems in the individual (e.g., sexual compulsivity) and/or in the relationship (e.g., lack of sexual communication). For instance, Schneider (2000) described a 36-year-old man who had engaged in compulsive masturbation and reliance on pornography for years prior to discovering the Internet. He said, "Cybersex did not cause my sexual addiction—it is just another way for me to act out sexually. I was using porn long before the Net."

The Internet can lead to an escalation of sexual difficulties, it may be a reflection of sexual problems in a relationship, or it can serve as a catalyst for new and different sexual problems for individuals or between couples. Personal inhibition levels, social controls, and the lack of willing partners and sexual scenes that may limit sexual activity in everyday contexts are obsolete in cyberspace. It is easy for latent desires to be realized in cyberspace. Internet sexuality may thus serve as a *catalyst*.

Although a crisis triggered by the Net sexual activities of a partner is taxing and threatening for a woman, it does represent an opportunity for intervention and it can lead to therapeutic change and eventual relationship enhancement for both the individual and the couple.

Therapists who are treating women whose partners are sexually active on the Net, may find it useful to help their patients anticipate and articulate the exact nature of their concerns. Is she worried that her partner will leave her? That his activities are deflecting attention from domestic or family responsibilities? That her partner is doing something illegal (e.g., viewing child pornography)? That he is acting on homosexual urges? By determining the nature of the woman's worries, it may be possible to intervene more effectively.

Finally, therapists should avoid joining the woman in assuming that a man's use of the Internet is necessarily either threatening or in need of control. In some instances, a partner's use of the Internet can have a positive impact. For example, heterosexual men who engage in Net sexual activities do not just consume pornography, engage in cyberprostitution, or cultivate sexual cyberaffairs; many also participate in sexual metadiscourse and exchange ideas with other men and women about how they might improve or enhance their love lives with their partners. Even cyberaffairs do not have to perforce imply a crisis in the relationship, but with the establishment of certain ground-rules (e.g., no face-to-face-meeting with the cyberlovers) may be the means of safely satisfying the thirst for sexual adventure without putting a real relationship on the line. The following case example illustrates this point.

Martin and Beth, both 41, have been married for 19 years and have four children. From the start of their relationship, Martin expressed regret about not having had more time for sexual experimentation prior to getting married. Early on in their marriage, he had an extramarital affair. The affair hurt Beth deeply, and Martin decided he never wanted to do it again. When Martin discovered Multi-User Dungeons/Domains (MUDs) he was thrilled. "I really am monogamous. I'm not interested in something outside my marriage. But being able to have, you know, a tiny romance is kind of cool."

Martin decided to tell Beth about his MUD sex life, and after reflection, she told him she did not mind. Beth made a conscious decision to consider Martin's sexual relationships on MUDs as more like his reading an erotic novel than like his having a rendezvous in a motel room.

To Martin, online affairs were a way of fulfilling what he felt were missed opportunities as an adolescent, since he married young and had not had much premarital sexual experimentation. He wanted a "safe" way of experiencing youthful fantasies without endangering his marriage (Turkle, 1995, p. 224).

While not all partners may be as reasonable as Beth, it is possible for a therapist to help clients take a less catastrophic view of the meaning of online sexual exchange than they might initially. For instance, all men and women have sexual fantasies that they typically do not verbalize but that enrich their sexual life. Sharing fantasies online may not be dissimilar in its impact; it may ultimately serve as a sexual stimulus for both partners.

Finally, it is also possible that the use of the Internet for sexual purposes by one partner may be integrated into a more mutual use (e.g., exchange of mutually received or produced cybererotica, participation in sexually orientated discussion and meeting forums for couples), be it simply as a sign of desire, curiosity, and expansion of ones horizons (see Levine, 1998) or explicitly as a part of therapeutic intervention (see Cooper, Scherer, & Marcus, chapter 11 of this book).

Forced Internet Sexuality

Early on, feminists and others hoped that cyberspace could be a social space in which individuals interacted with each other as equals via textual communications without respect to gender, age, race, or class. However, sexism and violence against women are not absent from cyberspace, and sex continues to be used in the service of power.

Cyberharassment

Women can have unwanted sex pushed onto them when using the Net in both sexually motivated as well as non-sexually motivated ways, and this harassment concerns both nonsocial (typically logging onto Web pages) as well as social Net use (e.g., chat or e-mail contacts).

The search for lesbian Net resources can lead to www.lesbian.org, a feminist Web portal, yet with the slightest typing error—www.lesbian**s**. org—one lands immediately at a porn site. Women who discuss political or personal aspects of sexualized violence in the newsgroup talk.rape are not infrequently confronted with pornographic tales of rape or open threats that are sent to the group by men. Feminists who question the patriarchal structure of society and raise their voices with their own Web sites are confronted with sexualized threats ("You're just a cunt"; see Kennedy, 2000), just as female users who simply enter into a sociable online chatroom and are immediately greeted with anonymous messages such as "Need a fuck?" or "How large are your boobs?" (Adams, 1996, p. 158).

Such cases can be (re)traumatizing and are experienced by many women and girls as akin to the sexist violence that may occur in other areas of their lives. It is unclear, particularly in the case of cyberstalking (Griffiths, 2000, p. 548), whether real violence will follow the threats ("I know where you live").

As sad as the existence of these various forms of cyberharassment is for women and girls, it must be recognized here that we are not dealing with a fundamentally new problem. And the terror of cyberstalking is not based upon the fact that a new quality of violence is occurring online, but rather that the dangers that have always existed for women of being physically violated are a possibility in cyberspace as well. It is at least inherent to the Net that, as a rule, harassment can be prevented and fought against more adequately than in real life with corresponding competence in Internet use (Spertus, 1996).

Instead of forbidding our daughters to go out into cyberspace, we would do better in educating them about virtual self-defense (Spender, 1996). Just because online search tools primarily return references to pornographic offerings under the keyword "women," we should no longer be intimidated, for this difficulty is as familiar as the effectiveness of alternative search strategies for women-related resources (Korenman, 2000). And even if we must reject the utopian vision of the Internet as a gender-equal paradise, the dystopian views of the Internet as a woman-hating, sexist, and violent environment are ill-suited: In both political and therapeutic contexts, dealing with and combating real (and virtual) violence can be very effectively organized by Internet-initiatives.

In Nigeria, Bene E. Madunagu, DAWN regional coordinator for Anglophone Africa and Chairperson of Girl Power Initiative in Calabra Cross River State, Nigeria, uses e-mail to create international support and solidarity for young girls taking action against female genital mutilation for themselves and their sisters, relatives, and peers. "The technology of electronic mail has been of immense use to us in our work. It has enabled us to share our work with others to mobilise larger groups . . . to break the cycle of reproducing decadent culture and tradition" (Harcourt, 2000, p. 695).

Our indignation at the fact that the organizers of these types of Net initiatives are confronted again and again with annoying e-mails should not be greater than our indignation at the fact that the corresponding forms of real physical violence are so widespread and often receive little attention outside of the Net.

Cyberprostitution

E-commerce abounds in the virtual commercialization of sex and often in the exploitation of women (Butterworth, 1996). Just as child pornography rings use the Net, so the organized trade of women uses this infrastructure (Hughes, 1997). And the boom of porn sites, of cybersex and telephone sex offers, and of Webcams and online sex shows requires female suppliers who are in part either urged or forced by their partners or third parties to participate. While these issues are primarily legal, criminal, and political matters, in clinical practice we are interested in dealing with the resulting trauma to women, assuming they are able to access professional help at all.

On the other hand, it should be noted that not all women who engage in sex work feel exploited (Alexander, 1996; Podlas, 2000). For example, a strong amateur movement has developed on the Net (Semans & Winks, 1999, pp. 55), which offers nude and sex photos, films, and Webcams where men, women, and hetero- and homosexual couples appear and along which a fluid boundary to the professional branch of sex work can be traced. Conflicts and problems that are associated with these types of semicommercial sexual expression should not be rashly traced back to the fact that offering cybersex services is necessarily detrimental to women, but rather that the participants' actual conditions of production, expectations, and opportunity of having a say in the matter have changed.

☐ Using the Internet to Promote Oneself

We do not know exactly how many women use sexually related Net offerings and which women, for whatever reasons, prefer, ignore, or reject particular sexuality-related Net activities. Nonetheless, forms of self-chosen sexually related Net activities that are especially important for women are worthy of consideration. The spectrum includes sexual metadiscourse and sexual interactions that occur in commercial as well as in noncommercial sectors.

Commercial Sex

From the feminist point of view, commercial sex is often equated with the exploitation of women, which also implies a sweeping discrediting of women who partially choose to work in this field and are concerned with improving their working conditions and position in society (Alexander, 1996). Apart from the danger of coerced cyberprostitution, there exists the possibility, especially on the Net, that women emancipate themselves from third-party-controlled prostitution and not only are economically better off with their self-controlled Web offerings, but also can shape their own work medically, socially, and psychologically (e.g., Podlas, 2000).

A former erotic dancer, big-breasted model, and star of soft-core videos, Danni Ashe gave up the strip-club circuit and moved her fan club online (Danni's Hard Drive: www.danni.com). The site's instant popularity, fueled initially by Danni's many fans on Usenet newsgroups, who spread the word about her site, convinced Danni that the Web was a superior way for erotic performers to pursue their trade, so she expanded her site to include photos and biographies of several dozen other models. Danni's models retain complete control of their online image: They write their own biographies and choose which photos to present. As a result, you won't find the "I'm horny for you, Daddy" tripe typical of many adult pay sites. Instead, viewers get a more authentic and interesting peek into the lives and dreams of real women (Semans & Winks, 1999, p. 58).

In addition to prostitute services, which are computer-mediated sexual interactions with customers, nonsocial offerings belong to commercial sex as well. Online shops selling sex toys, condoms, lubricants, lingerie, books, CDs, and videos are omnipresent on the Net (Fisher & Barak, 2000). Some online sex shops claim to be "women-friendly" and are often headed by women (Fisher & Barak, 2000, p. 576; Semans & Winks, 1999, p. 125). One example is the online branch of the feminist sex shop Good Vibrations (www.goodvibes.com). The online shop Toys in Babeland (www.babeland.com) is also run by women and contains, among other things a select assortment of books and videos for women and a lesbian e-zine; it describes itself as "S/M, transgender, queer, straight, vanilla, and bi friendly."

Potential new opportunities are arising through commercial online sex not just for female suppliers, but also for female customers. Only a few interested women have the opportunity to seek out the sex shop Good Vibrations in San Francisco personally. But through the online shop, they can survey the ambience, order appropriate products, and study instructional and informational material that belongs to the concept of the shop, for example, the online historical museum of vibrators. Online shopping is ideal for female customers who otherwise rarely have the opportunity to privately investigate the purchase of sex toys or other products or who might have special requests.

For example, one of our patients was extremely sexually inhibited. She entered therapy as a 42-year-old single woman who felt gravely deficient in terms of her sexuality. She had never experienced orgasm, and her goal in treatment was to become orgasmic with masturbation. While initially unable to even maintain eye contact or to talk directly about her sexual anxiety, over time she became increasingly comfortable. She was extremely computer literate and soon began surfing the Net to find sexual materials. At first, she bought self-help books at Amazon.com but then ventured onto Betty Dodson's homepage (www.bettydodson.com), where she was impressed and encouraged by the direct discussion of masturbation as well as every other conceivable sexual topic of interest to women. She gradually became more confident in conducting Net searches and found that she was not so unique in her sexual difficulties. She purchased vibrators, both vaginal and anal, and instructional materials as well as erotic videotapes online. She freely admitted that she could never have brought herself to explore sexual merchandise if it was necessary to walk into an actual store, but she had few reservations about shopping anonymously online (Leiblum, 2000).

When women appear in greater numbers as customers of sexual materials, not only can they experience sexual agency individually (which may have a positive impact on their real-life sexual relationships) but they can also influence the structure of the supply of sex products. Remember that videos were initially made popular because of their ability to satisfy the pornographic interests of men, but increasingly, women and couples have become consumers of this medium, which has led to noticeable changes in the depicted scripts (for example, a greater focus on woman's sexual satisfaction; Williams, 1999). Similarly, women's easier access to sex toys, erotica, or sex shows by way of online shopping might weaken the dominance of heterosexist scripts and gender models and might lead to more varied, woman-centered views of sexuality in general.

The availability of online shops may be used to assist or encourage female clients to expand their ideas about sexual options. Some women may feel gratified and encouraged by the large selection of vibrators or harnesses available online; it may suggest to a woman that it is, indeed, completely acceptable to gratify herself or to penetrate her girlfriend with a dildo. On the other hand, the selection of toys and underwear portrayed in online shops may lead women to feel more performance pressure to be sexually adventuresome and liberal and may increase a woman's feeling of sexual anxiety and insecurity. Research is necessary to evaluate how and in what ways women can benefit from the availability of online sex and sexual aids. It is also necessary to consider how to incorporate the plethora of cybersexual materials in a therapeutic way and to investigate possible consequences of the use of online sex shops systematically from the physiological, cognitive, affective, and imaginative processes that accompany their use (Fisher & Barak, 2000, p. 578), instead of assuming either pathogenic or salutary effects.

Sexual Information, Education, Discussion, and Support

Sexual and reproductive health information, sex education, and sex-related discussion and support groups are available in large numbers on the Internet in English (Leiblum, 2000, Semans & Winks, 1999; see also Ochs, Mah, & Binik chapter 13 of this book). Relevant sites are conducted by individual professionals or laypeople and also by teams. Some are reserved for girls and women, others have no access restrictions. Owing to the triple-A and triple-C factors, the Internet is the ideal medium for finding information relating to sexual questions and to exchange experiences with others. Especially for girls, who are usually more competent than their mothers, the Internet constitutes an important informational source for sexual questions (see Longo, Brown, & Orcutt, chapter 5 of this book).

The open exchange of one's own sexual experiences or lack of them is rare for women because of feelings of shame or embarrassment. The overabundance of sexual topics and images in the mass media should not hide the fact that most people, even in the closest of circles, only rarely and selectively relate personal sexual experiences, which, particularly in the case of problems, leads to feelings of helplessness, insecurity, and loneliness. Social support in the sense of emotional reassurance, information and materials, and practical help assumes first that social communication fields exist in which sexual topics can be revealed. Women's initiatives have made useful information and support available by way of womens' health information, resources, and discussion groups. Regrettably, these resources reach only a fraction of the women and girls who might benefit from them.

Relevant Net offerings are useful to those who have an especially hard time finding support in real life (e.g., women living in rural areas; girls from families who belong to certain religious groups; women and girls with marginalized sexual identities such as lesbians, transgenders, those

engaged in the practice of bondage/dominance/submission/sadomasoch-
ism [BDSM] or women who are affected by disabilities or illnesses that
have sexual implications; see Tepper & Owens, chapter 4 of this book).
Even with a superficial look at relevant mailing lists, newsboards, or
newsgroups, one encounters a large number of postings in which women
and girls express gratitude for the support they have received from various online forums.

The advantage of the Net in accord with the triple-C engine of allowing
the affected to express and link themselves also contains a dark side, in
which laypersons, either inadvertently or sometimes deliberately, disseminate incorrect information or react to delicate self-revealing statements
insensitively or disparagingly. Another danger is that the variety of perspectives that may be found in an online discussion can overtax and con-
fuse some individuals. Sometimes, those searching for help online are
disappointed if their statements or disclosures are misunderstood or ignored. While a real-life group provides both nonverbal and verbal feedback, online it is not easy to evaluate how others are interpreting or reacting to one's communications.

Here, as well, Internet competence plays a central role. One needs to
know how to separate information from disinformation (Morahan-Martin & Anderson, 2000) and how to become comfortable in an online community (Rheingold, 2000). These issues are not peculiar to the Net. In
other spheres (e.g., library, discussion group, TV shows), too, we are often confronted with contradictory and partially false information or are
contradicted or ignored.

In general, online support is not to be understood competitively, but
rather as an extension of the existing consultation and therapy infrastructure. Often the selection of the sexually related problem on the Internet
proves to be the first step to more extensive dealings with the topic. Laypersons encourage one another to take advantage of professional medical
or psychological help and exchange information about helpful clinical
services. Crisis intervention centers that offer e-mail or chat consultation
often arrange on-site consultation.

As clinicians and professionals, it is important to optimize these interfaces between online and offline help, between self-help and professional
help. Many Net initiatives are looking for voluntary professional support.
Such participation might benefit both professional educators and therapists, since it stimulates the quest for accurate information and expands
and extends our knowledge about the issues and concerns of particular
members of a virtual community. Closed online forums that do not want
the participation or observation of professionals are, of course, off-limits.

Because the medical and psychological discourse on sexuality has traditionally been dominated by men, women-oriented information and

communication offerings provide a useful and necessary counterbalance. Critical assessment of the quality of these Net offerings is necessary, however. For example, it is important to determine the professional qualifications of those responsible for the service and who the participants are, how appropriate and current the information or resources being offered are, and so on. When deciding on issues concerning the quality of online support, the use of all-women forums is often especially valuable for women and girls (e.g., Herring, 1994; Spender, 1996). For instance, online discussion about sexualized violence or lesbian lifestyles can occur in moderated and/or closed forums, so that participants are protected from inappropriate contributions.

It must be acknowledged that personally insulting contributions (so-called "flaming") do not come only from men. One should not automatically assume that women-only forums are always friendly and harmonious, because women are known to flame as well (Witmer & Katzman, 1998). In addition, particularly concerning questions of sexual advice and education, there exists interest on the part of heterosexual or bisexually identified women and girls to hear what men and boys have to say about the topics at hand. In online self-help groups that deal with menopause or breast cancer, men are encouraged to participate and share impressions. In general, the effectiveness of online groups is not solely dependant upon their gender composition, but rather on various other factors relating to the groups' composition and their setting of goals (Savicky & Kelley, 2000) which are in themselves worthy of further study. It is then particularly relevant, in connection with sexually related questions, whether and to what extent women consider these questions themselves in relation to gender aspects: While some women, for example, understand the exchange with other lesbians primarily as a sign of gender solidarity, for others, sexual attraction is the most important element. Relevant differences must be sorted out in the online forums and then lead into a determination of rules of conduct or the splitting up of the forum.

Sexual Self-Expression

Besides the exchange of advice and information concerning actual problems, the Net is also used to share erotic and sexual experiences. Different female users may offer diaries, poems, stories, drawings, or photographs on their personal homepages which express the personal and the sexual. Such individual initiatives are sometimes connected by "Webrings," for example, Femme Fatale (www.femmefatale.de) a German Webring for erotic self-expression by women, and BiFems (www.lunamorena.net/BiFem), an international webring only for bisexual women. Additionally, there exist communal projects such as e-zines (e.g., scarletletters.com) or Web portals. While in the mass media a large enough target group with enough buying power must exist in order to produce a media public at all, Net publications with comparatively little expense are readily feasible. These publications accommodate experimentation with new perspectives that do not correspond to any shine-and-gloss aesthetics or mainstream philosophy and give space to marginalized groups and forms of expression. The following is an excerpt from A Dyke's World (www.dykesworld.de/).

> Welcome in! These sites are dedicated to celebrate lesbian visibility and diversity—in all its dignity, its craziness and various colours. A DYKE's WORLD is a personal home page—a work of passion, done for free spirits, woven by Indina Beuche. It's quite a huge site—and still growing—call it web-pollution! This site is non-commercial and has no institution behind, its staff fits into one chair, its focus is global, it has no hidden traps, worships no political party nor message, charges no entry fees—rien comme ça. Simply said: It's a world that welcomes fun, wit, diversity and an open mind.

Between autobiographical and artistic self-expression, informational and entertainment offerings, lie these Net publications that admittedly find no mass public, but that not infrequently have small fan communities who rally around them, help to establish social contacts, and sometimes are reviewed by traditional media (e.g., magazines, television shows).

Although there exists relatively widespread agreement that women should be empowered to create more comfortable and self-defined sexualities, it often remains unclear in which social spaces this self-expression should occur. The Internet is well suited to such initiatives in accord with the triple-C model and can reach even the "marginalized among the marginalized" (Koch & Schockman, 1998).

Clinically, therapists may encourage the creative efforts (writing, painting, photography, etc.) of their female patients, which can be combined with Net publication. The documentation, archiving, and publication of ones own work on the Web may not only instill pride and motivate further creative activity, but can lead to the establishment of Web contacts. This special potential of the Net requires high Internet competence. It may include production, publication, and maintenance of personal Web pages and their promotion (e.g., registration with search engines and Webrings).

Cybersex and Cyberromance

The Internet offers ideal opportunities to initiate and cultivate sexual and romantic contacts and relationships. Two ways of meeting new people on the Net can be differentiated: the *casual meeting,* which takes place within the framework of social forums or discussion groups and the *deliberate partner search* through online personal ads (see Burke, 2000), forums for singles and sex chats.

Regardless of whether an erotic encounter occurs accidentally or deliberately, individuals can decide whether or not to meet in real life with the hope of forming a permanent partnership or marriage or whether to have a casual, noncommitted affair. Net relationships can, on the one hand, focus on emotional-romantic exchanges in which worlds of feeling and thought are reciprocally exchanged in detailed e-mails and hour-long private chats and support is provided when problems arise. On the other hand, cybersex can occur, in which one tries to arouse the other through explicit verbal or e-mail messages. Often, sexual talk is acccompanied by solo masturbation.

The unique quality of cybersex and cyberromance is accelerated self-disclosure in comparison with face-to-face-situations. One expresses thoughts and feelings more frankly and more quickly than is characteristic of face-to-face situations and often experiences more intense feelings of closeness and passion (Cooper & Sportolari, 1997; Döring, in print; Gwinnell, 1998). Individuals can spend many hours online and can begin to lose interest in what feels like mundane daily life. Imagination and projection often play a critical role in online love affairs, and online relationships can be ruled by illusory hopes and expectations. Since computer-mediated communication messages can be sent and received around the clock, it requires a considerable amount of self-discipline to distance oneself from preoccupation with online lovers and focus on other activities. Cybersexual addiction can develop not only in connection with the exchange of erotica and pornography, but also in the cultivation of online romantic and sexual contacts.

Besides overinvolvement, there exists the danger of deception and disappointment. In the online encounter, it is more difficult to develop a realistic picture of one's counterpart, which not only increases the probability of a false assessment, but also raises the danger of falling victim to intentional fraud.

Subject: love on the net ?
Date: 30 Dec 2000 14:07
From: Annette <anette@hotmail.com>
Newsgroup: soc.women.lesbian-and-bi

My name is Annette, I am an 18 yrs old girl (lesbian) and I have a question for those who could enlighten me a little.

I live in the Dominican Republic, a very closed-minded country. I've always been aware of my sexuality, but also of the fact that it is not something I could be open about. Also, I've been raised in a very quiet environment, so my need for anything outside my home wasn't big; my interests were not the same as most teenagers so I did not "fit" very well in groups. That is why, when I "discovered" the Internet and the chatrooms and IRC and all that, it was like a "perfect" world to me. . . . I didn't have to put up with people because it wasn't necessary. . . . If they liked me, they would message me, if not, they wouldn't . . . but there were no problems. And then, I started going to bi/les channels . . . and there I really felt free!

Eventually, as I grew older, I started to feel the need of something more than friendship, the Net was also my answer to it, or at least I thought it was.

At 15, I met a 27 years old woman who made the world look like heaven. . . . She wrapped me in lies and kept me in a phone/internet relationship until her girlfriend—who lived with her for 7 years—called me at my private number to insult me. . . . Even after that the woman I had met kept lying to me and I was so foolish to believe her lies and we were "together" for several months. That was my first "experience" on-line. After that one, I had many other experiences similar to this one, where I met women on-line who made me believe they loved me and that we would meet someday soon, but it never happened and I always ended with a broken heart and shattered dreams. . . .

Now . . . I know that I can't expect this to be "perfect" . . . but maybe I am expecting too much from an on-line relationship? . . . I've seen people who meet on-line and then meet in person and have a great relationship . . . so I am not sure what is my problem here. . . .

Please let me know what you think . . . and don't be too hard on me. . . . Believe it or not, I have only had one girlfriend off the net and it was over a year ago . . . I am what you could still call a naive virgin.

Best regards,
Annette

While this vignette is easy to dismiss as indicative of the gullibility of a young girl, many more mature or worldly women fall prey to the same kind of emotional rollercoaster, that is, believing that one has finally found a genuine soulmate, and then, either because of an actual face-to-face meeting or a chance discovery, find that their soulmate is actually married or has falsely represented critical aspects of himself. Of course, such disappointments are true of other venues as well, for example, personal ads, dating services, and pen-pals.

With some understanding of the reality of Net relationships, intentional fraud is detectable. People who are hoping to find a serious partner after meeting online should be told to conduct "reality checks" as soon as possible (exchanging photos, telephone calls, and face-to-face meetings) instead of remaining in a fantasy world for prolonged periods of time (e.g., months, years). Until recently, there have been few studies that systematically looked at which specific aspects of online encounters may be predictive of successful relationships offline. Recent research suggests that three factors are important (see Döring, in print):

1. The degree of cultural differences and geographical distance. In cyberspace, one usually meets individuals removed from one's immediate surroundings.
2. Differences in everyday habits and lifestyles. On the Net, relationships are based purely on communication and allow for no common or shared activities in real life.
3. Lack of genuine emotional and sexual intimacy. Intimacy and emotional closeness are often more difficult to sustain in real life than via e-mail or distant chatting.

Despite the various shortcomings of online relationships, they should not be dismissed as trivial. Often, for a socially isolated or inexperienced person, they activate repressed longings and desires and may stimulate valuable self-reflection. The special affinity of women for online relationships should be noted. Housewives or women who are restricted to the house or who are subjected to powerful social control may find meaningful social communities easily and inconspicuously. They may be able to cultivate and enjoy intimate relationships with both men and women without negative sanction from their immediate family or friends. Women have an opportunity to adopt a "new identity" which can liberate them from both heterosexual expectations and social conventions: They do not need to behave passively or modestly online, and if they are witty or wise or provocative or interesting, they will not be ignored.

In fact, women are often uniquely capable of cultivating online relationships since many women are especially competent in verbal exchange, that is, in sharing and expressing personal experiences, thoughts, and feelings. In some ways, Net relationships that consist solely of the exchange of intimate verbal messages over a period of time is a "female form of relationship." Similarly, for men, it is often easier to display emotional openness and vulnerability on the Net with the protection of anonymity, invisibility, and spatial distance.

The loss of inhibitions facilitated by computer-mediated communication is not just a new means for women to encourage men to become more emotionally expressive, but it permits women to reveal and express more aggressive and sexual aspects of themselves. Women and girls may use chat forums specifically to flirt and invite sexual contact, to verbalize their sexual preferences and fantasies directly, and to experiment with new sexual orientations, roles, and practices. Women who have an erotic affinity to words and are interested in sexual challenges (and who can also type rapidly!) find that the Net provides an ideal arena for a safe exploration of their desires in terms of social, psychological, and physical dimensions (see Döring, 2000).

Hamman (1996) described a single woman who uses cybersex to resolve the conflicts between her sexual desires and moral reservations; in so doing, she establishes a sexual identity and her own sexual agency. Odzer (1997, p. 117) described how she herself used a video conference with her cyberlover quite deliberately as a form of self-therapy:

> I was determined to seize the opportunity to overcome my gender conditioning. I wanted to break the barrier that made me embarrassed of my genitals. What a stupid emotion embarrassment was. After adjusting camera angle and lighting, I put on a wig to keep my face hidden—vanquishing shame didn't mean I was going to open myself up to blackmail or ridicule if the other person wanted to put a nude picture of me on the Web. That night I succeeded in further freeing my sexuality from the shackles of society. I let myself be the sexual being I am and let myself enjoy the pleasure my body was capable of without embarrassment or shame. What freedom! What power! I slew a dragon!

Whether cybersex and cyberromance are helpful and lead to satisfactory face-to-face relations or whether they simply provide temporary escape and avoidance of problems depends on a number of factors. If the appeal of text-based cybersex for a woman consists primarily of seeming desirable and sexually appealing to potential partners—a facade that contradicts a woman's real-life feelings—then they are probably of limited value. On the other hand, if cyberrelationships provide a needed boost to the woman's self-confidence and self-esteem, and thereby permit greater risks in face-to-face interactions, then they are therapeutically useful and should be encouraged. Often, this outcome is difficult to predict beforehand!

One divorced 48-year-old patient, for instance, was able to communicate with wit and assurance on a variety of discussion forums and chat rooms but could not be persuaded to make the leap into risking a face-to-face meeting with any of her chat buddies.

Another patient, a successful psychotherapist, chatted often and well with a variety of men, but found all of her face-to-face meetings disappointing and frustrating. "The men often talk a good game, but are so socially unskilled that meeting them in person shatters all of my illusions!" she remarked.

Sexual exploration in virtual communities of sexual subcultures (Palandri & Green, 2000) may be seen either as preparation for entry to offline scenes or as playful extensions of the existing sexual repertoire without any desire for offline realization. When women in committed relationships use Net meetings for clandestine romantic or erotic contacts, problems usually arise in the primary relationship. As therapists, we should explore and discuss with our patients the likely aftermath of the discovery of these activities on both their partner and on their relationship. If partners can successfully agree on how they want to incorporate Net sex exploration into their life together and can negotiate which Net sex activities are acceptable (and which are not!), problems will be averted, and in some cases, the universe of sexual options and paraphernalia available on the Internet may enrich and revitalize their relationship.

☐ Conclusion

Sexual exploration on the Internet does pose risks for women: Partners can use the Net to betray or to establish relationships that exclude them, women can be forced to participate in online sex or can be sexually harassed or insulted; and online romances can endanger primary relationships. But none of these dangers is unique to the Internet. On the Internet, these common risks, assuming the user possesses some degree of technical competence, may be avoided and dealt with more readily than in many face-to-face-contexts. In fact, real life poses greater risks for most women than the potential risks associated with Internet usage. In real life, sexual and physical violence is commonplace for many women, and gender and power inequities abound. Technology can not eradicate or heal the disappointment and bitterness of some feminists about the fact that computer-mediated communication does not abolish gender asymmetries or provide women an egalitarian cybertopia.

The sexual options available on the Internet offer women unique opportunities: Women can display themselves or their creations, find or establish supportive networks, engage in open sexual discourse, and explore sexual preferences and fetishes with other women and with men. These options provide genuinely new arenas for women to act assertively as sexual subjects and protagonists rather than as sexual objects. Over time, these opportunities for women to define and express their sexuality may have far-reaching consequences in enhancing and extending feelings of autonomy and empowerment. How and whether these goals are achieved will ultimately depend on a woman's unique circumstances, competencies, and goals.

☐ References

Adams, C. (1996). "This is not our fathers' pornography": Sex, lies, and computers. In C. Ess (Ed.), *Philosophical perspectives on computer-mediated communication* (pp. 147–170). New York: State University of New York Press.

Alexander, P. (1996). Prostitution: A difficult issue for feminists. In S. Jackson & S. Scott (Eds.), *Feminism and sexuality—A reader* (pp. 342–357). New York: Columbia University Press.

Benedikt, C. (1995). Tinysex is safe sex. *Infobahn Magazine: The Magazine of Internet Culture,* June 1995, from http://www.cwrl.utexas.edu/~claire/texts/thoughts.html

Burke, S. K. (2000). In search of lesbian community in an electronic world. *CyberPsychology & Behavior, 3*(4), 591–604.

Butterworth, D. (1996). Wanking in cyberspace: The development of computer porn. In S. Jackson & S. Scott (Eds.), *Feminism and sexuality—A Reader* (pp. 314–320). New York, NY: Columbia University Press.

Cooper, A. (1998). Sexuality and the Internet: Surfing into the new millennium. *CyberPsychology & Behavior, 1*(2), 181–187.

Cooper, A., Delmonico, D. L., & Burg, R. (2000). Cybersex users, abusers, and compulsives: New Findings and Implications. *Sexual Addiction & Compulsivity, 7*(1–2), 5–30.

Cooper, A. & Sportolari, L. (1997). Romance in cyberspace: Understanding online attraction. *Journal of Sex Education and Therapy, 22*(1), 7–14.

Döring, N. (in print). Studying online love and cyber romance. In B. Batinic, U.-D. Reips, M. Bosnjak, & A. Werner (Eds.), *Online social sciences.* Seattle, Toronto, Switzerland, Germany: Hogrefe & Huber.

Döring, N. (2000). Feminist views of cybersex: Victimization, liberation, and empowerment. *CyberPsychology & Behavior, 3*(4), 863–885.

Fisher, W. A., & Barak, A. (2000). Online sex shops: Phenomenological, psychological, and ideological perspectives on Internet sexuality. *CyberPsychology & Behavior, 3*(4), 575–589.

Fisher, W., Byrne, D., White, L. A., & Kelley, K. (1988). Erotophobia-erotophilia as a dimension of personality. *Journal of Sex Research, 25,* 123–151.

Griffiths, M. (2000). Excessive Internet use: Implications for sexual behavior. *CyberPsychology & Behavior, 3*(4), 537–552.

Gwinnell, E. (1998). *Online seductions. Falling in love with strangers on the Internet.* New York, NY: Kodansha International.

Hamman, Robin B. (1996). Cyborgasms. Cybersex amongst multiple-selves and cyborgs in the narrow-bandwidth space of America online chat rooms. MA Dissertation, Department of Sociology, University of Essex, Colchester, UK. Retrieved from http://www.socio.demon.co.uk/Cyborgasms.html

Kennedy, T. L. (2000). An exploratory study of feminist experiences in cyberspace. *CyberPsychology & Behavior, 3*(5), 707–719.

Koch, N. S., & Schockman, H. E. (1998). Democratizing Internet access in the lesbian, gay, and bisexual communities. In B. Ebo (Ed.), *Cyberghetto or cybertopia. Race, class, and gender on the Internet* (pp. 172–184). Westport, CT: Praeger.

Korenman, J. (2000). Women, women, everywhere looking for a link. *CyberPsychology & Behavior, 3*(5), 721–729.

Leiblum, S. R. (2001). Women, sex and the Internet. *Sexual & Relationship Therapy, 16*(4), 389–405.

Leiblum, S. R. (1997). Sex and the Net: Clinical implications. *Journal of Sex Education and Therapy, 22*(1), 21–27.

Levine, D. (1998). *The joy of cybersex. A guide for creative lovers.* New York: Ballantine Books.

Maheu, M. M. (2000). Cyber-affairs survey results. *Self-Help & Psychology Magazine*, Rubrik "Cyber-affairs." Retrieved from http://www.shpm.com/articles/cyber_romance/

McKenna, K., & Bargh, J. (1998). Coming out in the age of the Internet: Identity "de-marginalization" from virtual group participation. *Journal of Personality and Social Psychology, 75*(3), 681–694.

McRae, S. (1996). Coming apart at the seams: Sex, text and the virtual body. In L. Cherny & E. R. Weise (Hrsg.), *Wired women. Gender and new realities in cyberspace* (pp. 242–264). Seattle, WA: Seal Press.

Morahan-Martin, J., & Anderson, C. (2000). Information and misinformation online: Recommendations for facilitiating accurate mental health information retrieval and evaluation. *CyberPsychology & Behavior, 3*(5), 731–746.

Odzer, C. (1997). *Virtual spaces. Sex and the cyber citizen.* New York, NY: Berkley Books.

Palandri, M., & Green, L. (2000). Image management in a bondage, discipline, sadomasochist subculture: A cyber-ethnographic study. *CyberPsychology & Behavior, 3*(4), 631–641.

Podlas, K. (2000). Mistresses of their domain: How female entrepreneurs in cyberporn are initiating a gender power shift. *CyberPsychology & Behavior, 3*(4), 847–854.

Rheingold, H. (2000). *The virtual community: Homesteading on the electronic frontier* (revised edition). Cambridge, MA: MIT Press.

Savicky, V., & Kelley, M. (2000). Computer mediated communication: Gender and group composition. *CyberPsychology & Behavior, 3*(5), 817–826.

Schneider, J. P. (2000). Effects of cybersex addiction on the family: Results of a Survey. *Sexual Addiction & Compulsivity, 7*(1–2), 31–58.

Semans, A., & Winks, C. (1999). *The woman's guide to sex on the Web.* New York, NY: HarperSanFrancisco.

Spender, D. (1996). *Nattering on the Net—Women, power, and cyberspace.* Toronto: Garamond Press.

Spertus, E. (1996). *Social and technical means for fighting on-line harassment.* Retrieved from http://www.ai.mit.edu/people/ellens/Gender/glc/

Turkle, S. (1995). *Life on the screen: Identity in the age of the Internet.* New York: Simon and Schuster.

Witmer, D., & Katzman, S. (1998). You say that: Graphic accents as gender markers in computer-mediated Communication. In S. Sudweeks, M. McLaughlin & S. Rafaeli (Eds.), *Network and netplay. Virtual groups on the Internet* (pp. 3–12). Menlo Park, CA: AAAI Press, MIT Press.

Young, K., Griffin-Shelley, E., Cooper, A., O'Mara, J., & Buchanan, J. (2000). Online infidelity: A new dimension in couple relationships with implications for evaluation and treatment. *Sexual Addiction & Compulsivity, 7*(1–2), 59–74.

3

CHAPTER

Michael W. Ross
Michael R. Kauth

Men Who Have Sex With Men, and the Internet: Emerging Clinical Issues and Their Management

Most people use the Internet in moderation and experience few problems associated with online use (Cooper, Scherer, Boies, & Gordon, 1999). But about 1% of Internet users, mostly men, spend more than 40 hours per week in online sexual activities, often causing significant disruption in their lives. This chapter discusses (a) diagnostic terminology, (b) the role of the Internet in the exploration of male–male sexuality and identity development, (c) treatment approaches for extreme Internet use, and (d) other ways that the Internet impacts on gay and bisexual men.

☐ Cybersex Addiction, Compulsion, Hypersexuality, or What?

Writers do not agree about how best to characterize excessive use of the Internet for sexual pursuits (the primary clinical problem presenting with regard to Internet use) or what to call it. Each label has a different theoretical perspective and particular treatment strategy. (For reviews of theoretical models, see Coleman, 1990, and Rinehart & McCabe, 1997). In general, writers have emphasized the role of anxiety, depression, and difficulty with intimacy in excessive Internet behavior (Rinehart & McCabe,

1997). Carnes (1983, 1989) viewed excessive sexual behavior as a sexual addiction, similar to alcoholism, because the experience is mood-altering. Accordingly, sexual addiction is characterized by a time-consuming pre-occupation with the activity, ritualization to enhance their cognitive experience and prepare for sexual activity, out-of-control behavior in which sex is the most important aspect of life, and shame and despair following the sexual event, which prompts repetition of the cycle. Goodman (1992, 1993) described sexual addiction as an attempt to regulate affective states and offered diagnostic guidelines based on *DSM-III-R* criteria for addictive disorder. Mosner (1993), however, noted that Goodman's criteria would diagnose newly married couples as sexual addicts because they are preoccupied with sexual activities, engage in sex frequently, and often allow sexual activities to interfere with other social activities. Rinehart and McCabe (1997) also pointed out that Goodman's model fails to differentiate between normative and pathological sexual behavior. *DSM-IV* does not consider addiction to sexual behavior. Coleman (1990, 1991) viewed excessive Internet use for sexual pursuits as a sexual compulsion similar to obsessive-compulsive disorder (OCD). Here the anxiety-driven obsessive-compulsive behavior is sexual. Classic OCD involves intrusive, uncontrollable thoughts and engaging in rigidly repetitive behaviors to reduce distress temporarily. The obsessions and compulsions themselves, usually meaningless and unpleasant, cause marked distress and maintain the maladaptive behavior pattern. According to Coleman, sexual compulsives experience their sexual behavior as distressing, obstructive, and not pleasurable.

Quadland (1985) and Kafka (1997) saw excessive sexual behavior as a disorder of desire or hypersexuality. Quadland also argued that hypersexual behavior is anxiety-based, out-of-control, and not very pleasurable. Among gay men, hypersexuality is associated with greater numbers of different sexual partners, more sex in public settings, greater use of alcohol or drugs with sex, fewer long-term relationships, and fewer feelings of love and relaxation prior to sex. Barth and Kinder (1987), basing their conclusions on Quadland's (1985) study of gay men, suggested that the problem is one of impulse control. While Kafka (1997) offered a clear definition of male hypersexuality—seven or more sexual experiences per week for a minimum of 6 months after the age of 15—in a recent probability study, Laumann, Gagnon, Michael, and Michaels (1994) found that 3.1% of men ages 18–59 masturbated one or more times a day for the last year.

From all these definitions, the term cybersex is imprecise for its application to men who have sex with men (MSMs) and may include any online sexually related activity. For this reason, more precise definitions have been proposed in the introduction to this volume (chapter 1). In order to better describe and study this phenomenon, we need to agree on terms and have a common lexicon. Thus, for the purposes of this text we define online sexual activity (OSA) as use of the Internet for any activity (including text, audio, graphic files) that involves sexuality, whether for purposes of recreation, entertainment, exploration, support, education, commerce, efforts to attain and secure sexual or romantic partners, and so on.

Cybersex is a subcategory of OSA and can be defined as using the medium of the Internet to engage in sexually gratifying activities, such as looking at pictures, engaging in sexual chat, exchanging explicit sexual images or emails, and "cybering" (i.e., sharing fantasies over the Internet that involve being sexual together while one or both people masturbate).

Online sexual problems (OSPs) include the full range of difficulties that people can have due to engaging in OSA. Such difficulties include negative financial, legal, occupational, relationship, as well as personal repercussions from OSA. The "problem" may range from a single incident to a pattern of excessive involvement. The consequences may involve feelings of guilt, loss of a job or relationship, and HIV or other sexually transmitted disease (STD). Finally, online sexual compulsivity (OSC) is a subtype of OSP and refers to excessive OSA behaviors that interfere with the work, social, and/or recreational dimensions of the person's life. In addition, there are other indications of the "loss of control" of their ability to regulate the activity and/or minimize adverse consequences (Cooper, 1998).

Thus, cybersex broadly involves talking about sex online or talking about nonsexual subjects within sexual chatrooms, as well as responding to personal ads, receiving information about sexual matters from newsgroups, arranging to meet someone offline for a sexual encounter, downloading or trading sexual images, watching live sex spy cams, buying sex toys and videos, and masturbating while viewing images online. This term makes little distinction between OSAs, although these behaviors are not equivalent: Loosely used, the term cybersex will include getting information about STDs from a Web site as well as engaging in activity for sexual gratification, and thus any description of OSA for MSMs must distinguish the type and purpose of activity. Cooper et al. (1999) and Cooper, Delmonico, and Burg (2000) regarded number of hours online as one of the defining characteristics of cybersex and view cybersex compulsion as different from sexual compulsion. For stylistic consistency, the inexact term cybersex compulsion is used here.

Compulsive sexual behavior has been extensively described in the literature in the last decade and has been defined by Kafka (2000) as having as its hallmark, and the factor that gives it clinical status, the volitional impairment and the amount of time consumed by nonrelational sexual fantasies, urges, and activities, and the adverse personal and psychosocial consequences that accompany it. In his recent review, Kafka (2000) listed three characteristics that provide an operational definition. First, over at least 6 months, having recurrent, intense sexually arousing fantasies, sexual urges, or behavior involving culturally normative aspects of sexual expression that increase in frequency or intensity so as to significantly interfere with the expression of the capacity for reciprocal, affectionate activity. Second, these fantasies, urges or behaviors cause significant distress or impairment socially or occupationally. And third, these problems do not occur exclusively during an episode of another *DSM-IV* Axis I condition, substance abuse, or other medical condition. Thus, the condition must be long term, distressing or dysfunctional, and independent of other psychiatric disorders. It is important to consider what is not included. Episodic excessive use of the Internet is not included, nor is behavior of less than 6 months standing. It must interfere with the expression of reciprocal, affectionate activity, which is a problem considering the fact that such affectionate activity may not exist in some gay contexts such as "coming out" or in the case of geographically isolated individuals. Thus, when the context or the stage of the individual's gay identity formation has not enabled gay affectionate activity to develop, it is questionable whether this condition may have been met. For gay men, it is reasonable to assume that Internet use is subculturally normative: Ross, Tikkanen, and Månsson (2000) report that half of a conventionally recruited sample of men recruited from gay venues in Sweden had used the Internet in search of sexual partners or gratification, and 86% of Internet-recruited MSMs had; and this figure will undoubtedly increase over time as access to the Internet becomes more common. Where social or occupational functioning is not impaired, it is doubtful if the situation can be classified as a disorder. And finally, there must not be evidence of another Axis I psychiatric diagnosis.

These exclusions are emphasized because of the nature of Internet use in the gay subculture. As Ross, Fernández-Esquer, and Seibt (1995) have noted in their comprehensive review of the gay subculture as a culture, the identity of the individual may be centered upon sexual activity, and particularly when an individual is at the stage of exploring their identity: Part of that exploration may involve frequent sexual contacts. Indeed, for MSMs, frequent and anonymous sexual contacts may be their only outlet. Thus, we would specifically advise caution in labeling, as cybersex-compulsive men in geographically isolated areas, in social situations where disclosure of gay or a MSM would endanger their personal or occupational safety or social supports, or where the individual is in the process of "coming out" and uses online contacts as a means of identity construction or experimentation, unless there is clear disruption in functioning.

Further, with regard to the gay-subculturally normative aspects of sexual expression, it must be noted that levels of sexual activity are significantly higher than in the dominant heterosexual culture. We note this because the Internet has a number of positive functions in the gay subculture, especially for geographically or socially isolated individuals and because of the stigma still associated with being gay or having same-sexual contacts. Any assessment of extreme cybersexual behavior in this population must include balancing the wider context of the use of the Internet in the gay subculture and its possibly positive impact on identity formation or reduction of isolation.

Nevertheless, we believe that there will be clear cases where the individuals themselves will recognize that their sexual Internet use is dysfunctional, and it will also be obvious to the clinician that this is so. We are more dubious about cases in which an external source has labeled the behavior as pathological, for example, cases involving sexual Internet use at work or detected by an unsympathetic spouse. In such cases, the labeling of the behavior as deviant does not establish a diagnosis of sexual compulsion and clinicians should be wary of pathologizing perceived deviance and acting as social control agents.

☐ Cybersex and Gay and Bisexual Identity Development

Men who are attracted to men face numerous obstacles in homophobic-heterosexist cultures. Homosexuality may be widely visible in the media, yet still harshly stigmatized in society. American television programs have openly gay characters, but images in popular media do not mean greater tolerance at the community level. Twenty-seven states have sodomy laws that criminalize consensual adult same-sex erotic behavior (Lambda, 2000), and the U.S. Department of Defense's "Don't Ask, Don't Tell" policy has led to a large increase in the number of discharges for homosexuality (Human Rights Campaign, 2000). Conservative religious groups condemn homosexuality as a sin and the cause of the collapse of the nuclear family and encourage gay men and lesbians to change their sexual orientation (Family Research Council, 2000). The vast majority of gay men and lesbians report experiencing antigay harassment and discrimination, and a significant number experience antigay violence (Berrill, 1992).

For men who are attracted to men, large metropolitan areas offer greater anonymity for same-sex pursuits, social contact, and access to gay-positive information, legal and social services, bars, support groups, and organized community activities. Yet, many men are unable to access these resources, and for men in small towns and rural communities, such resources do not exist. Young, ethnic, religious, and rural gay and bisexual males may experience an enormous sense of alienation and pressure to conform to a heterosexual lifestyle. For these men, the Internet offers escape from pressures to be completely heterosexual and access to explicit images of male–male sexuality (Ross et al., 2000). Carey (1996), Egan (2000), and Schwartz and Southern (2000) speculated that access to and availability of sexual information and images may facilitate gay and bisexual identity development. (No comparable theory about lesbian identity development has been proffered, and lesbians appear to be less avid users of the Internet than gay men.)

Models of gay male identity development suggest an early stage of identity confusion in which the individual is aware of same-sex feelings and being different from others (Coleman, 1985; Troiden, 1989). Many gay and bisexual men are aware of same-sex feelings by early adolescence, although others recognize such feelings later in life. For men struggling with their sexuality, going to gay bars, bookstores, or support groups makes a public statement about self-identity that can be risky and frightening. However, accessing sexual images on the Internet or participating in male chatrooms entails less personal risk or stigma. On the Internet, one is not seen without consent, and identity can be disguised. Consequently, the role of physical attractiveness is diminished. Rather, certain types of Internet interactions emphasize similarity, rapport, and mutual disclosure (Cooper & Sportolari, 1997). Since most Internet service providers (ISPs) offer e-mail, often free, as well as access to chatrooms, personal ads, sex sites, and sexual images, cyberspace opens a virtual community that provides social support even to those who are marginalized, unattractive, or have masked their identity.

Egan (2000) described the experiences of gay teens who use the Internet to explore their sexual feelings, develop a support system, and test out intimate relationships. Most teens spend a great deal of time on the Internet and many describe themselves as "addicted," although they may mean something different. While gay or bisexual identity can develop independently of sexual behavior, for many gay and bisexual men, sexual experimentation and romantic relationships precede identity formation (Coleman, 1985). For men seeking sexual experiences with men, the Internet makes contact easy. Several writers (Schwartz & Southern, 2000; Tikkanen & Ross, 2000) refer to the Internet as the new "tearoom," a reference to Humphreys' (1970) book about quick, anonymous sexual encounters between mostly married men in public restrooms. Cruising online is anonymous, quick, and efficient. Regardless of the many similarities between tearooms and cyberspace, there is little evidence that male–male cybersex activities involve mostly married men. Furthermore, unlike tearooms and other public sexual encounters that involve no verbal exchanges, contact online is entirely textual, interactive, and nonvisual. Although some chat participants require picture exchanges, the received image may not be the sender's.

Despite the sexual nature of Internet contacts, for many gay and bisexual men, cybersex activities may function partly as social support or partly as a stage or level of experimentation in "coming out." Frequent participation in chatrooms and viewing explicit images may enhance social networks and stabilize identity, much like meeting gay friends in bars and having casual sexual relationships. The adaptation of sex for social networking may help account for the greater numbers of lifetime sexual partners among gay men. Sex is part of the culture, and gay male culture is immersed in sexually explicit language, behavior, and images. More than heterosexuals, gay and bisexual men are technologically skillful and likely to use the Internet for a variety of purposes (Cooper et al., 2000). Thus, clinically, the Internet may facilitate one of the early stages of coming out, exploring one's same-sex attraction and feelings, without the trauma of actual social or sexual experimentation. The uses of the Internet in MSMs can be well described by reference to the "quin-A" engine.

☐ The Quin-A Engine and MSMs

While there has been reference made to the triple-A engine (accessibility, affordability, anonymity) that drives sexual contact on the Internet, there are other factors operating for MSMs. Tikkanen and Ross (2000) have suggested that there are two other variables: acceptability (in the gay subculture) as being a normative way to meet other people and date, and approximation. Approximation refers to MSMs who are unsure of their sexual identity being able to experiment to determine their sexual identity by approximating being gay either through fictitious selves or by having virtual sex on the Internet, which enables them to experience the psychological concomitants without actually engaging in physical sex with another. These quin-A engines are likely to make MSM use of the Internet more common and serve important psychological functions as well. Thus, excessive Internet use may be clinically adaptive for many MSMs. Empirical data about gay and bisexual men's use of the Internet is limited. One study of men who visit men for men (M4M) chatrooms found that participants are more likely to identify as bisexual or heterosexual than gay (Tikkanen & Ross, 2000). Frequent chatroom visitors were more likely to live outside of major urban areas, and were younger and less educated than infrequent ones. The average age of frequent chat visitors was 30, compared with 40 for men who never visited chatrooms. Frequent chatroom visitors were most likely to report only having casual sex partners and more female sexual partners in the past 12 months. Men who lived with a steady male partner were less likely to visit chatrooms, although gay men in open relationships frequently visited chatrooms. A high proportion of chatroom visitors met their contacts for real-time sexual activity. In addition, frequent chatroom visitors were more likely to engage in unprotected anal intercourse with casual partners than were nonvisitors. Chatroom visitors were less open about their sexual identity than nonvisitors, although the two groups did not differ in attendance at gay bars and sex clubs. This study illustrates that "out" gay men, gay men in open relationships, and nongay men use the Internet differently. Furthermore, this study suggests that cybersex activity may be a stage of identity exploration for men who like men. Thus, any treatment approach needs to carefully distinguish between cybersex behavior which is destructive of personal relationships and is occupationally or socially damaging, and that which is adaptive in exploring or acculturating to the gay subculture and moving through the stages of "coming out" through observation, accessing information, or controlled exposure and experimentation. The distinction between adaptive and maladaptive cybersexuality is crucial for the therapist. Clearly, different norms need to be used when talking about different sexual subcultures, as Ross et al. (1995) have illustrated.

☐ Extreme Cybersex Behavior

Brad's Story

Previous writers have provided case histories of people in treatment for cybersex compulsions (Orzack & Ross, 2000; Slater, 2000). While informative, these histories tell only one side of the story. Understanding the various kinds of cybersex experiences presents a clearer picture of the phenomenon.

Brad (whose name and personal identifiers have been changed) is a 35-year-old, White male postgraduate who has been openly gay for many years (interviewed by M.K., 12/00). For 3–4 years, Brad engaged in daily cybersex activities between 30–45 hours per week. At that time, Brad was single and had started a new full-time job in a new city, where he had no friends. Brad had recently discovered America Online (AOL) chatrooms and saw the local M4M chat as an easy way to meet other gay men outside of bars and entertain himself. His activities mainly involved M4M chats, instant messages (IMs), and trading sexual images. Regulars in the M4M chatroom became friends, some of whom Brad met offline for social activities. It was a code of the M4M chat that regular members did not have sex with each other. Brad had multiple screen names, some for regular Internet use and others for cybersex cruising. It was not unusual for Brad to maintain multiple chats and IMs simultaneously. Sometimes, he and chat friends held telephone conversations about current chat activities while online. Masturbation during chat was "not arousing" because too many conversations and screens would be active at the same time. Brad denied experiencing any significant problems associated with his heavy online use but acknowledged that he "probably could have done more (offline) social stuff." When asked about who he encountered in M4M chatrooms, Brad described two kinds of men. "There were those who were social and had social lives offline, and those who had no social life offline. These guys were scary."

Brad met several online partners for sex. He preferred nonreciprocal oral sex with straight or bisexual men. Despite Brad's online prowess, he was often less satisfied with his offline sexual experience and noted that "sex wasn't so good." The excitement and challenge of seduction was more interesting than the sexual act. He added, "Eighty percent of the fun was the pursuit; 20% was the catch."

Brad became bored with his online and offline sexual activities. About this time, he took a new job in another city and moved in with roommates. His cybersex activities dropped sharply. He spent most of his time with roommates and friends and had less opportunity for online activity. Brad also found online chatrooms less entertaining. For the past 2 years, he has rarely participated in chatrooms. Brad spends less than 20 hours per week e-mailing friends and surfing the Web for recreation or work. He is single, not dating, socially active, and happy.

Research on Extreme Cybersex Behavior

Few studies have investigated excessive cybersex behavior. Cooper et al. (1999) described one large sample, and their findings warrant review. Most respondents were male (86%) and heterosexual (87%). Seven percent identified as gay/lesbian or bisexual, respectively. The majority (64%) were married or in a committed relationship.

A major finding of Cooper et al. (1999) was that most Internet users spent moderate amounts of time online and reported no significant problems associated with online activity. Ninety-two percent of respondents spent less than 11 hours per week engaging in cybersex behavior. Most cybersex participants accessed sexual sites for entertainment rather than sexual release. Only 20% reported being both excited and aroused. Furthermore, most cybersex participants were not distressed by their activities. Only 12% of the sample thought that they downloaded sexual material too often. A second major finding of Cooper et al. (1999) was that frequent cybersex participants (11 or more hours of use per week) preferred to talk about sex in chatrooms and via e-mail. This group also indicated that cybersex activities interfered with some important aspects of their life. Cooper et al. (1999) concluded that the most powerful and potentially problematic types of interactions take place in chatrooms with other users; this is typically online sexual gratification.

It may be clinically useful to distinguish between Internet "engagement" and Internet "addiction/compulsion" (we prefer the term "extreme cybersex behavior") as stages that may be points on the same continuum (with computer or Internet phobia as the other extreme) or not necessarily related. There is a danger that taking a solely statistical definition of time spent online (e.g., 2 or 3 SD above the mean of a distribution) will not distinguish between adaptive behavior, a stage of "coming out" and gay acculturation, maladaptive or disruptive behavior, or engagement versus addiction or compulsion. The nature, consequences, and context of the behavior are critical to making a clinical judgment in the case of MSMs. Further, any statistical decision would need to be made based on distributions of MSMs, since it appears that MSMs are more avid users of the Internet for sexual purposes than heterosexual men. From the data of Ross et al. (2000), gay men contacted on the Internet reported an average of 150 Internet visits per year, compared with an average of 100 for their sample contacted using questionnaires in gay venues.

Cooper et al. (2000) also categorized respondents by scores on a Sexually Compulsive Scale (Kalichman et al., 1994). Most people (83.5%) were not sexually compulsive. Sexual compulsives made up 4.6% of the sample. Sexual compulsives who also spent more than 11 hours online per week in sexual pursuits were labeled cybersex compulsives (1%). Of the 734 subjects who spent 11 hours or more online per week, only 13% were in the cybersex compulsive group. Thus, frequent cybersex behavior is not necessarily synonymous with sexual compulsion.

Cybersex compulsives spent an average of 15–25 hours online per week in sexual activities. Students were most likely to fall into this group. Cybersex compulsives were also likely to be women (21%), gay men/lesbians (16%), bisexuals (21%), and single/dating (26%). Male cybersex compulsives preferred accessing the Web, while females preferred chatrooms. Eighteen percent of cybersex compulsives reported that their online sexual behavior did not interfere with their life, while 24% viewed their online activity as interfering in all areas of their life. Thirty-seven percent of cybersex compulsives were gay or bisexual.

It is probable that for MSMs, pathological cybersex activity is defined too liberally. Factors unrelated to sexual compulsivity may support high

Internet use. A more appropriate cut-off for excessive cybersex behavior may be 20 or more hours per week, consistent with findings by Schwartz and Southern (2000). However, caution is warranted when drawing clinical conclusions from a single sample of self-selected Internet users. Since gay and bisexual men use the Internet more often and engage in more frequent sexual behavior than heterosexual men, if frequency of Internet activity is the single criterion for extreme cybersex behavior, then many gay and bisexual men will be pathologized for engaging in what, for their subculture, stage of coming out, or level of isolation, is healthy or normative sexual behavior. Without reliable data about how gay and bisexual men use the Internet and without clear definitions of what constitutes pathological online behavior, it is unclear that gay and bisexual men are indeed at greater risk of developing extreme cybersex behavior. If frequency of Internet use is not the sole criterion for extreme cybersex behavior, then online activities are not equivalent, and duration of heavy Internet use also becomes relevant. It is generally agreed that further research in this area is needed. Clinicians should be wary of definitions of extreme cybersex behavior based solely on the statistics of Internet use.

In contrast to online surveys, clinical samples report lower rates of gay and bisexual men seeking treatment for sexual compulsivity. Among 100 men in treatment for compulsive masturbation, chronic infidelities, dependence on pornography, and other paraphilia-related problems, 10% identified as gay and 12% were bisexual (Kafka, 1997). Nearly half (46%) of the sample was currently married. Another sample (Schwartz & Southern, 2000) described 40 patients who were in treatment for problematic cybersex activity that included compulsive masturbation. Most patients were online 20 hours or more per week for sexual pursuits. Of the men, 58% were married. Although sexual orientation was not reported, 11% and 5% of men explored gay or bisexual themes online, respectively. No doubt, some cybersex compulsive men are gay or bisexual. However, the extent to which these groups are at greater risk of cybersex compulsivity may be based on subculturally different norms. Clinicians should be wary of extrapolating heterosexually based norms to homosexual samples.

By many accounts (Carnes, 1989; Cooper et al., 1999; Cooper et al., 2000; Schwartz & Southern, 2000; and perhaps Coleman, 1990), Brad's 3-year behavior would label him a sexual addict or cybersex compulsive. Brad's experience begs the question of how long frequent cybersex behavior must occur to be problematic, and none of the addiction/compulsion models predict spontaneous and permanent termination of cybersex behavior. Some people may get bored, while others may habituate and escalate their behavior to obtain the same gratification as previously (classically, this is typical of an addiction rather than recreational use). Although Brad may have minimized the problems produced by his extreme cybersex behavior, it is also possible that his behavior was a convergence of circumstances, loneliness, novel technology, and entertainment that simply ran its course. Two years later, Brad engages in no cybersex behavior or compulsive sexual behavior. Brad's own observation about differences among chat participants suggests one possible explanation: He has social skills and real-life social activities. However, further clinical research needs to distinguish between varieties of cybersex behavior and to identify reliable features of extreme cybersex behavior, as well as the natural histories of extreme cybersex use.

☐ Assessment and Treatment of Problematic Cybersex Behavior

Even without good definitions of extreme cybersex behavior, men who experience excessive and disruptive online behavior will present for treatment. Prevalence estimates differ by an order of magnitude. The National Council on Sexual Addiction and Compulsivity (NCSAC, 2000) claims that 2 million Internet users are sexually addicted. Cooper and colleagues (1999) placed this figure at potentially 4.6 million (8% of 57 million) who displayed some of the features of Internet sexual compulsivity. However, Cooper et al. (2000) revised this figure to a potential 200,000 by including high scores on the Kalichman sexual compulsivity scale and other data.

Descriptions of people in treatment for cybersex behavior just using statistically extreme scores and psychological scales are general and essentially uses screening tools. We suggest that an assessment of the adaptive or maladaptive nature of the extreme Internet use, including the nature, consequences, and context of the behavior, are critical to making a clinical judgment in the case of MSMs. Schwartz and Southern (2000) stated that at-risk individuals lack a history of sexual compulsivity but are depressed and stress reactive and therefore "vulnerable to developing sexual addiction after discovering the access, affordability, and anonymity provided by the Internet" (p. 136). We would suggest that negative mood states may be associated with lack of access to gay support or to uncertainty about the individual's orientation, and thus significant Internet use may also be an adaptive response to negative mood states. This is a critical distinction. Patients may not first present with cybersex compulsivity. Problematic cybersex behavior may be identified only after addressing depressed mood, unhappiness, marital or relationship problems, compulsive masturbation, sexual abuse, fetishism, job performance related to Internet use, chemical dependencies, sexual orientation, and feelings of guilt and shame. A thorough assessment of all dimensions of functioning is necessary to identify problematic behaviors and their contingencies. Satel (1993) warned against labeling problems prematurely and ignoring significant coexisting conditions. As always, incapacitating symptoms, including suicidal ideation or severe depression require priority attention.

In his comprehensive review of treatment modalities for sexual paraphilia-related disorders (including compulsive cybersex), Kafka (2000) noted that relationship dynamics, where there is a primary sexual relationship, may have an impact on the course of treatment. He notes also that the sudden revelation of compulsive cybersex in a partner during a stable relationship may create relationship dysfunction, which may in turn exacerbate the extreme cybersex behavior as a result of a cooling or withdrawal of the relationship or disappearance of trust. Thus, relationship dynamics bear close examination, particularly when they are in flux from the recent impact of a disclosure or feelings of betrayal. In such cases, the relationship dynamics may serve to actually strengthen the extreme cybersex behavior through the withdrawal of emotional and sexual support. Attempting treatment in such a context before attempting to deal with the relationship crisis is not advisable. Kafka suggested that the quality of current sexual intimacy and interpersonal communication where there is an existing pair bond may profoundly influence treatment outcome.

Cybersex treatment approaches divide into two camps. The "addictions" people (Carnes, 1989; Goodman, 1993; Schwartz & Southern, 2000) take an Alcoholics Anonymous (AA)/12-step recovery treatment approach, which focuses on admitting powerlessness over the addiction, spiritual development, and peer support. Abstinence is a central feature of the AA model, although cybersex addiction treatment does not forbid computer use. Rather, cybersex treatment stresses time-limited abstinence or "celibacy contracts" (e.g., Carnes, 1989). Software programs (e.g., CyberPatrol, Disk Tracy, NetNanny, Surfwatch, Web Guardian, etc.) are used to block access to sexual sites, although these can be circumvented. Behavioral interventions, such as moving the computer to a highly visible area, help to reduce cybersex activity. AA models of treatment tend to discourage and distrust pharmacological interventions (Coleman, 1990).

Group psychotherapies, according to Kafka (2000), have been used successfully with gay and bisexual men. Quadland (1985) reported on the use of outpatient group psychotherapy with the goal of controlling repeated sexual contacts in these patients. The use of 12-step programs to deal with addictive or compulsive behaviors and the self-help nature of 12-step programs have a number of advantages. They may be accessible and the methods may be familiar to participants who are likely to have become familiar with the methodology through participation for chemical addictions: Schwartz and Southern (2000) reported that in their sample of 40 heterosexual cybersex compulsives, over 70% of men and 40% of women had a previous history of chemical dependence. Such therapy groups are not financially burdensome, they lessen the shame surrounding both sexuality and sexual compulsion by providing a supportive environment of peers in the same situation, they add a spiritual (though not necessarily religious) component lacking in most other treatment modalities, and they use "sponsors" who function as role models and provide important social-cognitive support to what is essentially a peer-led approach. They also have the advantage of being geographically widespread, providing long-term availability, and being accessible lifelong if necessary. As "healing communities" that utilize many of the effective aspects of peer-led social-cognitive therapy (Bandura, 1986), 12-step programs have some distinct advantages for stigmatized behaviors and social statuses, and in our opinion are underestimated and underutilized. Specifically, many gay-specific 12-step programs are available in major metropolitan areas. For men who have previously successfully attended 12-step programs for chemical addictions, this may be a treatment of choice given the amount of positive transfer of training available. Further, the group support that is a central part of 12-step programs will have the effect of meeting the gay community and affiliation needs of gay men.

The "compulsion/hypersexuality" camp (Coleman, 1990, 1991; Kafka, 1991; Quadland, 1985) supports a pharmacological treatment approach. Selective serotonin reuptake inhibitors (SSRIs) such as fluoxetine (Prozac), sertraline (Zoloft), paroxetine (Paxil), citalopram (Celexa), and lithium carbonate effectively reduce or eliminate obsessive-compulsive symptoms and sexual desire. SSRIs are used primarily to treat depression, and sexual performance problems are often an unhappy side effect. While the SSRIs reduce problematic sexual behavior, development of new healthy thoughts and behaviors are supported by cognitive-behavioral interventions that address stress management, social skills, communication, and healthy sexuality. Addiction programs usually include similar auxiliary psychotherapies (Orzack & Ross, 2000; Schwartz & Southern, 2000). Kafka (2000) noted that there are some encouraging data suggesting that pharmacotherapy for associated disorders such as depression and other mood and anxiety disorders is effective. Further, there appears to be some rationale for the fact that increased sexual arousal and disinhibited sexual appetites may be mitigated by pharmacological agents that enhance CNS serotonin. In particular, there are case reports of the effectiveness of SSRIs even in the absence of significant mood disorders. While there are insufficient data, according to Kafka, the use of SSRIs, psychostimulants, and sometimes also orally administered antiandrogens may have a significant effect in ameliorating nonpsychotic hypersexuality disorders.

Both treatment approaches to extreme cybersex behavior are more consistent with treatment of eating disorders than OCD or substance dependence, which may be a better model for cybersex treatment (Orzack & Ross, 2000). Similarly, cybersex treatment focuses on eliminating inappropriate behaviors—not banning sexual behavior or computer use, but promoting healthier sexuality and computer use. Computer use is a sufficiently important occupational skill in the 21st century that we must assume that it cannot be avoided entirely just because there is a disorder associated with it—just as one cannot entirely avoid eating even if one has an eating disorder. Treatment simultaneously addresses chronic associated problems—depression, low self-image, distorted body image, anxiety, loss of control, and conflicted sexuality—through behavioral interventions, skill development, and by challenging irrational thoughts. Like eating disorders, cybersex compulsions affect sexuality and intimate relationships. Associated therapeutic issues for gay and bisexual men in treatment for extreme cybersex behavior include unresolved feelings about sexual orientation, internalized homophobia and stigmatization, managing life in a heterosexist culture, spirituality, intimacy and communication with partner, safer sex, and the role monogamy plays in a committed relationship. For probably the majority of homosexually oriented men in North America, who live outside the major metropolitan areas that have organized gay subcultures, and who probably exist in an exclusively heterosexual milieu, the Internet may be one of the only opportunities outside of vacations to exist in an environment in which they can be themselves. High Internet use in such a circumstance may be the only opportunity to exist in a supportive context in a life that is otherwise hidden and stigmatized.

Cognitive–behavioral therapies, as described by Kafka (2000), evolved from relapse prevention programs for chemical abuse and eating disorders. They are commonly used in sex offender programs as well. They involve identifying cognitive distortions associated with hypersexual behavior, sensitizing patients to recognize and anticipate high-risk situations, identifying precursors to relapse, and implementing behavioral rehearsal of alternative behaviors as well as social skills training. Essentially, for men who have sex with men, it takes a similar approach to the classic work of Serber and Keith (1974), who embarked upon a treatment program with incarcerated homosexual men which started with the premise that their problems with their homosexuality were a function of their inability to make meaningful gay contacts rather than with their sexual orientation as such. Serber and Keith reported on a successful homosexual retraining program in which homosexual inmates were provided with retraining in social behaviors, using well-adjusted gay role models and social supports

Several treatment programs specialize in cybersex addiction or compulsion, but despite preliminary claims of treatment success, outcome data for these programs have at the time of writing not been published.

☐ Emerging Issues

Cybersex compulsion is one important new area of concern. Although for most people OSAs are not frequent or problematic, a few people experience excessive online behavior and significant distress.

A current area of concern is the Internet as a vector for the spread of STDs, including HIV. The San Francisco Department of Public Health (SFDPH) recently documented an outbreak of syphilis among participants of an M4M chatroom (Klausner, Wolf, Fischer-Ponce, Zolt, & Katz, 2000). Two gay men with new cases of early syphilis met most of their partners in a chatroom called SFM4M and knew only their partners' screen names. SFM4M chat participants received e-mail messages informing them of the syphilis outbreak and encouraging them to seek medical evaluation if they met their partners in the chatroom. The number of gay men evaluated at the clinic increased by 18% for the next month, and five additional cases were identified among SFM4M participants. These data suggest that at least some gay men who meet sexual partners in chatrooms engage in risky sexual activities and that disease prevention messages posted in chatrooms have some effectiveness in encouraging testing.

The Denver Public Health HIV Counseling and Testing Site compared risk of STD transmission among people who seek sexual partners online with those who do not (McFarlane, Bull, & Rietmeijer, 2000). Most study participants were White (77.8%), male (69.2%), heterosexual (65.3%), and 20–50 years old (84.1%). Of the 856 participants, 135 (15.8%) people sought sexual partners online, of which 88 (65.2%) met online partners for sex. Internet sex seekers were mostly male (90.4%) and gay (59.4%). One-third was heterosexual, and 13 were women. Internet sex seekers reported sexual contact with MSMs (65.4%), women (64.4%), HIV-positive partners (28.9%), anal sex (69.4%), and previous STDs (29.4%). Half of recent sexual encounters included a condom. None of the Internet sex seekers were HIV infected. While a small number of people who request an HIV test currently seek sexual partners on the Internet, gay men are most likely to do this, and STD transmission risk factors among Internet sex seekers are high. Together these two studies suggest that the Internet will contribute to the spread of STDs/HIV and that online disease prevention messages are needed. From the clinician's perspective, if patients have engaged in offline sexual activity, STD and HIV screening should be strongly encouraged.

A third area of interest, especially for MSMs, is how the Internet impacts sexuality development. As discussed earlier, gay and bisexual men may use the Internet to create a virtual support community and resolve conflict over sexual feelings. In chatrooms and e-mail, identity and sexual fantasies can be explored rather than in gay bars, public restrooms, or sex clubs. Thus, access to sexual materials on the Internet may facilitate healthy gay and bisexual male identity formation, increased self-esteem and mental health, and coming to terms with one's sexual identity at an earlier age. Heterosexual identity formation is also likely to be affected, and probably strengthened, by home access to sexually explicit images and materials, exploration of sexual fantasies, and occasional gender bending. This effect may first be observed among young people who are frequent users of the Internet. However, openness about sexuality, tolerance of less typical sexual practices, and reduction of homophobia as a result of online experiences may be limited by the number of people who engage in regular cybersex behavior and the extent to which private attitudes are expressed publicly. While in America, it has been argued that the ethnic technological divide will confine cybersexuality to a phenomenon among Whites, recent survey data suggest that African Americans are only a few years behind Whites in their Internet use, so studies based on race and ethnicity are urgently needed.

Greater societal and sexual openness often results in social discomfort with access to sexual information and the kinds of sexuality being exposed. Critics predict social disaster and call for greater regulation of behavior. In this context, the cybersex addiction/compulsion phenomenon can be seen as a reaction to greater access to sexual materials and the appearance of unrestrained sexuality. Several writers (Cooper et al., 1999, 2000; Schwartz & Southern, 2000) have portrayed cybersex behavior as widespread and out of control. Cooper and colleagues (1999) predicted that 4.6 million people may have a cybersex problem and stated that the public must be forewarned about "these modern day Sirens (the Internet) . . . luring them to the rocks." The NCSAC (2000) described cybersex as "dangerous." However, Cooper et al. (1999) also wrote about the enormous potential of the Internet in terms of its advantages as well as risks and the importance of leaders in the field educating the public and clients on how to realize the benefits of the Internet while avoiding its potential pitfalls. Orzack and Ross (2000) called cybersex an "extremely potent addiction" and compared it to crack cocaine; they characterized nonheterosexual behaviors are signs of addiction "escalation" (Sexual Addiction Recovery Resources, 2000). However, as Kafka (2000) noted, it is common to find that those with extreme cybersex behavior have previous histories of sexual compulsion or related addictions prior to their having access to the Internet; thus, the issue may simply be a new forum for the expression of the problem rather than the creation of a new source of pathology. The main point is not that extreme cybersex behavior is a reaction to social events or that addiction models are sex-negative (Coleman, 1990) but that some writers illustrate fears about unrestrained sexuality as a result of the Internet. What is more, homonegativism is evident in premature predictions that gay and bisexual men's sexual behavior is most out of control. Whether the Internet is ultimately a blessing or a curse, the technology has already impacted our thinking about sexuality and reignited old fears. Concerns about the negative, rather than the positive, aspects of MSMs' Internet use should not focus attention solely on its clinical problems but also on its clinical possibilities, discussed later in this chapter.

☐ Coexisting Disorders

It may not be uncommon for sexual compulsion to coexist with other disorders, and in such cases, it is important to treat these disorders at the same time. Kafka (2000) reported that in a large series of outpatient males with either paraphilia-related disorders or paraphilias, 86% of the paraphilic sample had at least one lifetime paraphilic-related disorder, most commonly compulsive masturbation or pornography dependence. Often, he indicates, there may be reduced sexual arousal to "conventional" partnered sex, especially when the initial infatuation has passed. Kafka also noted that because of this reduced sexual arousal, such conditions may initially present as sexual *hypo*activity. Schneider (2000) described the responses of spouses to the discovery of compulsive cybersex in their partner and noted the devastation and repugnance that seems to accompany this discovery. This can lead to sexual withdrawal, but Schneider also reported that the spouses indicated that in more than half the cases, the cybersex-compulsive partners were minimally interested in sex with them. Clearly, there will be interactive factors in such relationships, and Schneider noted the limitations of her self-selected sample, but in terms of the primary relationship, hyposexuality appears to be a common occurrence, combined with Internet hypersexuality. It is therefore essential to initiate the consultation with a full lifetime sexual history (Ross, Channon-Little, & Rosser, 1999).

☐ The Importance of Cybersex to Gay Acculturation

Given the fact that psychological treatments can be effective where the client or patient is significantly distressed and disadvantaged by his hypercybersexuality, it may also be important to consider the place that cybersexuality may play in the psychological adjustment of gay men and MSMs. Thus, removal or modification of an important part of an individual's sexual expression must also be considered as a potential negative step. The role of the gay cybercommunity is potentially important in the ability to "come out" at one's own speed and while maintaining a degree of control, and what is considered excessive use may in fact be psychologically advantageous to an individual who is geographically or socially isolated from accessible gay communities. "Lurking" in a gay chatroom may arguably be a safer way of learning about the gay subculture than doing the same in a gay bar. As Ross et al. (2000) have argued, sexual partner contact on the Internet may have both the advantage that explicit discussion about sexual safety and risk can proceed without many of the limitations and omissions of face-to-face verbal negotiation, and the disadvantage that sexual priming may occur. That is, when online sex has been "unsafe" (behavior that if carried out in person could transmit HIV or other STDs), then the subsequent real contact may have been scripted and this script may already be internalized.

The importance of gay acculturation should also not be underestimated. Ross et al. (1995), in their review of the importance of gay acculturation for social adjustment and avoidance of sexual risk behavior, note that the sense of belonging to a subculture, the social supports and psychological safety associated with being part of a community, and the importance of diffusion of safer sex norms utilizing role models and social support structures all reduce risk. Such risks are reduced with membership in a community, and to the extent that cybersexuality involvement adds to acculturation to such a community, it is advantageous. Further, it might now be argued that with the level of gay involvement in cybersexuality, the gay community is as much virtual as real.

☐ The Internet as a Treatment Modality

Consideration of use of the Internet and of treatment modalities would be incomplete without discussing the use of the Internet as a treatment modality itself. DeGuzman and Ross (1999) reviewed Internet technological capabilities for counseling and appropriate counseling models and concluded that client-centered, reality, and group therapies were all possible candidates for use of Internet-based counseling for HIV/AIDS issues, among others. Interviews with a licensed counselor in the field revealed that while there were concerns, including lack of visual and verbal cues, accessibility by the neediest, confidentiality, and increased client separation or isolation, there were also benefits. While Putnam and Maheu (2000) have argued that the Internet may be an inappropriate medium for treatment due to the relationship between the computer and sexual arousal, DeGuzman and Ross (1999) noted that for the isolated and those seeking information, such as MSMs isolated socially, geographically, or by sexual identity, the Internet may have significant advantages; indeed, excessive Internet use may in some cases be the equivalent of "self-medication." It is possible that initial advice and specific suggestions may be useful in attracting people who are concerned about excessive sexually related Internet use into self-help groups via chatrooms or inquiry into treatment. The use of the Internet to provide screening and self-help information (or even online self-help groups) may seem to be a paradoxical intervention, but it could act as a step toward limiting but not removing the inappropriate or damaging behavior, in much the same way as eating disorder programs seek to bring eating within normal bounds. From the point of sexuality and therapy, such an approach could contain aspects of the PLISSIT model (see Ross et al., 1999), by providing permission to see the behavior as problematic, limited information on the nature of the problem (perhaps with illustrative case histories), and some specific suggestions. After this point, if and when intensive therapy might be advisable, possible referral sources could be listed on the Web.

☐ Conclusions

Extreme cybersex behavior is poorly clinically defined and lacks conceptual support. The few self-selected online samples that are available inform but fail to identify the prevalence of problematic cybersex behavior. Studies based on clinical samples overly pathologize the phenomenon. Theory-driven hypotheses and methodological rigor are needed in future research.

While only a few people have difficulty regulating their Internet behavior, additional research is needed to reliably identify this group. Based on frequency of use and sexual compulsion scores, Cooper and colleagues (2000) believed that 1% of Internet users may have a cybersex compulsion and warn that gay and bisexual individuals are at increased risk of developing such problems. However, frequent cybersex behavior may be normative for gay and bisexual men, and for some, excessive cybersex behavior may be a phase of identity formation. For many gay and bisexual men, the Internet is a "safe" place to explore sexual feelings, discover others like them, and develop social and sexual relationships. Thus, the Internet may facilitate gay or bisexual identity development. One clear finding is that frequent Internet use is not necessarily synonymous with sexual compulsivity. Further research must distinguish between healthy and pathological cybersex behavior and how cybersex activity functions differently by age, sex, ethnicity, relationship status, sexual orientation, and the stage of acceptance of sexual orientation, as well as by geographical access to gay subcultures.

☐ References

Bandura, A. (1986). *Social foundations of thought and action: A social cognitive theory.* Englewood Cliffs, NJ: Prentice Hall.

Barth, R. J., & Kinder, B. N. (1987). The mislabeling of sexual impulsivity. *Journal of Sex & Marital Therapy, 13,* 12–13.

Berrill, K. T. (1992). Anti-gay violence and victimization in the United States: An overview. In G. M. Herek & K. T. Berrill (Eds.), *Hate crimes: Confronting violence against lesbians and gay men* (pp. 19–45). Newbury Park, CA: Sage.

Bingham, J. E., & Piotrowski, C. (1996). On-line sexual addiction: A contemporary enigma. *Psychological Reports, 79,* 257–258.

Boutin, A. (1988). *Biological and medical correlates of sexual compulsivity/addiction.* Paper presented at 2nd National Conference on Sexual Addiction/Compulsivity. Minneapolis, MN.

Carnes, P. (1983). *Out of the shadows: Understanding sexual addiction.* Minneapolis, MN: CompCare Publishers.

Carnes, P. (1989). *Contrary to love: Helping the sexual addict.* Minneapolis, MN: CompCare Publishers.

Carey, R. (1996). Betwixt and between: An organization's relationship with online communication. *SIECUS Report, 25*(1), 8–9.

Coleman, E. (1985). Developmental stages of the coming out process. In J. C. Gonsiorek (Ed.), *A guide to psychotherapy with gay and lesbian clients* (pp. 31–43). New York: Harrington Park Press.

Coleman, E. (1990). The obsessive-compulsive model for describing compulsive sexual behavior. *Journal of Preventive Psychiatry and Neurology, 2,* 9–14.

Coleman, E. (1991). Compulsive sexual behavior: New concepts and treatments. *Journal of Psychology & Human Sexuality, 4,* 37–52.

Cooper, A. (1998). Sexuality and the Internet: Surfing into the new millennium. *Cyberpsychology and Behavior, 1*(2), 181–187. Retrieved July 20, 2000, from http://www.sex-centre.com/internetsex_folder/sexual&internethtm%205

Cooper, A., Delmonico, D. L., & Burg, R. (2000). Cybersex users, abusers, and compulsives: New findings and implications. In A. Cooper (Ed.), *Cybersex: The dark side of the force* (pp. 5–29). New York: Taylor & Francis.

Cooper, A., Scherer, C. R., Boies, S. C., & Gordon, B. (1999). Sexuality on the Internet: From sexual exploration to pathological expression. *Professional Psychology Research and Practice, 30*(2), 154–164.

Cooper, A., & Sportolari, L. (1997). Romance in cyberspace: Understanding online attraction. *Journal of Sex Education and Therapy, 22*(1), 7–14. Retrieved July 20, 2000, from http://www.sex-centre.com/internetsex_folder/Romance%20in%20cyberspace2

DeGuzman, M. A., & Ross, M. W. (1999). Assessing the application of AIDS-related counseling and education on the Internet. *Patient Education and Counseling, 36,* 209–228.

Egan, J. (2000, December 10). Lonely gay teen seeking same: How Jeffrey found friendship, sex, heartache (and himself) online. *The New York Times Magazine.* Retrieved December 12, 2000, from http://www.nytimes.com/library/ magazine/home/ 20001210mag-online.html

Family Research Council. (2000). Position statement. Retrieved December 8, 2000, from http://www.trc.org/iss/hsx/index.cfm

Goodman, A. (1992). Sexual addiction: Designation and treatment. *Journal of Sex & Marital Therapy, 18,* 303–315.

Goodman, A. (1993). Diagnosis and treatment of sexual addiction. *Journal of Sex & Marital Therapy, 19,* 225–251.

Human Rights Campaign. (2000). *Discharges of gay and lesbian soldiers sky-rocket on eve of 5th anniversary of Don't Ask, Don't Tell, Don't Pursue policy.* Retrieved December 4, 2000, from http://www.hrc.org/hrc/hrcnews/1999/990122.html

Humphreys, R. A. L. (1970). *Tearoom trade: A study of impersonal sex in public places.* London: Duckworth.

Kafka, M. P. (1991). Successful antidepressant treatment of nonparaphilic sexual addictions and paraphilias in men. *Journal of Clinical Psychiatry, 52,* 60–65.

Kafka, M. P. (1997). Hypersexual desire in males: An operational definition and clinical implications for males with paraphilias and paraphilia-related disorders. *Archives of Sexual Behavior, 26,* 505–526.

Kafka, M. P. (2000). The paraphilia-related disorder: Nonparaphilic hypersexuality and sexual compulsivity/addiction. In S. R. Leiblum & R. C. Rosen (Eds.), *Principles and practice of sex therapy* (3rd ed., pp. 471–503). New York: Guilford Press.

Kalichman, S. C., Johnson, R. R., Adair, V., Rompa, D., Multhauf, K., & Kelly, J. A. (1994). Sexual sensation seeking: Scaled development and predicting AIDS-risk behavior among homosexually active men. *Journal of Personality Assessment, 62,* 385–397.

Klausner, J. D., Wolf, W., Fischer-Ponce, L., Zolt, I., & Katz, M. H. (2000, July 26). Tracing a syphilis outbreak through cyberspace. *Journal of the American Medical Association, 284*(4), 447–449.

Lambda Legal Defense and Education Fund. (2000). *State-by-state sodomy law update.* Retrieved December 4, 2000, from http://www.lambdalegal.org/cgi-bin/pages/documents/record?record=275

Laumann, E., Gagnon, J., Michael, R., & Michaels, S. (1994). *The social organization of sexuality: Sexual practices in the United States.* Chicago: University of Chicago Press.

McFarlane, M., Bull, S. S., & Rietmeijer, C. A. (2000, July 26). The Internet as a newly emerging risk environment for sexually transmitted diseases. *Journal of the American Medical Association, 284*(4), 443–446.

Mosner, C. (1993). A response to Aviel Goodman's "Sexual addiction: Designation and treatment." *Journal of Sex & Marital Therapy, 19,* 220–224.

National Council on Sexual Addiction and Compulsivity. (2000). *Cybersex and sexual addiction.* Retrieved November 9, 2000 from http://www.NCSAC.org/main.html

Orzack, M. H., & Ross, C. J. (2000). Should virtual sex be treated like other sex addictions? In A. Cooper (Ed.), Cybersex: The dark side of the force. *Journal Sexual Addiction & Compulsivity* (pp. 113–125). New York: Taylor & Francis.

Putnam, D. E., & Maheu, M. M. (2000). In A. Cooper (Ed.), Cybersex: The dark side of the force. *Sexual Addiction & Compulsivity* (pp. 91–112). New York: Taylor & Francis.

Quadland, M. C. (1985). Compulsive sexual behavior: Definition of a problem and an approach to treatment. *Journal of Sex and Marital Therapy, 11,* 121–132.

Rinehart, M. J., & McCabe, M. C. (1997). Hypersexuality: Psychopathology or normal variant of sexuality? *Sexual and Marital Therapy, 12,* 45–60.

Ross, M. W. (1977). Paradigm lost or paradigm regained? Behaviour modification and homosexuality. *New Zealand Psychologist, 6*(1), 42–51.

Ross, M. W., Channon-Little, L. C., & Rosser, B. R. S. (1999). *Sexual health concerns: Interviewing and history taking for health practitioners.* Philadelphia: F. A. Davis.

Ross, M. W., Fernández-Esquer, M. E., & Seibt, A. Understanding across the sexual orientation gap: sexuality as culture. In D. Landis & R. Bhagat (Eds.), *Handbook of intercultural training* (2nd ed., pp. 414–430). Beverly Hills, CA: Sage.

Ross, M. W., Tikkanen, R., & Månsson, S. A. (2000). Differences between Internet samples and conventional samples of men who have sex with men: Implications for research and HIV interventions. *Social Science and Medicine, 51,* 749–758.

Satel, S. L. (1993). The diagnostic limits of "addiction." *Journal of Clinical Psychiatry, 54,* 237.

Schneider, J. P. (2000). Effects of cybersex addiction on the family: Results of a survey. In A. Cooper (Ed.), *Cybersex: The dark side of the force* (pp. 31–58). New York: Taylor and Francis.

Schwartz, M. F., & Southern, S. (2000). Compulsive cybersex: The new tea room. In A. Cooper (Ed.), *Cybersex: The dark side of the force* (pp. 127–144). New York: Taylor and Francis.

Serber, M., & Keith, C. G. (1974). The Atascadero Project: Model of a sexual retraining program for incarcerated homosexual pedophiles. *Journal of Homosexuality, 1,* 87–97.

Sexual Addiction Recovery Resources. (2000). *Recovery resources on the Internet.* Retrieved December 4, 2000, from http://www.home.rmi.net/~slg/sarr/rroti.htm

Slater, L. (2000, November 19). How do you cure a sex addict? *The New York Times Magazine,* 96–102.

Tikkanen, R., & Ross, M.W. (2000). Looking for sexual compatibility: Experiences among Swedish men in visiting Internet gay chatrooms. *Cyberpsychology and Behavior, 3,* 605–616.

Tikkanen, R., & Ross, M. W. (2001). *Technological tearoom trade: Characteristics of Swedish men visiting gay Internet chatrooms.* Submitted for publication.

Troiden, R. R. (1989). The formation of homosexual identities. *Journal of Homosexuality, 17,* 43–73.

Mitchell S. Tepper
Annette F. Owens

4

CHAPTER

Access to Pleasure: Onramp to Specific Information on Disability, Illness, and Changes Throughout the Lifespan

All too often, sexual health is overlooked or ignored in the health care system (Tepper, 1992). The most common reasons for not providing sexual health care services from a provider's perspective include anxiety with regard to discussing sexuality with patients, inadequate training, lack of appropriate curriculum, and the health provider's belief that it is someone else's responsibility (Ducharme & Gill, 1990; Krueger 1991; Novak & Mitchell, 1988). Discomfort with and resistance to talking about sexual issues with people who have disabilities, chronic conditions, or are elderly is reinforced by societal attitudes that do not embrace the sexuality of those who are not young and healthy. Instead of routinely assessing patients' sexual health needs, many health professionals will wait for the patient to bring up a concern.

From the patient's or client's perspective, research shows that both men and women fear discussing sexual problems with their doctors because of concerns that physicians would be embarrassed with the topic (Partnership for Women's Health at Columbia, 1999). A telephone survey of 500 Americans over age 25 found that 68% of those polled worry that their physicians would be uncomfortable discussing sexual issues, with 75% of women expressing such concerns compared to 61% of men. Survey respondents also believe that sexual problems have an impact on a number of medical issues, including depression (91%), emotional stress (93%), poor self-image (88%), and extramarital affairs and marriage breakups (91%). Historically, men and women who interact with the health care system have had sexual concerns but felt they had nowhere to turn for help.

Silence about sexual health-related issues has made access to sexual health care from traditional sources difficult resulting in unnecessary suffering for many. This is especially true for the three discrete populations that are the focus of this chapter, namely, (a) people with disabilities, (b) people with chronic conditions, and (c) people who are in their later years. As noted, these groups have traditionally been sexually disenfranchised. Misconceptions about sexuality as they relate to these populations often add to the generally negative societal attitudes toward sexuality.

Now patients can turn to the Internet for help. The Internet has begun to bridge the sexual communication gap between provider and consumer. It offers a novel medium providing direct, private, and anonymous access to information about sexual health. The concept of sexual health includes treatment of underlying medical conditions that interfere with sexual and reproductive functions as well as freedom from fear, shame, guilt, false beliefs, and other psychological and social factors inhibiting sexual response and impairing sexual relationships.

In this chapter we will give a brief overview of previous research about sexuality and disability, chronic illness, and aging, provide demographic information on Internet use among the groups focused on, examine how people with disabilities, chronic conditions, and age after midlife have begun to utilize the Internet to gain access to sexual health information, and provide suggestions as to how the therapist can incorporate this phenomenon into his or her practice. We will discuss this in general terms and give examples of existing Web sites.

☐ Brief Historical Overview

A rapidly growing novel focus on sexual health in the late 1960s and early 1970s brought along several publications on sexuality in conjunction with physical disability and chronic conditions (Anderson & Cole, 1975; Diamond, 1974; Krieger, 1977). Pioneering studies on individuals with spinal cord injuries in the 1950s and early 1960s laid some of the foundations for this work (Tsuji et al., 1961; Zeitlin, Cottrell, & Lloyd, 1957). As reviewed by Kaplan (1990), some studies on sexuality and aging date back even further (Kinsey, Pomeroy, & Martin, 1948, 1953; Masters & Johnson, 1966, 1970; Palmore, 1970, 1974).

When reviewing past literature, it is striking how little progress has been made. Society's regard of physically disabled people as nonsexual beings is largely unchanged (Mona & Gardos, 2001). It is still widely believed that a physically disabled person is either unable to engage in sexual activity or does not have a need for sexual expression (Anderson & Cole, 1975). Sex primarily appears to be reserved for the young, healthy, and fertile population.

Why have attempts to abolish these myths and to educate the general public about the rich sexual experiences and potential of older people and those with disabilities or chronic conditions failed? One simple explanation may be that the information has yet to reach a wider audience. While articles can be found in academic journals and movement is underway within the disability community, within populations of specific chronic conditions, and among retired people, the mainstream media has not given much attention to this matter. Media portrayals of the sexuality of people with disabilities is sensationalized and still exaggerates the tragedy of lost sexuality after a devastating injury instead of producing plots that include people with disabilities as sexy and capable of healthy sexual relationships.

The Internet may prove a superior medium for dissemination of information on sexual health that heretofore has been relegated to academic journals and segregated identity movements. By providing access to information about sexual health to a broader population, including older people, people with disabilities, and people with chronic conditions, it may finally become obvious that sexual expression does continue after midlife and that it is an important part of life for people with chronic illness and disability.

☐ People With Disabilities, Chronic Conditions, and Natural Changes With Aging, and Their Use of the Internet

Adult Internet users with disabilities, chronic illnesses, and natural changes associated with growing older comprise a large and very broad demographic group. The U.S. Department of Justice, in its deliberations on the Americans with Disabilities Act, estimated that 20% of the American population has a disability that impairs a major life function. Within this group, an estimated 21.6% have Internet access (U.S. Department of Commerce, 2000). With 196 million adults in the United States in 2000 (U.S. census projection for persons over 20 years old, U.S. Census Bureau, 1996), these percentages give a figure of 39.2 million adults with disabilities, of whom 8.5 million have Internet access. Of course, the Internet is not limited to the United States, so the global number of people with disabilities is much larger.

Within this broad demographic group there are segments defined by specific disabilities and/or chronic conditions. These include spinal cord injury, multiple sclerosis, cerebral palsy, cancer, diabetes, arthritis, developmental disabilities, psychiatric disabilities, HIV/AIDS, and learning disabilities, to name just a few. The Internet offers opportunities for continuous tailoring of Web site content to specific needs and conditions.

The Internet provides individuals with chronic illness, disability, and/or age-related concerns access to pleasure by making professional information available to them. It also allows individuals to emerge from isolation and to establish contacts with others in similar situations, thereby providing each other with understanding and support (Cooper, McLoughlin, & Campbell, 2000).

Overlapping the disability and chronic condition populations is the aging population. A significant group that might be considered under this categorization is the baby boomer population. Over time, most individuals will develop some disabling conditions with possible repercussions on their sexual health. With the baby boomers moving into their older years, this population is growing much faster than that of the general population. While 22% of adults in the United States reported a disability in 1999, this figure increased to 50% for adults 65 years of age and older (Prevalence of Disabilities and Associated Health Conditions among Adults—United States, 1999, www.cdc.gov/mmwr, Feb. 23 issue).

The baby boomer population includes people born between the late 1940s and the early 1960s. Thus, today most boomers are nearly or already over 40. Boomers have transformed every stage of life they have reached. Retirement and old age are likely to be changed as well. Boomers created the sexual revolution as they reached adulthood. Never inclined to accept limitations, boomers are not likely to settle for less satisfactory sex lives just because they get older. Thus they are likely to be eager consumers of any product or service that helps them meet these needs.

The level of interest by boomers is likely to increase as they move into the older age groups, and as their Internet access and sophistication increases. U.S. population projections show an increase in the population over age 40 from 116 million to 137 million over 10 years (U.S. Census Bureau, 1996). During this same time, Internet access is projected to increase from 56% in 1999 to 90% in 2009, and the over-40 population with Internet access is estimated to nearly double over a period of 5 years, from 65 million in 1999 to 115 million in 2004. More than 1 billion people are estimated to have Internet access by year 2005 (eTForecasts, 2001), and a recent study by NetValue, a global leader in tracking and interpreting online behavior, shows that the number of retired people going online in the United States jumped by 28.1% in December 2000, to a total of 8.6 million unique visitors. This surge has the online retired population now representing 10.2% of the overall Internet population (NetValue, 2001).

☐ The Internet as a Useful Tool for the Described Populations

The driving force for the Internet with respect to sexual expression consists of three key factors: access, affordability, and anonymity. Cooper (1998) has termed these factors the "triple-A engine" of the Internet, which makes the Internet a unique forum for accessing information about sexuality, pursuing specific sexual interests, and establishing sexual contacts. No other more conventional medium such as books, magazines, TV, or video has a similar promise as the Internet (Cooper, Boies, Maheu, & Greenfield, 1999).

For the populations discussed in this chapter, accessibility is of major importance and carries special meaning. People with disabilities, chronic conditions, and who are retired regularly face architectural and attitudinal barriers to sexual health. As will be described in the following, people with disabilities, chronic conditions, or advanced aging may now access information about their specific needs and concerns through the Internet. Chatrooms, forum boards, instant messaging, and "ask the expert" columns are all mediums that have helped the sexual lives of these populations, as they do for all others.

The populations discussed in our chapter can use the Internet as a very positive tool. These sexually disenfranchised populations can benefit from the access, affordability, anonymity, and the virtual communities that develop around common sexual questions, concerns and shared experiences. The Internet enables previously isolated individuals to become part of such virtual communities, where they may find empathy, support, and a sense of community and belonging (Cooper, Boies, et al., 1999). This, in return, may have positive psychological effects on the individual. As a flip side, increased Internet use may expose some of these individuals to the dangers of the Internet.

The following case example demonstrates how the Internet helped a quadriplegic man to overcome a long-term fear of having sex. His adolescent sexual inhibition became compounded by a spinal cord injury acquired at age 20. Online communication served as a bridge to establishing and pursuing a successful offline sexual relationship for the first time in his life, 17 years after his accident.

Bruce (an alias) is a 37-year-old quadriplegic, who acquired a cervical (c4/5) spinal cord injury from a diving accident. He is college educated, interested in journalism, and lives in an addition to his parents' house with 24-hour personal care assistants (PCAs) who help with the activities of daily life. Bruce's preinjury sex life consisted of one occasion of heavy petting as a teenager. His injury left him with no sensation below his upper chest and with only limited function in one arm. He has reflex erections in response to touch but does not experience orgasm or ejaculation. He received no sexual education or counseling during his rehabilitation.

For years after his accident, Bruce was in unrequited love with his former best friend. Bruce contacted Dr. Tepper's Web site (www.sexualhealth.com) with the following comments:

> The lust I had for her and others, while never directly expressed, tortured me and drove me to selfish, hostile behavior that hurt very kind friends . . . I have little desire to attempt physical sex, and lots of reservations. I fear I might be more of a spectator than a participant. When prone, I have no arm/hand function, no sensation below my upper chest, and penetration is not feasible. All that works is my mouth. I know these problems aren't insurmountable for everyone, but it would be great to hear about any similarly (dys)functioning guys or women who have succeeded at an ongoing relationship.

In subsequent postings, Bruce expressed doubt that he would ever have a physical relationship. He relayed that he had several wonderfully close platonic women friends but was unable to appreciate some of them because of unexpressed sexual desires. In his own words:

> I lusted for them, feeling guilty and frustrated. It's not just society that emphasizes sex; it's biological urges too, especially with my massive libido. When one friend offered to listen to my repressed feelings about sexuality, presto! Everything changed! Discussing sexuality with women cured my unrequited lust, and freed me to find a great sex-oriented relationship online. I am very fulfilled now, just curious about crips like me who manage successful long-term relationships.

Bruce coined the term "hands-free whoopee" to describe sexual excitement and fulfillment through mental activity and without involvement of physical stimulation of sex organs. He was now able to describe fantasies to partners verbally over the phone and by e-mail exchanges. He later wrote:

> My experience with written sex doesn't seem typical of "cybersex." I feel that my circumstances are fairly unusual—lack of privacy, lack of in-person confidence, love of and talent for writing, hyper-horniness, and most of all luck in finding a couple of women whose needs matched mine. These relationships were also not typical of cybersex because they included a dimension of love. I have felt guilty and ashamed of my libido for years; so

have my disabled lovers, and we cured each other—sort of a self-help sex therapy. Maybe there are more lonely, isolated and horny disabled folks than I think, but a great majority of people online either have in-person sex lives or very much want them.

Reservations and fear contributing to little desire to attempt physical sex are predictable outcomes of disability when sexual education is lacking during rehabilitation and there are few role models to learn from (Tepper, 1996; Tepper dissertation 2001). The Internet had given Bruce an outlet for his sexual expression and a source of brief professional counseling. His relationships based on written online communications combined with a greater vision of his possibilities provided by Dr. Tepper gave him the confidence to overcome his reluctance about sex. Eventually, a chance for a physical love relationship developed, and in the following text, Bruce describes a physical encounter with Wendy (an alias), an acquaintance he had met online.

> Writer that I am, I'm not sure I can find the words to convey how wonderful Wendy's visit was. It can't be true that waiting till age 37 was worth it! And yet if I had it to do over again, I really don't think I could bring myself to choose a life that doesn't include every blissful second of our 16 hours in heaven. In the realm of physical love, I have been massively deprived of quantity but extraordinarily blessed with quality. It's almost as if those two extremes are inversely proportional! Wendy's visit provided so much incentive! Not just the obvious kind; she makes me feel so confident in areas unrelated to sex and love, too. . . . But probably our greatest discovery wasn't primarily sexual. As she stood next to the chair, I realized that I could get my good arm around her and hug her quite strongly. I can hold her, Mitch! She LOVED it! I loved it! Until we get a lot more extended time together (which probably will happen, though not for several months), a lot of the brief time we have is bound to go to holding each other. Then we'll break out the toys!

Wendy eventually relocated with her teenage daughter to be closer to Bruce, with the intention of eventually getting married.

☐ Scientific Studies

While there are some early studies outlining the demographics of cybersex users of the Internet (Cooper, Delmonico, & Burg, 2000; Cooper, Scherer, Boies, & Gordon, 1999) and a new study that seeks to understand user profiles in online sexual activity (Cooper, Morahan-Martin, Mathy, & Maheu, 2002), we are unaware of any published studies that quantify the number of people utilizing the Internet to gain access specifically to information about sexual health. Data from our own Web site offering general information about sexual health is briefly summarized below. Parts of this analysis have been previously communicated (Tepper & Owens, 2000).

Nearly 600 questions presented over a 4-month period in 2000/2001 to a team of over 40 sexual health experts at www.SexualHealth.com, were analyzed. About 75% of inquisitors were from within the United States, while most other continents were represented to lesser degrees. Men and women were equally represented, and a few individuals listed their gender as transgender or intersex. Visitors' ages ranged from teenagers to individuals over 59 years, with the mode in age range from 20 to 29 years.

Not surprisingly, women mostly asked about low sexual desire, sexual pain, and orgasm, while men's top concerns were masturbation, erections, and ejaculation, including premature and delayed ejaculation.

Roughly 20% of the questions were requests for basic information about items such as anatomy (3%), physiology (10%), medication effects (2%), sexual positions (1%), and terminology (2%). The remaining 80% of questions were requests for specific information on topics such as sexual problems related to age, chronic conditions, and disability.

From this small sample we conclude that whether otherwise healthy or challenged by chronic illness, age, or disabilities, online users are willing to use the Internet as a medium for seeking general advice and specific information about sexual concerns (Tepper & Owens, 2000). As a consequence, the Internet is a viable way for health professionals to provide information to a wide audience. Our analysis further reveals the broad range of sexual issues people have been struggling with, some heretofore in silence, and reflects the dire need for more and better sexual education and counseling.

☐ Different Ways of Utilizing the Power of the Internet to Gain Access to Pleasure

In the following, we have summarized different ways for clients and clinicians to utilize the Internet for specific purposes. The listed categories apply not only to sexual health information, but to many other areas of interest as well.

Specific Information

The Internet makes access to pleasure possible by making general as well as and disability- or illness-specific sexual health information easily available. Heretofore, this type of information was relegated to obscure journals targeted toward academics and was not accessible to consumers. Clarifying myth-information and finding accurate information is the first step toward sexual enlightenment.

Affordable, Anonymous Access

The triple-A engine (Cooper, 1998) allows Internet users easy access to credentialed health professionals who can inform and offer advice regarding sexual health and sexual problems one-to-one and in groups. There is a shortage of well-trained sexual health professionals with expertise in the intersection of sexuality and disability or illness. The Internet lets those with experience make themselves known and provides users with affordable, anonymous access to these health professionals.

Peer Support

Access to pleasure is also made possible by providing forums and chats for objective discussions of sexual matters among peers and facilitating interpersonal contacts. Potential pitfalls of using the Internet are noted elsewhere in this book. Also, if someone learns to rely too much on computer-mediated relating (CMR; Cooper, Boies, et al., 1999) as a way of fulfilling their sexual needs, there may be too little motivation to pursue in-person relationships. However, for disabled, chronically ill, and older Internet users, it is sometimes difficult to meet sexual partners in general, and online sexual contacts may be welcome additions to their lives.

e-Learning

The Internet increases opportunities for training and continuing education of health service personnel with respect to sexual health. Equipped with superior knowledge, these individuals will be better prepared and more likely to address sexual health–related concerns with their patients. The major sexuality organizations provide listservs for members, where difficult cases can be discussed in a professional forum and information and announcements may be posted on bulletin boards. Other educational resources are online seminars and courses. The field of e-learning is rapidly growing and will revolutionize the ways in which professionals will be able to receive continuing education.

e-Commerce

The Internet makes access to pleasure possible by making sexual health–related products easily available for purchase (Fisher & Barak, 2000). Clients may be more comfortable buying sex-related products online. Retail stores for such products tend to be located in major metropolitan areas, and only a minority of potential customers have direct physical access to these stores.

Links and Contacts

Finally, computer links to the disability community and information about other online as well as offline resources make up a sexual health network, which allows clients and clinicians to effectively navigate the broad field of sexual health. For people with disabilities, this network of sexual health information provides a true onramp to pleasure.

☐ How Clinicians Can Utilize the Internet to Better Serve Their Clients

In addition to taking advantage of the above-mentioned ways to keep informed and up-to-date, clinicians should become familiar with the best sites in their specific area of interest and use them to complement their therapies (Family Life Matters, 2001). Therapists and other health professionals may want to provide patients with a list of regularly updated, high-quality sites and help them navigate "the mean streets" by demonstrating how to avoid exploitive or pornographic sites (Gotlib & Fagan, 1997). Due to a rapidly changing market, it is advisable to periodically use the major search engines for newly developed sites. The Sexuality Information and Education Council of the United States (SIECUS) provides regularly updated lists of Internet sources at SIECUS.org. The American Association of Sex Educators, Counselors, and Therapists (AASECT) has a Web site, AASECT.org, with current information and links. Many organizations with a specific focus, such as the American Heart Association, the National Multiple Sclerosis Society, or the American Diabetes Association specifically address sexual health topics on their Web sites. University- or hospital-based sites and sites that have been approved by Health On the Net or Truste are likely to be reliable sources as well.

Clinicians also may find the Internet to be a useful tool for informing themselves in areas in which their clients are well versed, thereby gaining greater understanding of the patient perspective. They should find out what sites their clients are visiting and what types of support, chat, or newsgroups they frequent. Clinicians may then be able to assist their clients to better use these resources. Health professionals may even aid with specific tasks, such as helping their patients to write personal ads and assisting them in registering for community classes promoting computer skills and literacy. We recommend having informational brochures about such services readily available in the office. Clinicians may find useful information on these sites, or they may take online continuing education courses or join a professional listserv within their particular area of interest. At present, several organizations, such as AASECT, the Female Sexual Function Forum (FSFF), and the International Society for Sexual and Impotence Research (ISSIR) have listservs that offer professionals a forum and a network for discussing difficult cases. This is one particular area of communication between clinicians that is likely to expand considerably in the future.

☐ Telehealth: Implications and Special Considerations

The use of the Internet for telehealth applications provides a unique medium for distributing basic sexual health information, education, and specific advice to a growing population. The Telemedicine Report to Congress of January 1997 (U.S. Department of Commerce) defined telemedicine as the use of electronic communication and information technologies to provide or support clinical care at a distance. Telehealth is a broader concept that includes clinical care in addition to the related areas of health professional education, consumer health education, public health, research, and administration of health services. The World Wide Web has the potential of reaching users in remote and rural settings, where medical care and mental health assistance is not readily available. However, ethical considerations and concerns need to be carefully evaluated before telehealth is more fully adopted and utilized along with traditional healthcare models (U.S. Department of Congress: National Telecommunications and Information Administration, in consultation with the U.S. Department of Health and Human Services, 1997)

Some of these ethical issues have been addressed previously (Cooper, Boies, et al., 1999) and within this book (see chapter 12 of this book). In the following, we will summarize special considerations and issues of concern to health professionals who work with disabled and/or chronically ill and older clients. Many of these issues are covered more fully in The Telemedicine Report to the Congress (1997).

Licensure Requirements

Licensure requirements for health professionals vary between geographical regions. Licensure and malpractice concerns arise when a licensed health professional works across state lines or provides services on a multistate basis, as is highly likely using the Internet. The major issue is which state has the power to regulate or discipline a provider who "enters" a state to practice via telehealth technology, and in which state or jurisdiction the provider will answer a telehealth malpractice claim.

Anonymity

One of the driving factors of the Internet and part of the triple-A engine, anonymity, carries several negative implications for telehealth. The fact that Internet users have the option to remain anonymous may impact and limit the relationship between the sexual health professional and the client. The professional has no guarantee that the information provided is accurate. As a consequence, thorough exchange of information and in-depth therapy is often limited. However, basic guidance, and if necessary, encouragement to seek out health care providers within the client's local area can usually be given. Thereby, someone who has previously relied on self-help may be moved to consult a trained local provider.

Another consequence of anonymity is that the physical location of the person seeking assistance is often unknown. Possible legal implications of this fact are manifold. Consider a client acknowledging pedophilic tendencies or someone who confirms being sexually abusive to a child or a partner. How can the telehealth professional take the necessary steps to protect potential or actual victims if the physical location of those individuals cannot be revealed without involving major, ethically debatable efforts of tracing?

Privacy, Confidentiality, and Security

Privacy, confidentiality, and security issues unique to telemedicine, especially mental health records on conditions that carry a social stigma such as HIV, are other areas of concern, as are the verification of credentials by the consumer and verification of the consumer's identity by the provider. The Telemedicine Report to the Congress (1997 U.S. Department of Congress: National Telecommunications and Information Administration in consultation with the U.S. Department of Health and Human Services) noted that unlike standard medical record documentation, in which the health professional has discretion to selectively record his or her findings, most interactive telemedicine consultations are recorded in toto. This record usually is maintained as part of the documentation of the consultation. As a result, practitioners have less discretion to remove information that they might otherwise not record. Another concern is that the patient may not be able to "see" who else is viewing the session along with the clinicians on the other end of the long-distance consultation. Health Internet Ethics (HI Ethics) has defined ethical standards regarding privacy, confidentiality, credibility, reliability, and security at http://hiethics.com. Another Web site, National Board for Certified Couselors (NBCC) Standards for the Ethical Practice of WebCounseling at http://www.nbcc.org/ethics/wcstandards.htm recommends certain codes of conduct with respect to online counseling.

Treatment Concerns

Several implications relate to treatment concerns. Sex therapy has an enormous potential for client resistance and for failure to complete assignments given by the therapist. Providing supportive counseling may be possible, but trying to elicit significant behavioral changes may prove more challenging, especially in sexual areas. Only ongoing evaluation will determine how effective "full-fledged" sex therapy can be online and how well it will deal with clients with very complex issues. Furthermore, many clients with disability, illness, or changes with age have at least some biological etiology to their sexual dysfunctions and may need to undergo physical exams and treatments. Lastly, there is some concern about the ability to obtain an appropriate assessment without visual cues like facial expressions and body language. However, since visually impaired individuals are not barred from doing therapy, this challenge may be overcome if telehealth providers begin to develop and rely on different cues germane to the Internet. Also, there is the option of setting up cameras on both ends, which becomes more viable with the proliferation of broadband access.

Billing for the service may be difficult if the client remains anonymous or does not have an internationally accepted credit card. Reimbursement for services by third parties, managed care, Medicare, and Medicaid is a concern for the long-term growth of telemedicine and telehealth. Finally, the Telemedicine Report to the Congress (1997) highlighted the need to evaluate certain telemedicine projects. The questions of whether patients and providers can accept telemedicine-enabled care, and whether outcomes associated with the use of telemedicine are acceptable, can only be answered in the future and after pilot programs have been established and evaluated.

These general implications on telehealth all apply to the specific populations discussed in this chapter. As the Internet and telehealth evolves, access to information, education, counseling, and support regarding disability, chronic conditions, and aging will be expanded and become even more accessible and user-friendly.

☐ Conclusions

We hope to have given clinicians an overview of past and present efforts to provide sexual health information to those who are physically challenged by disability or chronic conditions and by normal and expected changes throughout the lifespan. We also have attempted to provide health professionals with specific tools to help them and their patients take the right exit from a potentially disturbing cybersex maze. We believe that as health care providers use the Internet to improve their clinical skills and expertise, the general sexual climate and interaction with their patients will benefit. Finally, looking into the future, as ethical guidelines with respect to telehealth are being developed, we invite clinicians to consider making their expertise available to future e-counseling services, thereby reaching out to a much broader group of clients.

The title of this chapter, "Access to Pleasure," reflects a positive approach to human sexuality based on the right to sexual information and the right to pleasure. The concept of sexual health includes treatment of underlying medical conditions that interfere with sexual and reproductive functions and freedom from fear, shame, guilt, false beliefs, and other psychological factors inhibiting sexual response and impairing sexual relationships. People with disabilities or chronic conditions and people who do not generally conform to the dominant culture's depiction of sexiness no longer have to suffocate behind a veil of sexual silence. The Internet as an onramp to specific information and related resources for heretofore sexually disenfranchised populations is one of the most positive aspects of the World Wide Web.

☐ References

Alpert, S. A. (1998). Health care information: Access, confidentiality, and good practice. In K. W. Goodman (Ed.), *Ethics, computing and medicine: Informatics and the transformation of health care* (pp. 75–101). Cambridge, UK: Cambridge University Press.

Anderson, T. P., & Cole, T. M. (1975). Sexual counseling of the physically disabled. *Postgraduate Medicine, 58*(1), 117–123.

Barak, A., & King, S. A. (2000) The two faces of the Internet: Introduction to the special issue on the Internet and sexuality. *Cyberpsychology & Behavior, 3*(4), 517–520.

Binik, Y. M., Cantor, J., Ochs, E., & Meana, M. (1997). From the couch to the keyboard: Psychotherapy in cyberspace. In S. Kiesler (Ed.), *Culture of the Internet* (pp. 71–100). Mahwah, NJ: Lawrence Erlbaum.

Cooper, A. (1998) Sexuality and the Internet: Surfing into the new millennium. *Cyberpsychology and Behavior, 1*, 181–187.

Cooper, A., Boies, S., Maheu, M., & Greenfield, D. (1999). Sexuality and the Internet: The next sexual revolution. In F. Muscarella & L. Szuchman (Eds.), *The psychological science of sexuality: A research based approach* (pp. 519–545). New York: Wiley Press.

Cooper, A., Delmonico, D. L., & Burg, R. (2000). Cybersex users, abusers, and compulsives: New findings and implications. *Sexual Addiction & Compulsivity, 7*, 5-29.

Cooper, A., McLoughlin, I. P., & Campbell, K. M. (2000). Sexuality in cyberspace: Update for the 21st century. *Cyberpsychology & Behavior, 3*(4), 521–536.

Cooper, A., Morahan-Martin, J., Mathy, R., & Maheu, M. (2002). Toward an increased understanding of user demographics in online sexual activities. *Journal of Sex and Marital Therapy, 28*, 105–129.

Cooper, A., Scherer, C., Boies, S. C., & Gordon, B. (1999). Sexuality on the Internet: From sexual exploration to pathological expression. *Professional Psychology: Research and Practice, 30*(2), 154–164.

Diamond, M. (1974). Sexuality and the handicapped. *Rehabilitation Literature, 35*, 34–40.

Ducharme, S., & Gill, K. M. (1990). Sexual values, training, and professional roles. *Journal of Head Trauma Rehabilitation, 5*(2), 38–45.

eTForecasts. (2001) *Internet users will surpass 1 billion in 2005.* Press release, Buffalo, IL, February 6. Retrieved from http://www.etforecasts.com/pr/pr201.htm

Family Life Matters. (2001). *Sexuality, education and the lure of the web.* Published by the network for Family Life Education, Piscataway, NJ, 42, pp. 4–5.

Fisher, W. A., & Barak, A. (2000). Online sex shops: Phenomenoligal, psychological, and ideological perspectives on Internet sexuality. *Cyberpsychology & Behavior, 3*(4), 575–589.

Goodman, K. W. (1998). Bioethics and health informatics: An introduction. In K. W. Goodman (Ed.), *Ethics, computing and medicine. Informatics and the transformation of health care* (pp. 1–31). Cambridge, UK: Cambridge University Press.

Gotlib, D. A., & Fagan, P. (1997). Mean streets of cyberspace: Sex education resources on the Internet's World Wide Web. *Journal of Sex Education and Therapy, 22*(1), 79–83.

Kaplan, H. S. (1990). Sex, intimacy, and the aging process. *Journal of The American Academy of Psychoanalysis, 18*(2), 185–205.

Kinsey, A. C., Pomeroy, W. B., & Martin, C. E. (1948). *Sexual behavior in the human male.* Philadelphia: Saunders.

Kinsey, A. C., Pomeroy, W. B., & Martin, C. E. (1953). *Sexual behavior in the human female.* Philadelphia: Saunders.

Korn, K. (1998). Computer comments. Disability information on the Internet. *Journal of The American Academy of Nurse Practitioners, 10*(9), 413–414

Krieger, S. M. (1977). Sexuality and disability. *ARN J., 2*(1), 8–10, 12–14.

Krueger, M. M. (1991). The omnipresent need: Professional training for sexuality education teachers. *SIECUS Report, 19*(4), 1–11.

Masters, W. B, & Johnson, V. E. (1966). *The human sexual response.* Boston: Little, Brown and Co.

Masters, W. B., & Johnson, V. E. (1970). *Human sexual inadequacy.* Boston: Little, Brown and Co.

Mona, L. R., & Gardos, P. S. (2001). Disabled Sexual Partners. In L. T. Szuchman & F. Muscarella (Eds.), *Psychological perspectives on human sexuality* (pp. 309–354). New York: Wiley.

NetValue. (2001, January 29). *NetValue study on: Retirees behavior online "Retired and Wired."* Retrieved from http://us.netvalue.com/presse/index_frame.htm?fichier=cp0024.htm

Novak, P. P., & Mitchell, M. M. (1988). Professional involvement in sexuality counseling for patients with spinal cord injuries. *American Journal of Occupational Therapy, 42*(2), 105–.112.

Palmore, E. (Ed.). (1970). *Normal aging.* Durham, NC: Duke University Press.

Palmore, E. (Ed.). (1974). *Normal aging II.* Durham, NC: Duke University Press.

Partnership for Women's Health at Columbia. (1999). *Adult attitudes towards sexual problems. National survey of American adults aged 25 and older.* Prepared for Gender and Human Sexuality: A Continuing Medical Education Conference presented by the Partnership for Women's Health at Columbia. Survey conducted by telephone by Bennett, Petts & Blumenthal, 1010 Wisconsin Avenue NW Suite 208, Washington, DC 20007, March 25–31, 1999.

Prevalence of Disabilities and Associated Health Conditions Among Adults—United States, 1999. (Feb. 23, 2001). Retrieved July 10, 2001 from http://www.cdc.gov/mmwr/preview/mmwrhtml/mm5007a3.htm

Promotion of Sexual Health. Recommendations for Action. (2000). Proceedings of a Regional Consultation convened by Pan American Health Organization (PAHO) and World Health Organization (WHO) in collaboration with the World Association for Sexology (WAS), Guatemala, May 19–22. Retrieved from http://www.rki.de/GESUND/ARCHIV/PSH.HTM#_Toc490155411

Starr, B. D., & Weiner, M. B. (1981). *The Starr-Weiner report on sex and sexuality in the mature years.* New York: McGraw-Hill.

Tepper, M. S. (1992). Sexual education in spinal cord injury rehabilitation: Current trends and recommendations. *Sexuality and Disability, 10,* 15–31.

Tepper, M. S. (1996). Hands-free whoopee. *New Mobility, 7*(37), 88–89.

Tepper, M. S. (2001). Dissertation, Lived experiences that impede or facilitate sexual pleasure and orgasm in people with spinal cord injury. University of Pennsylvania, Philadelphia.

Tepper, M. S. (2000). *Telemedicine and telehealth: Implications for sex counseling and therapy.* Paper presented at Sexuality and the Millennium: Integrating Tradition, Technique and Technology, American Association of Sex Educators, Counselors and Therapists Annual Meeting, Atlanta.

Tepper, M. S., & Owens, A. F. (2000, October). *Women's questions about sexual health using the Internet as a medium for information and advice.* Abstract for the Female Sexual Function Forum. New Perspectives in the Management of Female Dysfunction, Boston University School of Medicine.

Tsuji, I., Nakajima, F., Morimoto, J., et al. (1961). The sexual function in patients with spinal cord injury. *Urol. Int., 12,* 270–280.

U.S. Census Bureau. (1996, February). *Current population reports. P25-1130 Population projection of the United States by age, sex, race, and Hispanic origin: 1995 to 2050,* pp. 1–131. Retrieved from http://www.census.gov/prod/1/pop/p25-1130/

U.S. Department of Commerce (in consultation with the U.S. Department of Health and Human Services). (1997). The Telemedicine Report to Congress, January 1997. Retrieved January 11, 2000 from http://www.ntia.doc.gov/reports/telemed/index.htm

U.S. Department of Commerce. (2000, October). *Falling through the Net: Toward digital inclusion. A report on Americans' access to technology tools.* Economics and Statistics Administration; National Telecommunication and Information Administration, pp. 1–120. Retrieved from http://www.esa.doc.gov/fttn00.pdf

Zeitlin, A. B., Cottrell, T. L., & Lloyd, F. A. (1957). Sexology of the paraplegic male. *Fertil. Steril., 8,* 337–344.

Robert E. Longo
Steven M. Brown
Deborah Price Orcutt

5

CHAPTER

Effects of Internet Sexuality on Children and Adolescents

☐ Introduction

Today's children and adolescents live in a sexual world filled with messages about sex from a variety of media (Knowles, 1998). In addition to television, radio, magazines, newspapers, and billboard ads, children and adolescents now have access to the greatest information engine of our time: the Internet. The Internet is a double-edged sword. It is capable of bringing a world of information to its user within seconds without having to go to the library or leave one's home. Yet, as demonstrated throughout this book, it can have tremendous impact on individuals and organizations by damaging relationships, creating a variety of sexual problems, and/or negatively effecting employee productivity. With children and adolescents, there are enormous positive opportunities and equally devastating potential problems.

The number of children online is staggering. In 1996, approximately 4 million children accessed the Internet, double that of the previous year (SOC-UM Organization, 1999). Finkelhor, Mitchell, and Wolak (2000) reported that in 1999 the number of children online was estimated to be nearly 24 million youth ages 10–17. Finkelhor et al.'s research conducted between August 1999 and February 2000 revealed that nearly 29 million children log online to play games, meet friends, or research homework assignments. In addition, children and adolescents often have far more knowledge about computers and the Internet than do their adult caretakers.

The Internet provides an unparalleled opportunity for children and adolescents to explore the world, increase their potential for knowledge, and, with proper guidance from parents and caregivers, learn about human behavior and explore sexuality. We should not discourage our upcoming generations from using the Internet based upon the potential hazards. Instead, it is our responsibility as professionals and caregivers to assist and teach children ways to avoid inappropriate materials and Web sites. We need to encourage appropriate and safe use of this medium, while assisting children and adolescent to feel comfortable navigating the information highway.

☐ Adults' Role in the Sexual Learning of Children and Adolescents

Children and adolescents in the United States get ambiguous and widely conflicting messages about sexuality from the adult society around them. Movies, television, and other forms of popular culture trumpet a go-for-it attitude, yet rarely address the negative consequences of sexual involvement. Schools, churches, and federal lawmakers promote the idealistic, but no more realistic, message to teens of "just say no" and abstinence programs, which can be devastating to certain youth who have already engaged in sexual behaviors (Kreinin, 2000). Despite the obvious health risks posed by unprotected sexual intercourse, the majority of parents talk very little to their children about sexuality.

As a result, children and adolescents are often left to their own devices to learn and make difficult decisions about sexuality as well as to negotiate the tremendously complex task of attaining sexual health. Despite criticism of what teens learn about sexuality from the popular media around them, responsible adults rarely actively engage in teaching young people about these issues in a balanced manner.

There is mounting evidence that active parental involvement in educating children and adolescents about sexuality promotes healthy sexual development. As noted earlier, factors such as supervision and feeling warmth, love, and caring from parents and family are associated with delayed onset of sexual intercourse. According to a 1998 study, parental communication with teens about HIV decreased the likelihood that they would engage in unprotected sexual intercourse (*The Facts. Parent-Child Communication*, 1999). Evidence indicates that parent–child communication that starts early and continues through adolescence is more effective, more comfortable for both parties, and less contentious.

We encourage educators and professionals who work with children and families to explore and work toward becoming comfortable with their own sexuality as a first step in assisting parents, families, and especially children with growing up in a world where sexuality is so much a part of our culture. Talking with children about human sexuality opens the lines of communication for them throughout their development. It is "okay" for parents to not be the expert, but parents and professionals need to be "approachable/askable" (Mayo Clinic, 2000; Planned Parenthood, 2000). When children are told they are not old enough to be discussing a question they have about sex, we give them a clear message that they need to find their sources of information elsewhere. The end result is that children may "shut down" with parents and caregivers and/or seek the answers to their questions from sources that may not be reliable or accurate or, worse, that may be distorted and inappropriate.

As professionals and parents, we must have a working knowledge and understanding about child development, what constitutes appropriate and inappropriate sexual behavior in children and adolescents during the various stages of development, and how children's sexual knowledge, attitudes, and behavior can be influenced by accessing sexual materials online. Today, it is particularly important that we keep ourselves updated with the best ways to guide children, their parents, and their caregivers on how to use the Internet. We need to know the best age-appropriate sites for children and how to safeguard children and monitor their online activities.

☐ Children's Sexual Learning

Understanding sexuality in children is important if we hope to guide them through the childhood and adolescent years of sexual learning and experience (Kreinin, 2000; Johnson, 2000). Sexuality is an integral part of each person's life and development from the moment of birth. Sexual touch and play in children is normal and feels good (Planned Parenthood, 2000). By their first birthday, one third of all children have been observed stimulating their genitals. Boys typically pull at their penises, and girls rub their external genitalia (Mayo Clinic, 2000). As early as 3 years of age, children begin wondering about and questioning differences between boys and girls and are curious about the build and shape of their bodies. Toddlers are interested in their own bodies and the bodies of other children. To satisfy their curiosity and learn about their own bodies, they may begin to do such things as "play doctor" with other children. At this stage they begin to ask questions about "where babies come from." In describing healthy sexual development in children, Johnson (2000) stated:

Natural and healthy sexual exploration during childhood is an informa-
tion-gathering process in which young people explore each other's bodies
by looking and touching ("playing doctor") as well as by exploring gender
roles and behaviors ("playing house"). Children involved in healthy sexual
play are of similar age, size, and developmental status and participate on a
voluntary basis. . . . Children's feelings regarding their sexual behavior are
generally light-hearted and spontaneous. Children usually experience pleasurable sensations from genital touching. Some children experience sexual
arousal while some children experience orgasm. Sexual arousal and orgasm are reported more frequently in older children entering puberty.

Planned Parenthood (1993) suggested the following guidelines in educating children about sexuality. These guidelines suggest the age by which
children should have particular knowledge and skills related to human
sexuality.

By age 5 children should

- use correct terms for all sexual body parts, including reproductive organs.
- be able to understand and identify concepts of "maleness" and "female-
  ness."
- be able to talk about body parts without a sense of "naughtiness."
- be able to ask trusted adults questions about sexuality.
- know that "sex talk" is for private times at home.

At ages 6–9 children should

- be aware that all creatures reproduce themselves.
- have and use acceptable vocabulary for communication about body
  parts, including their own and those of the opposite sex.
- be aware that sexual identity includes sexual orientation: lesbian, gay,
  straight, or bisexual.
- understand the basic facts about AIDS.

At ages 9–13 children should

- have an understanding of human sexuality as a natural part of life (ages
  12–13).
- view their sexual feelings as legitimate and normal.
- understand that sex is pleasurable as well as the way to make a baby.
- realize that sexual acts can be separated from reproductive acts.
- know about how male and female bodies grow and differ.
- know about contraception (ways of preventing pregnancy and diseases).
- know about changes they can expect in their bodies before puberty,
  i.e., menstruation and wet dreams (ages 9–11).
- know about sexually transmitted diseases.

☐ Trends in Adolescent Sexual Development and Behavior

Compared to past generations, today's adolescents reach puberty earlier, have sexual intercourse earlier, and get married significantly later. There is a wide gap between the onset of puberty and the age of marriage during which adolescents and young adults often have sexual intercourse outside of the context of marriage (*Facing Facts*, 1995).

In recent years the number of adolescents who report having had sexual intercourse has leveled off and perhaps declined. According to one source, in 1990, 55% of females reported having sexual intercourse, and in 1988, 60% of males aged 15 to 19 reported having sexual intercourse. In 1995, 50% of young women and 55% of young men reported having sexual intercourse. (*The Facts. Adolescent Sexual Behavior: II*, 1997). Factors associated with a delay in the onset of intercourse by teenagers include: (a) a feeling of warmth and caring from parents and family, parental supervision; (b) two-parent household; (c) parents who graduated high school; (d) involvement in athletics for girls; and (e) academic success, involvement in religion (*The Facts. Adolescents and Abstinence*, 1998).

Sexual behavior, generally defined, is almost universal among American adolescents. Eighty-five percent of American teenagers have had a boyfriend or girlfriend, 85–90% have kissed someone romantically, and 79% have engaged in "deep kissing." The majority also move to more intimate sexual behaviors during the teenage years. More than 50% of all 14-year-old boys reported having touched a girl's breast and 25% touched a girl's vulva. More than 75% of 18-year-olds had engaged in heavy petting (*Facing Facts*, 1995).

Lesbian, gay, bisexual, and transgender youth, largely due to societal homophobia and heterosexism, suffer higher rates of suicide, violent victimization, risk behavior for HIV infection, and substance abuse than their heterosexual peers. At the same time, there is greater access to information and support services for these youth, and the age of "coming out" has been dropping in recent years (*The Facts. Lesbian, Gay*, 1997)

☐ Assessing the Sexual Health of Adolescents

Assessing what is healthy and what is not when it comes to teen sexuality is often difficult to do. This is due, in large part, to the narrow research and public discussion about adolescent sexuality, which focuses solely on what is unhealthy about adolescent sexuality (unplanned pregnancy, out-of-wedlock birth, sexually transmitted diseases, including AIDS, and sexual abuse) rather than what is sexually healthy for teenagers. Moreover, professionals doing the assessing have little empirical guidance from research and therefore often fall back on viewing adolescent sexual behavior through the lens of their own personal backgrounds and values.

Our belief is that when evaluating the sexual behaviors of adolescents it is critical to avoid dichotomous thinking and to view them on a continuum from healthy to problematic. It is also critical to view adolescent sexual behaviors not as isolated behaviors, but in the context of the whole person. There is clearly a big difference between a 15-year-old who has initiated sexual intercourse with a partner and is functioning well in other realms of this life (family, peers, academics, etc.) and a 15-year-old doing the same behavior whose parents recently divorced, who is cut off from his family, and who is abusing alcohol. Similarly, we believe it is important to assess the function that the sexual behavior serves for the particular teen. All people engage in sexual behavior for complex reasons and to meet a variety of needs, both sexual and nonsexual. However, an important indicator of sexual health for teenagers is the degree to which the sexual behavior is in the service of developmentally appropriate sexual needs as opposed to primarily nonsexual needs. A 16-year-old gay boy from a rural community who is experimenting with cybersex online may be quite healthy if he has had little opportunity to explore or express his sexuality in other ways. Contrast this with a 16-year-old boy who is engaging in cybersex because he has few friends and it momentarily helps him to escape his painful depression.

☐ Contrasting Adolescents' Healthy and Problematic Sexual Behavior

It is beyond the scope of this chapter to discuss all of the complex characteristics that describe healthy and problematic sexual behaviors in teenagers. In this section, we will focus on areas that seem most relevant to the topic of Internet sexuality. Again, it is important to note that, although we are contrasting healthy and problem behaviors, these characteristics are not simply present or absent, but rather exist on a continuum.

Exploring Personal Identity Through Sexuality

Exploring personal identities is a critical developmental task of adolescents. Sexually healthy adolescents with positive feelings of self-worth explore their personal identities in ways that are growth enhancing and do not place them at serious risk for danger or negative consequences.

This pursuit of an authentic and genuine sense of self manifests in a myriad of ways ranging from choices about dress to which peer group to socialize with, to explorations about sexual orientation. These teens may "try on" many identities to see which ones feel authentic; this experimentation serves primarily to help teens know themselves better. For healthy adolescents, surfing the Web, participating in chatrooms, and engaging in Internet sex may be ways of trying on multiple identities to see which fit.

This is in contrast to teens who tend to explore their personal identities in more extreme ways, which are often dangerous, self-destructive, and compensatory for core feelings that they are bad or unlovable. These teens may cut themselves off from family and get involved in high-risk sexual behaviors to act grown up. They may allow themselves to be sexually misused in relationships, sometimes by significantly older partners, because any attention is better than none. Their identity exploration could also take the form of preoccupation with creating fantasy personalities on the Internet that mask their feelings of inadequacy and provide a feeling of pseudointimacy to others (Freeman-Longo, 2000). Rather than taking risks of connecting in real relationships where they could be hurt, they escape into a fantasy world, where they can portray themselves as anyone they want to be.

Managing Negative Feelings

Adolescents who engage in healthy sexual behaviors are better able to tolerate negative feelings that arise in their lives without using sexual behavior as a primary way of coping with these feelings. Being in romantic relationships and engaging in sexual behavior serve the function of expressing closeness to another, learning what it is like to be sexual with another, and feeling pleasure. These young people cope with feelings of boredom, emptiness, loneliness, and helplessness that are common in adolescence in healthier ways, such as seeking out supportive adults, talking to friends, writing in a journal, or getting exercise.

In comparison, teenagers with sexual behavior problems may engage in sexual behavior and/or use sexual stimuli to help them deal with negative feeling states (Saakvitne, Gamble, Pearlman, & Lev, 2000). These youth often get overwhelmed by their feelings because they are less able to soothe themselves or to move from a state of intense anxiety to feeling better. Sexual behavior and sexual pleasure is a powerful way to feel better in the moment, to make feelings of emptiness or numbness go away, to feel in control when they feel out of control. The desperate need to rid themselves of negative feelings takes precedence over any thought about consequences. This can manifest in promiscuous and random sex, sexual offending, compulsive use of pornography, or compulsive masturbation. For adolescents with these type of difficulties, the Internet can be a seductively easy avenue to accessing sexually explicit stimuli as a way of coping with difficult feelings. Regularly masturbating to explicit sexual material on the Internet often serves to reinforce and perpetuate the behavior as well as this method of coping.

Developing Age-Appropriate Social Skills

Sexually healthy adolescents have or are engaged in the process of developing age-appropriate social skills. This includes such skills as making and maintaining friends; having friendships with both males and females; communicating effectively with friends; and respecting others' confidences (*Facing Facts*, 1995). It also often includes actively learning and practicing courtship and dating skills with romantic partners. Healthy teens, for example, communicate desires to engage or not engage in sexual behaviors, to talk about sexual behaviors before they occur, and to take measures to protect themselves from unintended pregnancy and diseases. Less healthy teens struggle to negotiate the world of friendships and romantic relationships and sometimes avoid it altogether. These teens may be at particularly high risk for compulsively using the Internet because it permits them to escape facing real-life social interactions. Some might argue that the Internet is a way for less socially skilled teens to learn in a less threatening way about relationships. But this would only seem to be healthy if cybersocializing or cybersex eventually led to more authentic real-life relationships. The Internet provides a virtual practice place for girls or kids with difficulties being assertive to learn to say no, to click someone away, and to be more assertive in sexual situations (it is easier to start these behaviors online than in real life or with offline friends who you have to see everyday).

Distinguishing Fact From Fiction About Sexuality

Adolescents who are sexually healthy are able to seek out accurate information about sexuality when they need it and can distinguish between realistic and distorted media messages about sexuality (*Facing Facts*, 1995). Teens with a positive sense of self who have internalized positive modeling about sexual values, gender roles, and developmentally appropriate sexual behavior are somewhat inoculated from the impact of the media, including the Internet, which so often portrays sex in an extreme, stereotypical manner. Teenagers who are less sexually healthy tend to have few positive and realistic role models to help them learn about sexuality. They are more vulnerable to adopting as fact misinformation and distorted media messages about, for example, how men and women are supposed to act, what is a healthy relationship, and what is involved in a mutually plea- surable sexual relationship, areas seldom addressed in sexually explicit materials on the Internet.

For young people who can filter out accurate from distorted informa- tion, the Internet can be an incredibly rich source of information, par- ticularly about topics generally not discussed with parents or in sex edu- cation classes, such as falling in love, breaking up, orgasms, and how to sexually pleasure a partner. A recent content analysis of questions sub- mitted to a sexuality information Web site for teenagers, sxetc.org, found just that. The kind of questions most frequently asked by teenagers per- tained to issues related to sexual pleasure; exactly those areas that adults and schools omit talking about (D. Sorace, personal communication, Sep- tember 22, 2000). However, for those teenagers less able to tell fact from fiction, the Internet, with its vast amount of distorted sexual stimuli (por- nography and otherwise), may only serve to propagate more misinfor- mation and reinforce exaggerated beliefs about sexuality. America Online and other Web sites have teen monitors for teen chats. This monitoring gives teenagers a chance to be "experts" and take positions of responsibil- ity and ownership for more prosocial mores.

Comfort With Sexual Orientation

Sexually healthy adolescents are comfortable with their sexual orienta- tion, or at least comfortable exploring feelings and attitudes related to their sexual orientation (*Facing Facts*, 1995). Unfortunately, for gay, les- bian, bisexual, and transgender individuals and young people question- ing their sexuality, this is an extremely difficult task because they live in a society that regards them as deviant, stigmatizes them, and often ren- ders them invisible. For these young people, as is true with other isolated and disenfranchised members of various groups, the Internet offers a way to connect easily with like-minded others, to learn about the issue, and to feel accepted. Less healthy adolescents feel extremely conflicted about or totally repress feelings related to their sexual orientation. Often this is due to the hatred they have internalized from the world around them. These young people can be at risk for being exploited on the Internet by adults who offer desperately needed acceptance, attention and escape from isolation and invisibility.

Web sites such as Queer Youth Webring and youth.org can be helpful to gay, lesbian, bisexual, transgender, and questioning teenagers.[1] Information about living in the world as a gay, lesbian, bisexual, transgender person, about coming out, about difficulties and negative social experiences that gay, lesbian, and bisexual youth may experience, and personal accounts of how young people have addressed these concerns can easily be found online. For young people living in rural areas, in communities lacking resources, or who are more socially withdrawn or isolated, the Internet may be one of the few and most valuable resources available to acquire such information.

☐ Children and Teens Online: Potential Opportunities

The Internet provides children and adolescents with a tremendous opportunity to learn and to experience communication that is instantaneous. There are many benefits that should not be overlooked by parents and others overly cautious about the Internet's potential to expose children and adolescents to undesirable images of violence and sex. The Internet is a powerful medium that can teach people, including children, and increase social skills (Cooper, Putnam, Planchon, & Boies, 1999). As Cooper and Sportdori (1997) noted, the Internet is a triple-A engine that has changed how people relate to and communicate with the world around them. The Internet is affordable, easily accessible, and can provide anonymity (to some degree) for the user.

The Internet is the most revolutionary method developed during our lifetime for people to learn virtually anything they want without having to travel outside of the home, office, or school. Human sexuality can be explored by children and adolescents through the use of age-appropriate Web sites (see Appendix A for a partial listing). Educational sites are filled with accurate and scientific information and can actually help youth work through difficult issues. For example, a *New York Times* article (Egan, 2000) described the trials and tribulations a gay youth experienced to further understand his sexual orientation. Despite some very rocky roads one may cross on the Internet, children and adolescents can turn negative experiences into positive ones and learn from them. These experiences and the learning can be further enhanced through careful support and monitoring of Internet use by parents, educators, and caregivers.

Through the use of monitored chat rooms and bulletin boards, children

---

1. http://www.youthresource.com/queeryouth/queeryouth.htm 1/27/01; http://www.youth.org 4/9/01

and adolescents can safely explore real information they want and need about sex that they can't get from schools, parents, etc. (info about feelings, actual sexual behaviors, how to be a good lover, etc.). This can be best accomplished by going online with children and helping them explore safe and monitored web sites dedicated to the appropriate age group (see Appendix A).

☐ Children and Teens Online: Potential Hazards

As early as age 2, many children are beginning to learn about computers. By the time they enter kindergarten, they may be quite skilled in computer use and could even begin to explore going online. During their school age years, many children become quite adept at surfing the Web. By early adolescence, many teens are more knowledgeable and skilled than most of their parents or caregivers about the Internet and the Web.

There are many dangers on the Internet that parents, educators, caregivers, and others must take into account when guiding children and adolescents in its use. A recent national survey of children ages 10–17 (Finkelhor et al., 2000) looked into children's activity and experiences online. The study, a call to health care professionals, educators, parents, caregivers, and others who work with youth, revealed that many children have distressing experiences online that range from unwanted e-mails and harassment to aggressive sexual solicitations. In their report Finkelhor et al. noted that risks to children include:

1. unwanted sexual solicitations and approaches,
2. unwanted sexual material,
3. threatening and offensive behavior directed at children.

Based on telephone interviews with a nationally representative sample of 1,501 youth ages 10–17 who use the Internet regularly, Finkelhor et al. (2000) found that:

1. one in five received an unwanted sexual solicitation or approach over the Internet during a 1-year period;
2. one in thirty-three received *aggressive* sexual solicitations;
3. one in four had unwanted exposure to pictures of naked people or people having sex;
4. one in seventeen was threatened or harassed.

It is not difficult for children and teens to come upon pornographic Web sites and sexually explicit materials. According to Aftab and Polly (1997) children can inadvertently view sexually explicit content in several ways.

1. Mistaken or mistyped URLs: A simple mistyped word such as "playstatio<u>m</u>.com" instead of "playstation.com" can take a child to adult-oriented materials. Even simple and basic search words such as "whitehouse," "toys," "pets," "boys," "girls," "Barney," or "fun" can lead a child to sexually explicit materials online.
2. Misdirected searches: Many search engines use computer codes to iden- tify sites. Innocent searching can lead to adult-oriented materials.
3. "Push," pornography and e-mails: Children can open e-mail that di- rectly links them to pornographic Web sites.

   We have long been aware that when children observe violent images on television, modeling behaviors can and do occur. We can assume that sexual images and violent sexual images that are conveyed on a com- puter can have the same detrimental effects. Children spend a large part of their time learning about life through the media. In fact, recent studies suggest that 63% of children ages 9–17 indicated they preferred the Internet over television and thus may spend more time on the Internet than they spend watching television (America Online, 1999). In addi- tion, the potential for a child to view violent images and specifically sexual images and violent sexual images on the Internet is far greater than that of television viewing (Baby Bag Online, 2001).

☐   Indicators of Problematic Internet Use

According to Cooper et al. (1999), the following are indicators of addic- tion to online activity. These indicators below (based upon adults) may serve, in the absence of scientifically validated studies on youth, as po- tential indicators for online sexual problems for youth or sexual addic- tion in youth.

1. excessive use of the Internet, including neglect of personal relation- ships and isolation;
2. acute/chronic depression;
3. seeking repeated mood-altering experiences that have brought about "highs";
4. sense of pseudointimacy;
5. Internet serves as an outlet for unresolved sexual difficulties and un- focused sexual energy;
6. a history of sexual behavior problems;
7. lack of or little engagement in peer-related social activities.

☐ Parents'/Caregivers' Guide to Safety and Prevention

Several authors and organizations (Aftab and Polly, 1997; Elam, 1997; Freeman-Longo, 2000; Gaines, 1999; Shepler, 2000; Smith, 1996; SOC-UM, 1999; U.S. Department of Justice, 2000) note that there are several steps parents, educators, and others can take to maximize a child's or teen's fun and learning on the Internet while avoiding most of the associated risks of online activity. There are various publications and Web sites outlining safety and the basic principles to teach children about the hazards of being online (see Appendix A). The following principles can be used by parents, caregivers, educators, and others in guiding children through online activity.

1. Talk with your child, long before adolescence, about sexuality. Part of the reason sexual content on the Internet is so compelling for children and teenagers is because so few adults are willing to talk openly with them about sexuality.
2. Don't put computers with Internet access in a child's room. Instead, keep the computer with Internet access in a public place where there is lots of activity at home and where the use can be easily monitored, such as a family room or kitchen.
3. Use software that provides the best security and precaution against accessing adult-oriented Web sites, including those that will track the child's use of the Internet and sites visited. Look for updated versions and newer and/or improved software periodically. Test software that claims to block children's access to adult-oriented materials on the Internet. When it comes to software and blocking devices, be a good consumer. What are the comparative ratings? Which programs are the most popular? See if you can beat the software and blocking programs; if you can, your child may be able to as well. Ask other parents what they use. There are several software packages, such as Cyber-Patrol, Internet WatchDog, SurfWatch, SafeSurf, CYBERSitter, and Net Nanny, that serve as blocking software, filtering software, and tracking software.
4. Provide children and teens with age-appropriate alternatives. Help children explore what is out there in cyberspace. Visit a variety of sites with the child while he or she is online. You are bound to come across undesirable sites, and that can become a valuable "teaching moment" as you discuss what is good and bad about the site.
5. Teach children and teens to keep their identity private and to never give out personal information on the Internet. Medaris (2000) dem-

onstrates that within 45 minutes of identifying a child with an e-mail address only, a sexual predator can discover the child's home address, phone number, where the child goes to school, and other particulars.

6. Get to know your child's online friends. Advise youth to *never* meet people in person that they have met online.
7. Advise youth that there is never complete privacy on the Internet.
8. Make sure the child's computer time is limited. Help children find a balance between computer time and other activities. People, not computers, should be their best friends.
9. Set and discuss online rules with children about computer times, usage, and so on. When a child violates the rules and conditions set by parents and caregivers for using the Internet, remove the child's privilege of Internet access, including, if necessary, prohibiting him or her from going to friends' homes, libraries, and schools that have Internet access.
10. Learn enough about computers so you can enjoy them with children.
11. Make sure children feel comfortable coming to you and asking you questions. Encourage discussions between you and children when they are online. Ask children to show you where they go online.
12. Keep children out of chatrooms, or monitor their involvement in youth-oriented chat rooms.
13. Teach children, teens, and others about the incidence of credit card fraud on the Internet.
14. Teach children to never respond to e-mail, chat comments, or newsgroup messages that are hostile, belligerent, inappropriate, or in any way make them feel uncomfortable.
15. If your child is being pursued or harassed by someone online and/or is engaging in sexual activities with a person online, report the information to Cybertipline: 800-843-5678.

☐ What Therapists and Professionals Can Do

While we are still learning about the Internet, youth who use the Internet, and what happens to youth who explore human sexuality via the Internet, we are not helpless in addressing youth when we detect problems or see warning signs that problems may be occurring. The literature has clearly outlined the problems adults face when sexuality becomes a primary purpose for going online (Cooper & Sportolari, 1997; Cooper et al., 1999; Young & Rogers, 1998). To better assist youth, and to begin to look at how to use and apply our knowledge, we can (a) apply what we have learned from the adult world of online sexual behavior problems and addiction, and (b) use a development and contextual framework regarding youth. In order to assess if a child or adolescent is experiencing problems and/or engaging in sexual activities online, assessment areas may include but are not limited to the following:

1. Take a complete developmental history of the child, including a detailed sexual history.
2. Assess problem areas for the young person in a holistic way, including sexual behavior problems. Address social behaviors. Is there evidence the child is withdrawing or isolating from family, peers, and social activities? Do parents and others notice a detachment from others on the part of the child?
3. Assess how much time daily and/or weekly children are spending online.
4. Assess places the youth is visiting on the Internet (parents or caregivers may already be using tracking software).
5. Assess the child's sexual knowledge (is it age appropriate, over or underdeveloped), orientation, interests, and concerns? Is the youth addressing or struggling with homosexual/bisexual lifestyle choices? Does he or she have concerns about sexual knowledge and experience? Is he or she experiencing peer pressures?

If the child appears to be dealing with sexual concerns or there is evidence that there are sexual problems including a problem with online sexual activities, the following may be helpful. It is important to note that the suggestions below should be followed using age-appropriate language and teaching and that for some younger children, these activities may need to be done at a later age.

1. Work with the child, parents, and educators to develop a list of age-appropriate Web sites he or she can visit.
2. Advise the child, caregivers, parents, and educators of screening and filtering software they can use.
3. Discuss with the child what his or her knowledge is regarding human sexual behavior. Explore what the child has learned about human sexuality online and offline, and correct misinformation.
4. Discuss with the child the difficulties children and teens experience with human sexuality and sexual experiences, that is , homosexuality, criminal sexual behavior, sexual harassment, sexual development, and so on.
5. Teach the child the differences between healthy sexuality and unhealthy sexuality and what constitutes healthy sexual practice. Explore differences between intimacy without sex, intimacy with sex, love and sex,

consent, and so on. Help the child become comfortable with his or her sexual orientation.

6. Go online with the child and explore the Internet together. Look at appropriate Web sites and, when found, discuss why some Web sites are inappropriate.
7. Talk to the child about the potential risks and harm of the Internet while underscoring the benefits of its proper use. Explain the ways in which they can be abused and exploited online, that is, through chatrooms, unwanted e-mails, and so on. Using the principles addressed earlier in this chapter, help the child develop appropriate online activities and ways to avoid or get out of the pitfalls and problems they may experience.

☐ Summary

Scientific research and information regarding children, teens, and sexual activity on the Internet is just now emerging. We are uncertain about the potential for youth to become sexual compulsives or even sexually addicted if they engage in online sexual activities. The American Psychological Association has determined that exposure to excessive amounts of television violence is impacting children and their aggressive behaviors in negative ways. We should be equally cautious about children's exposure to large amounts of inappropriate sexual materials on the Internet.

To uninformed persons, the potential harms of the Internet appear to outweigh the many potential benefits from engaging in online sexual learning. This chapter serves as a call to recognize the potential problems and the best ways we know at this time to help children avoid problems online or deal with these disturbing incidents when they occur. Time and further research into understanding the sexual interests and behavior of youth who use the Internet will only further serve our understanding of youth on the Internet, their needs to learn about human sexuality, and our efforts to encourage them to use the Internet in safe and responsible ways. Dedicated research into this new form of media and its impact on youth in both positive and negative ways will better assist us in preventive efforts to help children, teens, parents, teachers, and others understand the potential risks and benefits to children who explore human sexuality via the Internet.

There are additional issues that warrant further research in this area. First, in a population of children exposed to online pornography and adult-oriented materials, can we differentiate factors of emotional vulnerability and other personality traits that would predispose some to become sexual compulsives and, potentially, sexual addicts? Second, does online sexual behavior/activity predispose some children and teens to act out sexually and/or engage in sexually abusive behaviors? Third, are there effective ways that professionals and others can prevent children and teens from accessing such materials or minimizing the extent to which they do, and to help them cope effectively with these situations when they arise? Certainly there are many more issues to be addressed as we learn more about the use of the Internet by children and adolescents. In the meantime, we as professionals should continue to encourage youth and their parents, educators, and caregivers to understand the potential risks while enjoying the many benefits of the Internet—a phenomenal learning tool.

☐ References

Aftab, P., & Polly, J. A. (1997). Child safety online. Internet online summit: Focus on children. Washington, DC. Retrieved October 13, 2000, from http://www.prevent-abuse-now.com/summit.htm

America Online. (1999). *NUA Internet survey: Children prefer the Net to TV.* Retrieved November 12, 1999 from http://www.nua.net/surveys/index.cgi?f=VS&art_id=9053554028&rel=true.

Baby Bag Online. (2001). *Facts about media violence and effects on the American family.* Retrieved from http://babybag.com/articles/amaviol.htm

Cooper, A., Putnam, D. E., Planchon, L. A., & Boies, S. C. (1999). Online sexual compulsivity. *Sexual Addiction & Compulsivity: The Journal of Treatment and Prevention, 6*(2), 79–104.

Cooper, A., & Sportolari, L. (1997). Romance in cyberspace: Understanding online attraction. *Journal of Sex Education and Therapy, 22*(1), 7–14.

Egan, J. (2000, December 10). Lonely gay teen seeking same. *New York Times,* pp. 112–127.

Elam, P. (1997). *A parents guide to safe surfing.* Retrieved September 15, 2000, from Webnovice.com. 9/15/2000.

Facing facts: Sexual health for America's adolescents. (1995). Report of the National Commission on Adolescent Sexual Health. New York. Sexuality Information and Education Counsel of the United States.

The Facts. Adolescents and abstinence. (1998, September). Washington, DC: Advocates for Youth.

The Facts. Adolescent sexual behavior: I. Demographics. (1997, September). Washington, DC: Advocates for Youth.

The Facts. Adolescent sexual behavior: II. Demographics. (1997, September). Washington, DC: Advocates for Youth.

The Facts. Lesbian, gay, bisexual, and transgender youth: At risk and underserved. (1997, September). Washington DC: Advocates for Youth.

The Facts. Parent-child communication: Promoting healthy youth. (1999, February). Washington, DC: Advocates for Youth.

Finkelhor, D., Mitchell, K. J., & Wolak, J. (2000). *Online victimization: A report on the nation's youth.* Alexandria, VA: National Center for Missing and Exploited Children.

Freeman-Longo, R. E. (2000). Children, teens and sex on the Internet. *Sexual Addiction & Compulsivity, 7*(1–2), 75–90.

Gaines, S. (1999). Keeping kids safe on the Internet. (Providing guidance for online use; includes Web sites with information for parental guidance). Retrieved September 15, 2000, from http://www.findarticles.com/cf_0/m1041/8_77/55198581/p1/article.jhtml

Johnson, T. C. (2000). Children with sexual behavior problems. *Seicus Report, 29*(1), 35–39.

Knowles, J. (1998). How to talk to your child about sexuality: A parent's guide. Retrieved September 28, 2000, from http://www.plannedparenthood.org/GUIDEPARENTS/howtotalkchild.html

Kreinin, T. (2000). Stopping the cycle of sexual abuse. *Siecus Report, 29*(1), 4.

Mayo Clinic. (2000, July 24). Discussing "birds and bees." Retrieved September 20, 2000, from http://www.mayohealth.org/mayo/9909/htm/kids.htm

Medaris, M. (2000, December). Workshop: Online victimization: Hype or fact? Paper presented at *Justice for Children: A vision for the 21st century.* OJJDP National Conference, Washington, DC.

Planned Parenthood. (1993). *Human sexuality: What children should know and when they should know it.* Retrieved September 28, 2000, from http://www.planned parenthood.org/Library/SEXUALITYEDUCATION/ whatchildrenshould.html

Planned Parenthood. (2000). *National family sexuality education month.* Retrieved September 28, 2000, from http://www.planned parenthood.org/Library/SEXUALITYEDUCATION/nfsem.html

Shepler, J. (2000) John Shepler's writing in a positive light: Safe surfing. Retrieved September 15, 2000, from http://www.execpc.com/~shepler/safesurfing.html

Saakvitne, K. W., Gamble, S., Pearlman, L. A., & Lev, B. T. (2000). *Risking connection: A training curriculum for working with survivors of childhood abuse.* Lutherville, MD: The Sidran Press.

Smith, K. (1996). *Who's talking to your kids in cyberspace: The online threat to children.* Retrieved September 29, 2000, from http://www.soc-um.org/stips2.html

U.S. Department of Justice. (2000). *A parent's guide to Internet safety.* Retrieved September 15, 2000, from http://www.fbi.gov/library/pguide/pguidee.htm

Young, K. S., & Rogers, R. C. (1998). The relationship between depression and Internet addiction. *CyberPsychology & Behavior, 1*(1), 25–28.

☐ Appendix A

Internet Web Sites That Address Youth Online

www.siecus.org: SIECUS
www.opentalk.com: Open Talk
www.familyguidebook.com: Addresses risks in cyberspace
www.cyberangels.org: Safety quiz for kids
www.childrenspartnership.org: Offers helpful safety tips
www.smartparent.com: Children's pledge for online safety
www.edc.org: Centers for Children and Technology
www.cdt.org: Center for Democracy and Technology
www.cme.org: Center for Media Education
www.childlures.com: Child Lures
www.childnetint.org: Childnet International
www.childrenspartnership.org: The Children's Partnership
www.edc.org: Education Development Center
www.enough.org: Enough is Enough
www.ed.gov: U.S. Department of Education
www.advocatesforyouth.org: Advocates for Youth
www.plannedparenthood.org: Planned Parenthood

www.kaiser.org: Kaiser Family Foundation
www.cdc.gov: Centers for Disease Control

Internet Web Sites That Address Human Sexuality

www.sxetc.org: Sex, Etc.
www.teenwire.com: Planned Parenthood Foundation
www.kidsheaqlth.org: Kid's Health
www.teenpregnancy.org: National Campaign to Prevent Teen Pregnancy
www.Iwannaknow.com: American Social Health Association
www.youthresource.org: Youth resource for gay, lesbian, bisexual and transgender
www.youth.org: Youth.org
www.positive.org/cps: Coalition for Positive Sexuality
www.ncb.org.uk: National Children's Bureau
www.looksmart.com: Sex Ed for Youth
www.plannedparenthood.org/libraray: Planned Parenthood
www.nnfr.org: National Network for family Resiliency
www.cyfernet.org: Cyfernet Youth

Internet Web Sites for Female Adolescents

www.agirlsworld.com: Started in 1996, this is the only free online magazine with daily,
    weekly, and monthly features written and edited entirely by girls and teens from all
    over the world.
www.cybergrrl.com: A site that informs, inspires, and celebrates women.
www.cybergrrlz.com: This site is described as one that provides a place for girls to share
    their experiences and present their views about current events and other topics of
    interest to girls, in an open and entertaining way.
www.diaryproject.com: This is a site where girls can go to get or give advice and talk to
    other girls.
www.girlzone.com: A site committed to doing what is best for girls.
www.gURL.com: Founded in 1996 as a school project. It began as an irreverent online
    magazine and has developed into a leading Web site for teenage girls.
www.health.org/gpower/index.htm: Girl Power! is the national public education campaign
    sponsored by the U.S. Department of Health and Human Services to help encourage
    and motivate 9 to 14-year-old girls to make the most of their lives.
www.maximag.com: A friendly environment for girls to empower and inspire themselves.
www.razzberry.com: An online community of teen girls aged 13–17 which provides a place
    for girls to talk about issues they choose, open each other's minds, and grow into
    strong women.
www.smartgirl.com: An interesting site with lots to offer girls. GIRLS stands for Getting
    around, Issues to discuss, Reviews, Love and friendship, and Speak out.

CYBERSEX PROBLEMS: THERAPEUTIC CONSIDERATIONS

Al Cooper
Irene McLoughlin
Pauline Reich
Jay Kent-Ferraro

Virtual Sexuality in the Workplace: A Wake-Up Call for Clinicians, Employers, and Employees

☐ Introduction

Overview of Online Sexual Activities

The Internet has become the technology blitzkrieg of the new millennium. Electronic communications are dramatically changing the workplace, as e-mail, Intranets, the Internet, and the World Wide Web are fast joining the fax machine and voice mail as indispensable tools for doing business. In fact, about 50% of all Internet users use accounts supplied by their employers. The explosion of the Internet into the workplace has put temptation squarely in the face of millions of employees. With just a few keystrokes, they may all too easily travel to areas that are implicitly and even explicitly forbidden and/or at odds with their companies' mores and mission. This phenomenon raises a host of new legal and practical issues for any employer.

Organizations are thus being forced to deal with mushrooming ethical dilemmas, such as workers frittering away a morning shopping online or secretly viewing sexually explicit Web sites. Every day, companies face unexpected twists in the world of virtual morality. This new spin on the old concern of employees engaging in nonwork activities while on company time is called cyberslacking (Greenfield, 1999), but as with all things, the computer greatly magnifies the possibilities. For one thing, the Web can be insidious in its power, seductively lulling users to click from screen to screen for any number of non-work-related purposes, from online shopping to researching a vacation, to engaging in online gambling or looking for a husband. With so many temptations it is not surprising that employers are concerned that productivity will suffer.

When adding sexuality to the mix the concern rises to a whole new level. Sexuality is a powerful stimulus and the temptation to engage in one of the many forms of online sexual activity (OSA) is something that employees are finding themselves engaged in with increasing frequency. In addition, those individuals both with and without prior proclivities of this sort might find this activity so gratifying that they eventually develop problems with sexual compulsivity (Cooper, Putnam, Planchon, & Boies, 1999).

While the research on sexual compulsions and its treatment has burgeoned in recent years, little has been written from the perspective of a clinician or an employer interested in comprehensively managing the impact of this problem in the workplace. Some notable exceptions are discussed below. Carnes (1999), in an important study of nearly 1,000 sexual addicts, found that "by far the biggest losses recorded were in the workplace" (p. 87). The main loss was time. Most of the sex addicts studied reported not being able to work up to their potential, with 80% reporting a loss of productivity and 86% reportedly acting out in some way in the workplace.

In another study, Lybarger (1997) found that sexual harassment continues in spite of federally mandated training, reporting, and disciplinary action. According to Lybarger, training and other prophylactic measures on how to deal with sexual issues in the workplace are woefully inadequate, and those suffering from a range of sexually addictive tendencies may frequently be participants in harassment scenarios.

In the first large-scale study of the online sexual behavior of 9,265 men and women, Cooper, Scherer, Boies, and Gordon (1999) found that as many as 20% of the men and 12% of the women reported they had used computers at work for some sexual pursuits. This corroborates data from other sources reporting that adult content sites are the fourth most visited category while at work (Goldberg, 1998), and that 70% of all adult content traffic occurs during the 9 to 5 workday (Carnes, 2001).

In a recent larger and even more comprehensive study, Cooper, Scherer, and Mathy (2001) surveyed almost 40,000 adults, gathering responses to 76 questions pertaining to their use of the Internet for sexual pursuits. Of those surveyed, 20% report going online for sexual activities while at work. Of those who go online at work, 55% report they do it for distraction, 13% for education, 6% for coping, and 9% because they spend so much time at work. In addition, 63% of all respondents report that their workplace forbids OSA, while 14% report that their workplace does not forbid it, and 22% do not know. Also of interest is the fact that 48% of the respondents report that their company or workplace does not take steps to block access to sexual sites.

Another survey by Greenfield (1999) attempted to measure the extent of Web diversion at work and reported that about two out of three companies have disciplined employees for misusing the Internet on the job. In addition, one out of three companies participating in the survey reported firing individuals for Internet misuse. Pornography topped the list of abuses meriting corporate reprimands, with a 41% share, followed by chatting at 12%, games at 11%, and sports at 8%.

In Greenfield's (1999) study of 224 mid-sized companies, 83% report having a written Internet use policy. Only 34% of these firms reported that they were "not concerned" about Internet use in the workplace, while 56% acknowledged concerns that workers use it inappropriately. But employees' penchant for visiting online sex sites can do more than just monopolize bandwidth and waste company time. It can also portend sexual discrimination and harassment concerns for a company. Employees who encounter computer screens with pornographic images or receiving sexual e-mails could file a hostile work environment lawsuit if they raise concerns with the company and there is an inadequate response by management.

Cooper et al. (2001) found that 4% of those accessing online sex sites in the workplace report getting caught but experience no serious negative consequences, while only 0.4% get caught and incur serious negative consequences. The numbers of those individuals who engage in OSA versus those who are caught is vastly different; this discrepancy could well be explained by the fact that companies continue to be uncertain whether or not to get involved with the sticky issue of their employees' sexual habits. And for those companies that do want to take action, many face the dilemma of how they should best go about confronting and addressing the issue. Therefore, the purpose of this chapter is to argue that avoiding this issue is the worst possible strategy for an organization and to outline general questions and ways to begin to think about dealing with OSA in the workplace.

Negative Consequences

Allowing employees to visit sexually explicit sites via the company Internet system may be problematic in a number of ways. Employees who display or download offensive material may well be creating a *hostile work environment* under Title VII, thereby increasing the employer's exposure to liability. In addition, such employees expose the company to adverse publicity if their habits are discovered. For instance, a Nielson Media Research Inc. survey reported in *The Wall Street Journal* (2000) that, employees at AT&T, Apple, and IBM accessed Penthouse's Web site 12,823 times during a single month in 1996 (that is more than 347 eight-hour days, based on an average visit of 13 minutes). It was also nationally reported that a county commissioner in Washington used the county computer to visit more than 130 Internet sites depicting nude women and couples engaging in sex. Employees in increasing numbers are downloading sexual images, using their corporate e-mail addresses to do so.

Employees visiting sexually explicit sites may be costing their company money due to

- lost productivity, including the cost of firing and rehiring, human resources (HR), employee assistance programs (EAPs), legal counsel, and management time involved in dealing with a simultaneously sensitive and explosive situation;
- subscriber and access fees charged by such sites;
- online time charges, if the company pays by the hour for access;
- the myriad of ways that someone with a serious sexual compulsion is a less effective employee: deteriorating relationships with coworkers, loss of employee credibility and trust, becoming unhappy, secretive, ashamed and guilty; and spending more time on their problematic behaviors and less time for other healthy activities like exercising, socializing, and being part of the team at lunchtime or during breaks.

In addition, what employers often don't realize is that employees who engage in some forms of OSA could be committing criminal acts. Although the First Amendment generally protects all forms of speech, there are exceptions for certain forms of sexually explicit materials. The dissemination of obscenity and child pornography is completely prohibited in most states. Conversely, the communication of material considered "indecent" may be regulated but may not be completely banned. Although most employers will probably want to prohibit their employees from accessing even indecent materials, all employers need to be particularly concerned about those employees using workplace resources to access obscene materials or child pornography, which might violate both federal and state laws and leave the employer with some degree of legal exposure.

☐ Legal Implications for Employers

The use of the Internet at work opens the door to employer liability for the inappropriate behavior of its employees, with respect to both coworkers or the world outside the workplace. While we often find that traditional law and policy must be modified for the new issues raised by the Internet, employees should bear in mind that whatever is not permitted in the workplace (e.g., use of the workplace phone for personal calls, reading other material when one is being paid to do assigned work, posting sexually explicit pictures in the workplace, harassing other employees, etc.) is just as unacceptable when it involves the Internet as when it involves the telephone or other media. Naturally, employers should clearly explain their policies in personnel manuals that are made available to employees upon hiring and again on a periodic basis during the course of their employment. These need to be updated as circumstances require, particularly as new federal and state laws are adopted or case law evolves. Ongoing training by experts in this area for the company's management, attorneys, HR and EAP staff is also essential to keep both employees and employers out of trouble. It is important for those counseling clients with sexual acting out problems to know what legal issues might arise for those engaging in nonprotected sexual behavior in the workplace. A brief look at employment law involving Internet use at work, as well as the ramifications for those who demonstrate inappropriate workplace behaviors, follows.

Employee Privacy Expectations

On February 28, 2000, the U.S. Court of Appeals for the Fourth Circuit held that a government worker did not have a legitimate expectation of privacy with respect to the record or results of his or her use of the Internet at work in light of his or her employer's policy (*United States v. Simons,* 2000). The defendant was an employee of the Foreign Bureau of Information Services, a division of the Central Intelligence Agency. In June 1998, the employer instituted a policy stating that employees were to use the Internet for official government business only. Accessing unlawful material was particularly prohibited. Employees were informed that the employer would conduct electronic audits to ensure compliance. The employer hired a contractor to manage its computer network and to monitor for any inappropriate use of its computer system. In July 1998, the contractor entered the word "sex" into the "firewall" database and found a large number of "hits" originating from the defendant's workplace computer. The contractor noted that such sites were not visited for work-related purposes and reported the usage to the employer's representative. The employer had the defendant's computer examined by another employee at the workstation. The other employee printed a list of titles from downloaded files and copied all the files from the hard drive of the defendant's computer. Later, two representatives from the CIA Office of Inspector General viewed the files from a copy of the defendant's hard drive and found that they included pictures of minors. The computer's hard drive was removed and replaced with a copy, and a week later a warrant was issued and the defendant's office and computer were searched in his absence. Copies were made of the contents of the computer, diskettes in a drawer, files stored on the zip drive, and various documents, including personal correspondence.

The defendant was subsequently indicted on one count of knowingly receiving child pornography that had been transported in interstate commerce in violation of 18 U.S.C. Section 2252A(a)(2)(A) and one count of knowingly possessing material containing images of child pornography that had been transported in interstate commerce in violation of 18 U.S.C. Section 2252A(a)(5)(B). The defendant moved to suppress the evidence, arguing that the searches of his office and computer violated the Fourth Amendment of the U.S. Constitution. After a hearing, his motion was denied. At trial, he was found guilty on both counts and sentenced to 18 months in prison. The court held in denying his appeal that he did not have a legitimate expectation of privacy with regard to the fruits of his Internet use at work due to the clearly stated employer policy. As for the warrantless search of his office to retrieve the computer hard drive, the court concluded that the defendant had a reasonable expectation of privacy in his office. However, the U.S. Supreme Court's decision in *O'Connor v. Ortega* (1987) established that "a search by a government employer pursuant to the investigation of work-related conduct will not be in violation of the Fourth Amendment if the search is reasonable in its inception and scope."

Courts have found that there is no reasonable expectation of privacy in e-mail sent, stored, or received at work. Since the computer equipment belongs to the employer, so does the material on it. In one private sector case, for example, a court upheld the termination of an at-will employee based on a review of e-mail transmitted over the company network. The court found that, "even assuming the employer had promised not to read employee e-mail, and not to fire someone based on the contents of e-mail alone, the employer is within its rights to do so" (*Smyth v. The Pillsbury Corp.*, 1996). The existence of a company e-mail policy was significant in *Bourke v. Nissan Motor Corp.* (1993), in which the employee had signed a policy agreeing to restrict all use of company e-mail to company purposes. The policy also stated clearly that, by signing and returning the form, the employee had been given notice and understood that workplace e-mail might be reviewed by persons other than the intended recipient. In that case, the court found that no privacy rights had been violated, even when the employer read personal e-mail, including correspondence of a sexual nature, that had been sent over the company's e-mail system. Generally speaking, employers have the right to access employee e-mails. Congress enacted the Electronic Communications and Privacy Act as a protection against wiretapping, and in 1986 its coverage was expanded to apply to nonvoice and digital messages. While the Act prohibits the interception of e-mail messages while they are being transmitted, it does not prevent employers from accessing e-mail that is stored on *their* computer systems, including messages in an employee's in-box. The same act also permits employers to access employee e-mail with the employee's consent. In practice, this means that if an employer has a policy that the employer will monitor e-mail and the employee continues to use employer system e-mail after learning about the policy, then the employee has consented to the monitoring. The take-home lesson is that anything you do on your workstation can be examined by your employer and used against you if deemed necessary, particularly if you have been notified of this possibility.

In their personnel policies, employers may reserve the right to periodically monitor employee use of the Internet and e-mail. It is also possible to install programs that block employee access to undesirable and discriminatory Internet sites or to warn employees that a site is inappropriate for the office. Technology also enables employers to track and monitor those sites that are accessed and how much time is spent at each. Intermittently notifying employees that this will happen can be a very effective deterrent and a form of primary prevention.

Sexual Harassment

Methods of harassing people in the workplace have increased with the advent of employee use of the Internet. For example, an employee might be subjected to unwelcome sexual advances through the exchange of messages on an Intranet as well as through e-mail from outside the workplace. The dissemination of sexual jokes and other sexually oriented material, for example, on a coworker's computer screen or downloaded, may form the basis of a hostile work environment claim. Sexually oriented or harassing e-mail messages may serve as evidence in court of a hostile environment. Even messages that have been erased may be retrieved later for use as evidence in court. Employers may be required to produce existing hard copies of e-mail, new printouts, or computer disks in court.

In *Coniglio v. City of Berwyn* (1999), an Illinois court held that a hostile work environment claim existed when the defendant's comptroller used his work computer to access pornographic sites and download and print pornographic images and also when the defendant called the plaintiff into his office while the images were displayed on the screen to elicit a reaction to them. Once the plaintiff complained about the conduct, she began receiving unsolicited e-mails from pornographic Internet sites.

Employers may be held liable for the behavior of their employees under theories including *respondeat superior* and negligent supervision, however it may be possible for them to defend themselves by having had a preventive program in place, properly and promptly investigating claims and formulating/disseminating an electronic communications policy. If an employer exercises reasonable care to prevent and to correct sexually harassing behavior and the employee fails to correct the behavior, the employer may sometimes be able to defend itself from liability for the employee's workplace-based acts. In addition, the taking of early remedial measures such as employee discipline as soon as the behavior is known and implementing a policy to stop the use of company computers for the dissemination of inappropriate material unrelated to employment may be useful defenses (*Farragher*, 1998; *Burlington Industries*, 1998; *Spencer*, 1999; *Daniels*, 1998; *Rudas*, 1997).

Cyberstalking

Many states and municipalities report a surge in stalking in which e-mail is the weapon. About 20% of the 600 cases reviewed in 1999 by the Los Angeles Stalking and Threat Assessment Team involved e-mail or other electronic communications, according to a Los Angeles Deputy District Attorney. As of June 2000, 22 states had enacted cyberstalking laws over the previous 3 years, and another 15 state legislatures had cyberstalking bills pending, according to the National Conference of State Legislatures. Therapists should also be reminded of the classic Tarasoff case, in which a client's statements to a therapist were not protected by confidentiality when there was a duty to warn the intended victim, who was subsequently murdered. Therapists should contact their malpractice company and/or a knowledgeable attorney to determine the status of state protection of confidentiality when, for example, a client informs the therapist of intent to commit a sexual assault either in real life or via the Internet.

The Americans With Disabilities Act: No Protection

On March 25, 1997, the U.S. Equal Employment Opportunity Commission (EEOC) issued its *Enforcement Guidance on the Americans with Disabilities Act and Psychiatric Disabilities*. The Guidance does not have the force of regulations issued by EEOC, and it will take time to see how courts interpret it. The Guidance raises certain concerns, including the broadening of the definition of mental impairment, by "suggesting" that conditions not identified in the *Diagnostic and Statistical Manual of Mental Disorders* (*DSM*) may qualify for treatment as mental impairments. Many forms of problematic sexual behaviors (including those involving the Internet) are not officially listed in the *DSM*, and at least one court has determined that Congress intended the ADA to apply only to mental disorders recognized in the *DSM*. Even if it were so recognized, Section 511 of the Americans with Disabilities Act, the definitions section, excludes from the definition of disability "homosexuality and bisexuality, transvestism, transsexualism, pedophilia, exhibitionism, voyeurism, gender identity disorders, not resulting from physical impairments, or other *sexual behavior disorders* [emphasis added]" (*Public Law 101–336*, 1990). As a result, even a documented diagnosis of sex addiction would not result in protection for the employee under the Act, unlike the coverage of other forms of addiction, for example, alcohol or drug addiction, which fall under the Act if the employee is participating or has participated in a rehabilitation program and is not engaging in illegal use.

It should be noted that the Americans with Disabilities Act does not preempt any state law, if that state law provides protection for individuals with disabilities at a level greater than or equal to that provided by the ADA. It is important to consult with an attorney licensed to practice in one's own state to determine if the particular problematic sexual behavior is protected under the state's disability law and included among the definitions of disability under that law.

☐ Assessment of OSA

In order to effectively address sex-at-work issues, therapists, EAP personnel, and managers need heuristic assessment tools that assist them in distinguishing the range of OSA that a person might engage in. These might range from illegal or dangerous activities requiring immediate intervention (e.g., cyberstalking) to those representing an issue or concern that is benign and does not violate company policy (e.g., searching for information on a new form of birth control), as well as a myriad of issues in between.

How do clinicians and employers differentiate among OSAs in the work environment? When such behaviors do occur, how do supervisors and clinicians qualitatively assess and distinguish among various types of sexual conduct so that interventions and/or level of discipline is appropriate to the infraction? While there are no hard-and-fast rules to follow, clinical experience and emerging guidelines are being used to support prudent and issue-specific interventions for OSAs at work. The following section will outline important considerations and types of questions to ask in assessing sex-at-work problems. It is important to note here that it is not the employer's (or their designate's) role to do the clinical assessment, but rather to determine whether expectations regarding job performance and behavior are being met.

Guidelines for Assessing OSA

According to Carnes (1989), the first step in assessment and intervention is to understand and acknowledge the strength of the addictive system. It is important to assess for chemical or other addictive behaviors. For example, more than 70% of cocaine users may be sexually addicted (Washton & Stone-Washton, 1990), either premorbidly or as a result of their cocaine use. During the assessment phase it is advisable to get as much information as early as possible from the referral source. When meeting with the employee, listen to the presenting problem from their perspective and listen for "identifiers" of a sexual problem. According to Turner-Shults and Shults (1997), the following are some identifiers of sexually compulsive behavior that might be observed in the workplace prior to OSA being identified:

- continual violation of rules of conduct regarding the opposite sex at work,
- constant talk about sexual matters,
- suggestive remarks,
- inappropriate comments and compliments of a sexual nature to others,
- inappropriate sexual joking,
- refusal to take prevention efforts seriously,
- inappropriate dress or personal grooming in order to be seductive,
- nonaccountability for time and/or money.

There are several other important factors to consider when making an assessment decision regarding OSA at work. An initial step in the assessment process is to ask whether the behavior you are judging falls under one of the three distinct profiles of individuals who engage in OSA: recreational, compulsive, and at-risk (Cooper, Putnam, Planchon, & Boies, 1999). Recreational or nonpathological users are those who simply aim to satisfy their curiosity about available online sexual material, to occasionally experiment with or engage in some form of OSA, or to search for specific sexual information. Compulsive users are described as individuals who have an ongoing pattern of sexually compulsive traits and who find the Internet to simply be another venue in which to pursue these activities. At-risk users include online users without a prior history of sexual compulsivity, but who, since discovering the Internet, have experienced problems in their lives from their OSA.

Once there is a clear indication about the type and profile of OSA, it is important to consider several of the following factors in making a determination as to the best way to respond:

- *Does the behavior constitute sexual harassment?* Clearly an important consideration is to what degree the OSA constitutes illegal behavior, thereby exposing the organization to liability under Title VII laws. Therefore, a first step in assessment is to inquire whether or not the OSA in question represents an unwelcome sexual advance, a request for a sexual favor, and/or another form of verbal or physical conduct of a sexual nature.
- *What is the severity of the conduct in question?* It is paramount to make a distinction between what is a *concern or an undesirable* OSA and what is an *intervention-worthy problem* that is potentially litigious and/or dangerous to employees and the company. Failure to do so often contributes to unnecessary collateral problems quite secondary to the original offense. There is a significant difference between an employee who sends a steamy e-mail message to his wife on their anniversary and an employee who spends 2 to 3 hours daily downloading pictures from teensex.com and storing them on the company hard drive. Questions to help distinguish between an undesirable behavior or concern and an intervention-worthy problem include the following:

  How egregious or severe was the conduct in question?
  Was the conduct physically threatening or humiliating?
  Does the conduct in question interfere with the employee's work performance or that of another employee?
  Does the behavior only involve the OSA participant? If there is another person, what is the nature of that relationship, and is it mutually consensual?
  Was the conduct in question confined to the Internet or did it involve a crossover from virtual/cyberspace to reality? If so, did it involve physical contact or assault? Was it nuisance behavior or stalking?
  If there were victims, what type of harm did they suffer?

- *What Is the frequency and pattern of conduct involved?* Here, it is important to distinguish between those behaviors that are generally regarded as normal, acceptable, or tolerable given the particular work culture and that conduct which can involve legal sanctions and is clearly indicative of a more chronic, problematic pattern and/or compulsive behavior. Following are some guidelines in making that assessment and determination:

Is the behavior in question an isolated incident or similar to one that has been the subject of attention/observation in the past?

Is the OSA pervasive, involving a good deal of time and/or use of other company resources (e.g., other Internet environments such as e-mail, asynchronous chat forums, newsgroups, etc.), thereby interfering with productivity and performance?

Conversely, is the conduct in question an incident when a person demonstrated particularly bad judgment? Again, is this poor judgment atypical or part of a pattern?

Again, what is the degree of both actual and perceived threat? Does any physical threat (to self or others) exist? Are there any humiliating behaviors involved?

- *What is the potential for change?* While it is unrealistic to expect clinicians and/or EAP personnel to have a crystal ball, it is reasonable to execute sound clinical judgment in determining whether the employee is a good candidate for disciplinary procedures and/or some type of counseling intervention as opposed to immediately discharging them. Failure to establish a method for making these decisions propagates the same problematic practices in dealing with online sexual behaviors at work that many zero tolerance policies have created, namely, minimizing litigation exposure while missing opportunities to enhance employee development or support effective dialogue about sensitive interpersonal issues such as sexuality. Employees who minimize or deny their OSA, who display little or no remorse, and who remain defensive in the face of a confrontation are more likely to be chronic violators of company policy and are poor candidates for change. These employees may be more appropriate for disciplinary procedures and close supervision rather than treatment. Conversely, an employee who recognizes there is a problem, can articulate a willingness to cooperate in addressing it, and appears sincere in correcting problematic OSA, including that of a more compulsive or addictive expression, may be an ideal candidate for treatment, with disciplinary stipulations dropped following successful completion of a corrective action plan. Consider the following questions in the assessment:

What is the employee's response to the confrontation regarding OSA? Is the response solely motivated by fear of reprisal (company discipline), or is there any sign of subjective discomfort due to violation of a personal norm or value or recognition of other adverse effects on his or her life?

What defense mechanisms are salient in the employees' response to questions about OSA at work (e.g., rationalization, denial, blame-not-ownership, projection, deception)?

What is the employee willing to do about the conduct in question? How willing are they to invest the necessary resources (time, money, etc.) to end it? Are they willing to participate in a corrective action plan if indicated?

☐ Treatment Models and Intervention Strategies

The workplace is in a unique position to assist employees in addressing problems associated with OSA issues, in addition to other personal problems. It not only holds the necessary leverage to move an employee toward seeking appropriate help, but it can also provide long-term support, facilitating growth and/or recovery. No other system outside the family (or legal system) has the degree of ongoing contact and influence that would allow this. In looking at EAP effectiveness with substance abuse, there is evidence that (a) constructive confrontation and referral by supervisors may improve outcomes, (b) long-term follow-up support by EAP staff may improve outcomes, and (c) initial referral to intensive treatment followed by AA attendance produces better outcomes than referral to AA without other treatment when the EAP provides long-term support and monitoring of the clients (Stone, 1993).

Due to the complex nature of the OSA and other problematic sexual behaviors and the legal ramifications for corporations and organizations, it is necessary for clinicians and HR/EAP professionals to conceptualize treatment approaches from a multivariate rather than a linear perspective. What we propose in this section are guidelines and suggestions in various arenas of treatment attention. Interventions that include several of these domains, in a coordinated effort, significantly increase the chances of a better outcome.

Treatment of OSA in the Workplace

As stated earlier, sexual behavior in the workplace can range in severity from relatively benign joking or flirting to a means of recreational avoidance/procrastination and stress reduction, to a full-blown compulsive pattern. Fundamentally, OSA, regardless of where it lies on this continuum, has the potential to be misused by employees as a predictable, easily accessible, and pseudoanonymous source of sexual gratification. In addressing OSA at work, it is imperative to accurately assess and diagnose the nature, severity, and degree of problematic potential in addition to the concerns about how this behavior represents a risk to the organization or company within which it is detected.

Compulsive behaviors often involve a relational attachment to an experience that is mood altering. It is the reliability of this experience providing access to a state sufficiently different than one the person finds intolerable that often results in the behavior being increasingly used and thereby becoming a problem. The problematic potential of OSA can be found in the context of the person's life as well as in how that interacts with the culture of the organization. An employee may be particularly vulnerable to getting involved in inappropriate OSA when there is a significant lack of job satisfaction or an absence of connectedness and relationship with colleagues and coworkers, mounting stress with few if any identifiable means of reducing it, or lack of sufficient support for ongoing growth and development within their job role. Thus, in these situations it is also necessary to look closely at the organizational culture and its relative health or dysfunction to ascertain the influence of the social milieu upon an individual employee. Any treatment solutions must contain a combination of individual self-awareness, new coping skills, and modifications in the work environment that are supportive of healthy choices. Sexual behaviors are especially complex and therefore must be approached as such. In dealing with OSA, it is important to pay attention to such life domains as:

- *Interpersonal relationships with family and friends.* Is your personal life satisfying? Do you have friendships that are supportive? Do you have a network or community that you are a part of? Can you truly be honest and intimate with others in your life? Are there sexual issues that are unresolved within your primary relationship? Are there sexual issues that you have been unable to acknowledge even to yourself?
- *Personal values, purpose, and meaning.* What are the core values that best define who you are and what is important to you? Which principles do you rely on to guide your choices and express what you care about? Who are you and what is your purpose in life? What is your personal mission for your lifetime? What gives you meaning and satisfaction in your life? Do you consider yourself part of a group or community? Are there any causes you are passionate about or involved in?
- *Satisfying career and work life.* What meaning does the work you do hold for you? Do you have satisfying relationships with your coworkers and boss? Do you feel as if you are qualified and competent to perform at work? How do you deal with stress and anger at work?
- *Awareness of and capacity for dealing with emotions.* How aware are you of your emotions? Are you able to feel and express a full range from happiness to sadness? Can you share them with others as appropriate? Can you contain and/or divert the ones that would be better to not express in the workplace? How well do you deal with anger and frustration? Is sexuality a common way you deal with difficult emotions?

- *Self-care priorities.* How do you take care of yourself? Are you happy? What do you do for fun and relaxation? Do you have enjoyable hobbies and leisure activities? Can you, and do you, take time fully away from work and still feel content? Can you get joy from activities other than work and sex?

Workplace sexual problems that are of such a magnitude that they require intervention are rarely isolated or accidental events. Instead, they are more typically reflective of an employee with difficulties coping with some internal state. Clinicians and EAP professionals alike are advised to pay attention to how the work environment is either conducive to or prohibitive of addressing the emotional needs of the employee. It is also important to attend to the corporate culture with commensurate interest to that of the individual assessment. If the approach to sexual problems and other compulsive patterns fails to consider such things as contextual antecedents, situational triggers, and cues within the work environment, then clinicians working with OSA will miss an opportunity to make more systemic interventions for both the employee and the organization as a whole. In addition, professionals need to recognize that while punishment and sanctions alone may indeed ameliorate symptoms and may make organizational sense, they are at best a partial solution. Problematic behaviors occur when a person does not have a better alternative for fulfilling needs not being met in other ways, and if new coping strategies are not somehow learned, then while the behavior may not be seen, it is surely not gone. For a more in-depth discussion of treatment issues, the reader can consult chapter 7 of this book on treatment.

Strategies

Clearly, employers, and EAP and HR personnel will need to decide what steps should be taken when they find someone engaging in OSA at work—incidents which might range from a secretary looking up breast cancer support groups during her lunch hour or a software engineer e-mailing her husband a steamy sexual invitation for that evening, to an inside sales agent who was identified by the company's monitoring software as visiting five adult Web sites for 30 minutes each over the past 2 months, to a senior VP who spends 2 hours in chatrooms every day finding new partners to have cyber- or phone sex with, to an independent contractor who sends anonymous and threatening sexual messages to the new marketing intern. How should these various situations be handled? Successful interventions must approach such issues with a graduated series of responses, the involvement of several personnel with different areas of responsibility, proper documentation, follow-up and supervision, possible sanctions, and so on. The PLISSIT (permission, limited information, specific suggestions, intensive therapy) Model (Annon, 1976) is an approach with sequentially more intense levels of intervention and has been used for a variety of sexual issues. It might also have practical applicability for issues surrounding OSA in the workplace.

In the case of the secretary, she may be given permission to do educational searches during her breaks. For the software engineer, a manager should provide limited information about company policies, for example, that e-mail (particularly of a sexual nature) should not be used for personal purposes. The inside sales agent might be called to a meeting with the HR representative and his supervisor to assess (as outlined previously) whether this is merely an isolated instance of curiosity or part of a more pervasive pattern. The outcome of this evaluation might lead to a decision to provide limited information, stating that this type of surfing violates company policy and that reoccurrences will lead to serious sanctions. However, if the evaluation finds that the sales agent has a history of sexual problems, serious marital strife, or something similar, then more specific suggestions would be warranted. For example, the employer may recommend that a further evaluation and triage be conducted by the EAP counselor or an independent clinician with expertise in this area to further determine the degree of concern for the employee (as well as risk to the company). In this latter case, a formal letter would be put in the employees' file, outlining the results of the assessment or meeting, suggesting possible sanctions if the behavior were to be repeated, and requiring a 6-month reevaluation. For the senior VP, the situation would call for stronger action, such as intensive therapy or a higher level of intervention, such as meeting with HR personnel and the president or CEO and requiring a more formal evaluation and comprehensive remediation plan. This might include limiting her access to the Web and particular sites, installing a program that monitors the types of activities she engages in on her computer, and/or mandating that she obtain therapy and a psychological evaluation from someone who specializes in issues of compulsive sexuality. Similarly, the independent contractor scenario would need to be handled carefully, ensuring both his safety and that of the other employees. In a situation as serious as this, HR and legal consultation should be sought on the advisability of the continuation of employment with close supervision, versus termination with some consideration of continued benefits for counseling. Of course, in each of these situations, documentation, consulting with appropriate legal counsel, and finding ways to consider the interests of *both* the employee and the company are critical.

☐ **Awareness and Prevention Programs**

One of the most potent constituents of any initiative addressing OSA problems in the workplace includes a primary prevention component in the
form of issue-focused education and awareness and group interventions.
Today's organizations require competent employees who possess the
knowledge and the skill base to consistently perform in real-life situations and cope with complex choices, but at the same time the employer
must recognize them as people, with their own personal strengths and
vulnerabilities. The goals of these types of educational efforts are twofold:
to help personnel to maximally achieve their workplace potential and to
provide a safe and litigiously prudent corporate culture that maximizes
fair and equitable treatment to all personnel.

Ideally, the competencies taught would be part of an ongoing, multi-
tiered approach that includes very clear policy and procedure statements,
which become a part of the corporate culture, rather than a single training event approach. This type of strategy requires ongoing training and
in-service programs for all levels within the organization (front-line employees, middle and executive management, as well as HR and EAP personnel) and dialogue structures built into the organization that support
the employees' ability to discuss issues related to power, gender, socialization roles, and sexuality. The following are some examples of what
needs to be addressed in such prevention and awareness programs and
the specific competencies to be learned.

- Corporate policies specifically regarding OSA and the reasons that type
  of behavior is of concern to the organization.
- The various types of OSA (e-mails to lover, searches on health-related
  sexuality topics, visiting adult Web sites, etc.) and discussion of why
  people engage in them as well as what to do if a supervisor, supervisee,
  friend, or family member is found to be engaging in these activities.
- Core gender differences in employee sexual behavior and use of strategies with each gender.
- Basic assessment strategies for differentiating whether an "event" is an
  isolated concern or an indication of a more serious OSA problem.
- Methods of designing and implementing appropriate action (including
  how to involve HR, EAP, legal counsel, etc.), risk management plans,
  and intervention strategies that are EEOC compliant.
- Ways to coach, counsel, or discipline subordinates regarding acceptable
  workplace behaviors, including those that foster more healthy choices,
  skills, and lifestyles.

- The ability to understand and evaluate sexual behavior and its varying expressions such as OSA; this is necessary but, in itself, not sufficient to effectively address the issue. Organizational leaders and clinicians must become competent in translating their assessments and evaluations into action plans. When problems arise they need to be able to (a) review actual details of an employee's specific case, determine if a problem exists, and if so design an EEOC compliant plan; (b) identify when a referral to an outside mental health professional is necessary; (c) cooperate with EAP or others with expertise in OSA issues in designing intervention and remediation plans.

☐ Conclusion

The research cited earlier in this chapter is a wake-up call to clinicians and EAP and HR personnel that Internet abuse among employees while on the job is on the rise. For compulsive users who have access at work, upwards of 2½ hours per day may be spent engaged in OSA at work (Cooper et al., 2001). The problem is not as yet so visible that the business community feels sufficiently motivated to devote the necessary resources to fully dealing with it. However, caught off guard by the geometric growth of such issues and without adequate policies in place, many managers, EAP personnel, clinicians, and legal counsel are scrambling to learn how to avoid Internet problems and better understand the nature of OSA and the risks involved. It goes without saying that issues of sexuality, particularly those that manifest themselves in the workplace, are generally private, sensitive, and awkward issues to discuss. In addition, employers and managers clearly prefer to follow a policy of benign neglect, the rationale being that they are "treating employees as adults." This results in these issues getting a wide berth in all but the most egregious situations. It is significant to note that similar rationales were originally used with regard to sexual harassment issues, but it soon became clear that avoidance provided no cover in the courts, and as a result a whole industry now exists devoted to early and prophylactic intervention in this area.

However, despite the great technical advances in policing and blocking employees' cybersex use, little has been implemented in the area of corporate training to educate workers in general about healthy sexuality, healthy sexual boundaries, and the consequences of sexual boundary violations in the workplace. Ideally, the workplace should not be the primary forum for education in healthy sexuality, but with few other venues doing an adequate job, the employer has no choice but to fill this void when sexuality enters the workplace. Employers are realizing that they may literally be paying the price of this neglect in the form of large sexual harassment lawsuits and/or lost productivity. The cost of ignoring it may actually be greater than the expense of addressing it. Now, with the first of a wave of 88 million young adults of the Internet generation entering the workforce, and with research showing that 20% of men and 12% of women admit to going online for sex at work (Cooper, Scherer, et al., 1999), corporations are starting to recognize the need to reinvent themselves for a new corporate culture. The next task at hand for our nation's employers, with the collaboration of mental health professionals, is education, training, and public awareness about healthy sexuality and the consequences of its dysfunctional counterpart. Organizations need to collaborate and participate in increased research, as well as contributing to the funding that make it possible, on the risk of OSA in the workplace and prevention strategies. Training programs need to be designed and delivered and then evaluated for their effectiveness in terms of the impact on the performance of workers and the decrease in OSA. These issues are not about to evaporate, and those employers who cling to that hope will find themselves paying the price of neglect in the near future.

☐ References

Annon, J. S. (1976). *The behavioral treatment of sexual problems: Brief therapy*. New York: Harper and Row.

Bourke v. Nissan Motor Corp., Case No. B068705, California Court of Appeal, 2d App. District (July 26, 1993).

Burlington Industries Inc. v. Ellerth, 524 U.S. 742 (1998).

Carnes, P. (1989). *Contrary to love: Helping the sexual addict*. Minneapolis, MN: Compcare Publishers.

Carnes, P. J. (1999). Editorial: Cybersex, sexual health, and the transformation of culture. *Sexual Addiction & Compulsivity, 6*(2), 77–78.

Carnes, P. (2001). Cybersex, courtship, and escalating arousal: Factors in addictive sexual desire. *Sexual Addiction and Compulsivity, 8*, 45–78.

Coniglio v. City of Berwyn, No. 99-4475, 1999 WL 1212190 (N.D. Ill. Dec. 16, 1999).

Cooper, A., Putnam, D. E., Planchon, L. A., & Boies, S. C. (1999). Online sexual compulsivity: Getting tangled in the net. *Sexual Addiction & Compulsivity, 6*(2), 79–104.

Cooper, A., Scherer, C., Boies, S. C., & Gordon, B. (1999). Sexuality on the internet: From sexual exploration to pathological expression. *Professional Psychology: Research and Practice, 30*(2), 154–164.

Cooper, A., Scherer, C., & Mathy, R. (2001). Overcoming methodological concerns in the investigation of online sexual activities. *Cyberpsychology and Behavior, 4*(4), 437–448.

Curtis v. Citibank, No. 97-1065, 1998 WL 3354 (S.D.N.Y. Jan. 5, 1998).

Daniels v. Worldcom Corp. No. A.3:97-CV-0721-P, 1998 WL 91261 (N.D. Tex. Feb. 23, 1998).

Farragher v. City of Boca Raton 524 U.S. 775 (1998).

Greenfield, D. N. (1999). *Virtual addiction: Help for netheads, cyberfreaks, and those who love them*. Oakland, CA: New Harbinger.

Goldberg, A. (1998). *Monthly users report on adult sexually oriented sites for April 1998*. Washington DC: Relevant Knowledge.

Kimberlin, D., & Headley L. H. (2000). ADA overview and update: What has the supreme court done to Disability Law? *19 Review of Litigation 579*. University of Texas at Austin School of Law.

Knox v. State of Indiana, 93 F. 3rd 1327, 1332, 1337 (7th Cir. 1996).

Lybarger, J. S. (1997). Sexual addiction: A hidden factor in sexual harassment. *Sexual Addiction & Compulsivity, 4*, 77–90.

McCarthy, M. J. (2000, January 10). Web surfers beware: The company tech may be a secret agent. *Wall Street Journal*. Retrieved from http://wsj.com

McGraw, D. K. (1995). Sexual harassment in cyberspace: The problem of unwelcome e-mail. *Rutgers Computer and Technology Law Journal, 21*, 491–518.

McVeigh v. Cohen, Civil Action No. 98-116 (D.D.C., January 26, 1998).

Oneglia, S. (1999, February 22). Transsexuality ruled disability. *The Gainesville Sun*. Retrieved from http://www.usdoj.gov/crt/foia.tal051.tx

Public Law 101-336 July 26, 1990, 104 Stat. 327, page 133. Retrieved January 11, 2001 from http://janweb.icdi.wvu.edu/kinder/pages/ada_statute.htm

Rudas v. Nationwide Mutual Ins. Co., No. 96-5987, 1997 WL 634501 (E.D. Pa. Sept. 26, 1997).

Scott v. Plaques Unlimited, 46 F. Supp 2nd 1287, 1289 (M.D. Fla. 1999).

Simpson, D. (2000). *Feds find dangerous cyberstalking hard to prevent*. CNN.com. Retrieved from http://www.cnn....ing/06/12/cyberstalkers.idg.index.html

Smyth v. The Pillsbury Co., 914 F. Supp.97 (E.D. Pa., 1996).

Spencer v. Commonwealth Edison Co. No. 97-7718, 1999 WL 14486 (N.D. Ill. Jan. 6, 1999).

Stone, W. (1993). *Employee compliance system*. Dallas, TX: Compliance Corporation of America.

Strauss v. Microsoft Corp., 814 F. Supp. 1186 (S.D.N.Y. 1993).

Tarasoff v. Regents of the University of California, 17 Cal. 3d 425, 551 P.2d 334, 131 Cal. Rptr. 14 (Cal. 1976). Retrieved from http://plague.law.umkc.edu/cphl/cases/privacy/tarasoff.htm

Turner-Shults, N., & Shults, C. (1997). Sexual addiction in the workplace: An EAP perspective. *Sexual Addiction & Compulsivity, 4*(2), 179–192.

United States v. Mark L. Simons, Case No. 99-4238 (4th Cir., February 28, 2000) O'Connor v. Ortega, 480 U.S. 709 (1987).

Washton, A. M., & Stone-Washton, N. (1990). *Sex and drugs: The intimate connection*. Realizations, P.O. Box 555, Woodstock, NY 12498.

David Greenfield
Maressa Orzack

The Electronic Bedroom: Clinical Assessment of Online Sexual Problems and Internet-Enabled Sexual Behavior

☐ A New Phenomenon

Behavioral health clinicians are now encountering new problems and difficulties in their patients' lives that may, in part, be due to the their use and/or abuse of the Internet for sexual behavior. Greenfield (2000) referred to this phenomenon as Internet-enabled sexual behavior (IESB), however in order to remain consistent, the term online sexual activity (OSA) will be used in this chapter.

The purpose of this chapter is to provide clinicians with information about the definition, description, and assessment of OSA. First, the current definitions of OSA are augmented. IESBs are described and conceptual issues related to the development of the "disorder" are explored. Finally, evaluation and assessment issues are reviewed, along with specific information on how to conduct an examination of OSA.

☐ Online Sexual Activity

OSA is the use of the Internet for any type of sexual behavior which includes text, graphic files, or audio sites. Further, this activity may be used for recreation, entertainment, exploration, support, education, commerce, and efforts to attain and secure sexual or romantic partners, and to relieve stress. There are three subcategories included in this definition.

1. *Cybersex and its own subcategory of cybering.* These include using the Internet to engage in sexually gratifying behaviors such as pornography, sexual chats, e-mails, and instant messaging. Cybering is the direct use by two people who share the same fantasy while one or both masturbate. Online cameras often augment this.
2. *Online sexual problems (OSPs).* This includes the full range of difficulty that people can have as a result of their use of the Internet for sexual purposes. They range from a single incident to severe patterns. The repercussions can vary from guilt, financial ruin, loss of family, and divorce to jail sentences for viewing and/or transmitting inappropriate sites. Many people follow up Internet contact with phone and/or real-life connections.
3. *Online sexual compulsivity.* A subtype of OSPs, it is the most serious OSA because it indicates loss of control and even diminished capacity to regulate activities of daily living.

Problematic online sexual experiences appear, at least in part, to be the result of the synergistic relationship between the psychoactive elements of the Internet, including reinforcement, disinhibition, excitement, and anonymity, and the level of stimulation provided by the specific sexual material. In addition, there are undoubtedly numerous comorbid factors that impact the potential toward developing OSPs. These include but are not limited to preexisting sexual compulsion/addiction problems, as well as numerous other sexual, impulsive, and affective disorders and biosocial problems.

An example of this is MC, a 40-year-old man who has never been able to achieve orgasm except by compulsive masturbating. Described as having a nonparaphilic sexual disorder, Joe has a history of depression, low self-esteem, shyness, and socially avoidant behavior. Before the Internet, he used magazines and videos to sooth himself. Now he uses the Internet. Joe can now distance himself and safely engage in sexual stimulation on the Internet. For Joe his sexuality and sexual expression has become inexorably linked to Internet behavior. The three psychoactive elements of the Internet, known as the triple-A engine of affordability, accessibility, and anonymity (Cooper, 1998), serve to both maintain and contribute to Joe's nonparaphilic sexual problem.

A comprehensive assessment is dependent on the accuracy of the information about the patient's sexual activities and behavior. One way to analyze the role online sexual behavior plays in the patient's life and the nature of the impairment or distress caused by the behavior is self-monitoring. The use of self-monitoring of daily behavior assists in uncovering an individual's cycle of online sexual behavior and provides clues to why a person continues to engage in the behavior. The self-monitoring form includes a record of the time of day, thoughts, feelings, and behaviors that precede and follow every incident of online sexual behavior. The more detailed the patient's account is, the more likely that antecedent stimuli that trigger the behavior will be able to be identified. Reinforcing consequences of the behavior will also be able to be identified. Self-monitoring can provide a realistic psychophysical snapshot of sexual behavior problems, along with the contributing triggers and consequences.

The patient's awareness of the connections to the online sexual behavior is enough to decrease them. Self-monitoring helps the patient identify behaviors and situations that may serve as triggers of OSA. These are often completely unrelated to the sex. For example, depressed or irritable feelings from a bad day at work may trigger going online to escape these negative emotions. Self-monitoring is helpful for relapse prevention. Clinicians find that reactivity to self-monitoring may serve therapeutic purposes. An acceleration of desirable behavior and suppression of undesirable behavior often occurs. Finally, despite concerns regarding accuracy, self-reporting is often the only way to get a full account of behaviors that are difficult to observe, such as online sexual behavior. It is worth noting that individuals may often present for treatment in relation to problems associated with sexual compulsivity or relationship difficulties without identifying their online behavior as a problem. Due to denial and feelings of shame and embarrassment, it is common for sexually compulsive people to not acknowledge the problem. Thus, it is increasingly important that clinicians ask about sexual use of the Internet when related problems are apparent. More typically, presentation for clinical treatment is requested due to secondary problems arising from the use and abuse of the Internet or due to pressure received from another person. It is important to note that the distress the patient is experiencing may not be directly related to the sexual activities, but rather to the negative consequences of such. The sexual behavior itself may very well be ego-syntonic.

Conceptualizing compulsive sexual behavior as an addictive disorder with features consistent with substance dependence or gambling (i.e., addiction) has implications for how the behavior is assessed and treated.

The issue of online sexuality encompasses a wide range of behaviors including, but not limited to, answering sexual personal ads; chatrooms/message boards; Webcam sites; private member chatrooms; adult online sex shops and catalogs; e-mail, flirting and sexual innuendo; actual overt sex talk with the goal of arousal/orgasm; telephone sex; and actual, real-time sexual encounters. In some cases, online sexual encounters extend to more pathological forms of sexual behavior known as paraphilia; one can easily experiment with sadism, masochism, bondage, discipline, gender roles, playing personas, bestiality, fantasy, and many other paraphilic sexual activities. Most imaginable sexual preferences or desires can easily be viewed and experienced via the Internet. Because it is easy to search and view sexual material, which often leads to engagement in sexual behavior online, the potential for compulsive Internet use is significantly increased. Accessibility, affordability, and anonymity, (the triple-A engine) combine with the instant gratification and stimulating content of the Internet to make OSPs more probable than sexual problems caused by other media (Cooper, Delmonico, & Burg, 2000; Greenfield, 1999a).

A thorough assessment of general sexual behavior should routinely be performed. Further evaluation of the specifics of online sexual behavior and possible maladaptive patterns should follow. Finally, an assessment of potential compulsivity with such behaviors should be completed. Sexual compulsivity may not be present even with OSP and IESB. The presentation of a sexual problem may in fact be independent or interdependent of the (Internet) medium in which such behaviors are engaged. The questions of how the Internet serves to synergize, amplify, and maintain an individual's sexual behavior (compulsive or otherwise) becomes an additional focus in evaluating such individuals

☐ The Sexuality of the Internet: Sex in the Virtual Modality

Sexual content is found in every area of online service, including Web sites, newsgroups, chatrooms, Web cams, personals, e-mail, and Bulletin Board Services (BBS). Online sexual material comes in a variety of forms and ranges from viewing of visual sexual material to fully interactive mutual masturbation, complete with video, sound, and text (Putnam, 1997a). The content of online sexual material includes photos of partially clothed people as well as explicit images of people engaged in deviant sexual behavior, including a full range of paraphilic sexual preferences. It is now nearly impossible to discuss the issue of sexual function and dysfunction without mention of the Internet.

Clinicians increasingly report patients who have had a non-Internet problem with compulsive/addictive sexual behavior (with pornography or masturbation) that were exacerbated in their subsequent use of the Internet. Research supports the fact that less than half of the Internet compulsives report sexual behavior as their primary Internet focus (Greenfield, 1999). Compulsive Internet users surveyed often do engage in cybersex, and nearly one-third report (31%) having had real-time sex with someone they met online. Often these real-time sexual encounters begin as virtual online explorations. In many cases such individuals may have only fantasized about some of the paraphilic and non-paraphilic behaviors prior to going online. The online experience then seems to cata-lyze their newly discovered paraphilic desires.

For example, Jane, a 31-year-old mental health professional, complained of difficulty with intimate relationships, career problems, and interpersonal conflicts. During therapy, Jane admitted to a long-term paraphilia involving a spanking fantasy with autoerotic stimulation. Prior to her online use, the paraphilic behavior was limited to magazine use and some personal ads. Once accessing the Net she began to actively seek, advertise, and meet individuals whom she could have real-time spanking sessions with; this was occurring regularly when she first came in for treatment. Her diagnosis was a combination of paraphilia NOS, impulsive control disorder NOS, as well as a V-code for partner relational problem. Her compulsive Internet use developed conjointly with her growing and expanded paraphilic behavior.

Assessment focused on developing a clear and concise history of her sexual arousal patterns and behavior, both pre- and post-Internet use. Treatment then naturally focused on the sexual issues themselves and how her use of the Internet facilitated her paraphilic behavior.

☐ When Does Online Sexual Behavior Become Problematic or Compulsive?

There are numerous indications that a large majority of sexual compulsives use the Internet as a modality for achieving sexual stimulation and grati-fication (Carnes, 1999). There is little agreement among the psychiatric and psychological communities with regard to compulsive sexual behavior and even less when it comes to the Internet as a mediating or enabling factor. Regardless of how it is defined, many practicing clinicians have witnessed patients presenting with a variety of sexual problems integrated with their Internet use. In most, if not all, cases, patients presenting for evaluation or treatment are doing so because of negative effects second-ary to their use/abuse of the Internet for sexual pursuits.

The key questions that should be asked are as follows: (a) Does the patient utilize Internet-enabled sexual pursuits to alter their conscious-ness or mood? and (b) Does this behavior interfere with the major spheres of daily living (e.g., work, children, school, health, social and family rela-tionships, etc.)?

The overall clinical context, within which a patient presents him- or herself, should be seriously considered when assessing online sexual behavior. In many cases the use of the Internet for sexual stimulation and gratification may not be the core psychological issue. The history, learned behavior, and biological factors in combination with the potent availability of Internet-based sexual material, contribute to compulsive behavior. Clinical experience suggests that a majority of problems associated with online sexual activity revolve around the interference and compromises this behavior causes in marital and other significant relationships as well as other dimensions of life (e.g., work, legal problems).

To complicate this further, many cybersurfers believe that online flirting, cybering, or masturbating does not impact their personal relationships, They often think of them as totally separate behaviors. Many spouses and significant others feel distrust, betrayal, and rejection. This betrayal is exacerbated because the violation of their relationship often occurs in the same bedroom or family room that is used for their family activities.

The clinician should pay particular attention to whether the Internet is being used as a means to achieve stimulation (arousal) and/or as a method of achieving gratification (orgasm), and specifically how this activity is affecting the patient's life. Some patients justify their behavior by saying they use virtual sex to achieve arousal before actual sex. Others eliminate the connection with their spouse entirely. This distinction will be helpful in determining the degree of potential impact on real-time relationships and assist in ruling in or out other sexual arousal/orgasm disorders. If the Internet is being utilized to achieve arousal but the patient continues to maintain active sexual relations with his or her partner, then this requires more of a focus on the assessment of the relationship. In other words, this may not be a sexual disorder at all, but rather an issue on how this couple communicates and manages their sexuality. If the Internet is used primarily for sexual gratification, then the assessment focus should be more inclusive.

It is important to note that many sexual activities available on the Net may not interfere with a person's functioning in any way. For many people, adult Web sites, personals, purchasing sexual aids and materials, and the wealth of educational information and resources can actually enhance a person (and/or couple's) life and functioning. The Net can be a valuable, safe, and judgment-free source of sexual information, which in many cases may not be available elsewhere. Although some people (about 6%; Greenfield, 1999) become compulsive in the sexual use of the Internet, the majority does not. The Internet then remains yet another potent tool, just as medication for sexual dysfunction, vibrators, and adult videos.

☐ What Defines Online Sexual Problems?

Greenfield (2001a) delineates two types of compulsive Internet-enabled sexual behavior: primary and secondary. The primary type typically consists of a sexually compulsive pattern of behavior that predates the use of the Internet for achieving sexual satisfaction. The Internet functions as an alternate and perhaps more efficient means of achieving sexual arousal and satisfaction. This Internet-enabled pattern can accelerate the development of compulsive sexual behavior in those who may be vulnerable.

A typical example of this is JS. Over a 15-year period he meticulously collected X-rated videotapes, which he used for self-soothing during flashbacks of his childhood. He was forced to stop using tapes when he got married. Coincidentally, about this time his family bought their first computer. It did not take him long to find that the enormous number of sexual sites on the Internet allowed him to sooth himself more effectively than the videotapes. JS used this sexual activity as a means of coping with a variety of stressful situations at home and at work. Finally, he was caught looking at sexual Web sites at work. His supervisor told him that he would need to see a therapist and that if he engaged in this activity again, he would be fired.

The secondary type of patient often has no prior history of compulsive sexual behavior, but the development of the compulsive pattern seems to occur almost concurrently with the introduction of the Internet. There appears to be a synergistic process, where the stimulating content of sexually related material is amplified and enhanced by the potent nature of the Internet medium itself. It is almost as if an arousal/compulsion cycle spontaneously ignites. This is often borne out of the seeds of curiosity, sexual desire, and ease of availability of the Internet. It, in essence, seems to lower the threshold for certain people who go on to develop more consistent problems, further complicating their lives. There is little difference between thought and Internet-enabled action. Now, whatever the sexual fantasy or other paraphilic behavior, there is a relatively easy way to satisfy it. The Internet provides immediate gratification that affects one's ability to inhibit previously managed drives and desires. Hence, a compulsive pattern is born!

An example of the secondary type is VR, a divorced woman, who bought her computer in order to find sex and romance in chatrooms. She instantly became addicted to chatrooms, instant messaging, and personals. Prior to her computer use she had exhibited no compulsive sexual behavior, however she had been treated for severe depression. She began neglecting her child and her household obligations. The minute she arrived home VR turned to her computer and stayed on until the early morning hours. In addition, because of the easy availability of potential sex partners, VR took many risks. She gave online contacts her home address, she met many people offline, and she disappeared for days at a time without telling anyone where she was. She ended up losing custody of her child. This case sadly illustrates the dissociative and addictive power of the Internet when combined with potent sexual arousal.

☐ A Review of Assessment and Evaluation of Online Sexual Behavior

Two major elements must be considered when assessing online sexual activity. The primary concern should be to evaluate the nature and extent of the compulsive sexual behavior pattern irrespective of the modality in which the compulsive behavior is practiced. Secondarily, although the Internet may be the focus of the presenting problem, the first stages of the evaluation should always consist of a standard psychiatric intake evaluation along with an expanded sexual history.

This evaluation should include a complete bio-psychosocial history, mental status exam, and general medical and psychiatric history. Care should be taken to utilize interview techniques to minimize defensiveness and increase collaboration and comfort of the patient. Asking questions in a gentle, nonconfrontational manner is critical. Assume more than is revealed, but be careful while probing for details. Do not be accusatory or judgmental. This can be difficult when dealing with powerful forms of sexual behavior. When asking about the sexual history and the addictions history, care should be given to assessing what attempts had been made previously to address the problem. Questions should be formulated to ascertain the nature and extent of the sexual problem. What circumstances arose that made them decide to seek help; in other words, why now? Health care professionals should pay special attention to the context of the patient's presenting problem. The motivation for seeking treatment is often promulgated by the significant impact compulsive online behavior has on relationships. This reason for seeking treatment should be used to help assess prognosis and overall readiness for change.

Assessment of OSA presents clinicians with new and unique challenges. There are several general questions that should be included in a typical work-up for sexual concerns.

Sexual History

1. This should include early sexual awareness, age of onset of puberty, and emotional associations with sexual experiences. Specific focus should be on arousal patterns, masturbatory behavior (included methods of achieving arousal), fantasy patterns, use of role-play and personas, and use of audio/visual (pornography) or manual aids in arousal, stimulation, and gratification.
2. Clinicians can assess how the patient experiences their sexuality. In many cases patients who present with online sexual problems have prior histories of sexual problems, but there is evidence that there are a large number of individuals for whom the Internet seems to be the catalyst for a compulsive sexual process. This includes the use of explicit sexual media e.g., magazines, film, video, Internet, photographs, and so forth, frequent masturbation, use of 800/900 phone sex, sexual chatrooms, cybersex, cyberaffairs, utilizing prostitutes, indiscriminate and high-risk sexual behavior, and other forms of hypersexual behavior. One should further assess their personal pattern of Internet use and what contributes to changes in their online sexual behavior. In addition, the degree of tolerance as the result of withdrawal from the Internet for OSA should be assessed. Attention should be paid to experienced and expressed emotional distress regarding the problem and their subjective degree of impairment.
3. It is critical to address what stimulates the behavior or a relapse of the behavior after a period of abstinence. The knowledge of these triggers can be used to construct a relapse prevention plan. More specific questions include, when and where are the behaviors engaged in? Are they solitary or interpersonal? Is there shame attached to their behavior? Are they secretive about their online use and abuse? What seemed to start the pattern (when and where)? What has been done to stop it? Again, it is important to always be conducting the assessment with potential treatment issues in mind; the clinician is continually evaluating potential resources, underutilized skills, motivation, and readiness to change.

Early and Current Social Development

1. It is important to address intimacy patterns, early social and relational experiences, and interpersonal relationship patterns and styles. What is sought is a sense of the patient's interpersonal history, their social affiliation needs, social skills, and social dynamics, with an eye toward

their sexual patterns of behavior. Significant family experiences and perceived levels of family-of-origin discord and interaction should be noted, as well as any instances of precocious or premature sexual arousal or stimulation. This should include an assessment of any overt or covert aspect of sexual abuse.

2. This is also an important place to address the therapeutic relationship, transference, and countertransference. The potential for strong inter-personal reactions in patients, along with countertransferential feelings in the clinician is very clear when dealing with sexual material. It is important to be aware of these strong, and at times uncomfortable, emotions. The key is recognition of such feelings and reactions, and understanding their meaning, not eliminating them.

Marital and Intimate Relationship History

This is a key component in assessing online sexual problems. The vast majority of clinical presentations of OSPs appear to involve problems with significant intimate relationships (Greenfield, 2001b). In many cases a spouse or significant other has discovered the problematic behavior, which frequently has had significant negative effects on the relationship. Clinical experience suggests that the online sexual problem serves as both a cause and an effect in impacting such intimate relationships; there are undoubtedly relational issues that may contribute to the sexual behavior, and the sexual behavior clearly re-contributes to further relationship dynamics. We are talking about a recursive and reciprocal loop of interaction.

Life Interference

It is essential to address the consequences of OSA on work, family relationships, parenting, friendships, and other life obligations. The reason is that these interferences tell us a lot about the nature and extent of the problem, as well as the real impact it may be having on the patient's life. For example, problems in the workplace may result in disciplinary actions because of viewing, downloading, or distributing adult images or content. There have been countless disciplinary actions and terminations from jobs because of these activities. In the home, there are frequently marital and relationship concerns, parenting problems, and potential legal and financial consequences. Examine the degree of discomfort with the problem (or the effects of the problem), which can be utilized to determine level of motivation for treatment, as well as an assessment of overall judgment and insight. These factors become important in developing a viable and practical treatment plan.

Addictions and Impulsive Behavior History

1. Assess whether there have been other instances of addictive, impulsive, or compulsive behavior. Often there is an overlap between a history of other addictive and impulsive behaviors and the presence of online sexual problems (Greenfield, 1999a; 1999b). There is also a strong correlation between the full affective spectrum of problems and subsequent sexual problems (American Psychiatric Association [APA], 1994). Conditions and disorders could be identified that require treatment prior to (or concurrently while) addressing the sexual compulsivity.
2. Histories of frequent abuse of mood-altering behaviors or substances become useful in personality and behavioral assessment as well as treatment planning. Information can be derived about coping skills and strategies, support systems, and personal resources—all of which are important in developing a therapeutic plan. Based on the premise that all addictions follow similar neurochemical patterns (elevating seratonin and dopamine levels), it becomes less critical what behavior is engaged in, and more important how, when, and why the behavior occurs. In addition, a history of previous treatments and attempted solutions is critical in creating a solution-focused treatment plan; it is important not to repeat interventions that have been proven ineffective.
3. It is useful when assessing the biological factors which might be contributing to a patients' problems to ask the patients to fill in a genealogy chart of their family going back two generations.

☐ Diagnostic Factors in OSPs

Assessment of online sexual compulsivity, in addition to the factors discussed above, requires a thorough evaluation of psychological, social, and sexual history, including current functioning. As a result of such an assessment, preexisting, contributing, or comorbid psychiatric disorders and conditions should be evaluated and ruled out. It is clear that there are many psychiatric disorders that can impact, effect, and even include sexual disorders and problems as a lesser part of the symptom constellation. In assessing compulsive or problematic sexual behavior, one must look at questions that address and rule out a variety of Axis I disorders, including affective disorders and manic or hypomanic states; this can be done during a thorough patient and family history. A medical work-up is often recommended to rule out physiological problems. Hypersexual behavior can certainly be a corollary of such manic states as well as the result of certain hormonal and metabolic disturbances, such as hyperthyroidism, endocrine imbalances, and head trauma.

One must also address the patient's history of compulsive and impulsive behavior, both with regard to sex as well as in other areas of life. There is a strong tendency among those individuals with a sexual disorder history to develop and expand problematic sexual behavior online. For example, it is far easier for a patient to develop a mild nonparaphilic fantasy/interest into a more pronounced compulsive pattern once online.

An example of several of these points is illustrated in PT's case. He was referred by a sex therapist; PT had never had a complete sexual relationship. In order to have an orgasm during intercourse, he typically had to discontinue intercourse and masturbate. This problem put significant strain on the relationship. His partner became angry with him each time this happened, but they did not communicate about it. As a teenager and later as an adult, he used adult magazines and videos for self-gratification. Then he turned to the Internet because it was accessible, affordable, and anonymous. Most of his connections with the few friends he had were through the Internet, as he was highly uncomfortable with his large physical size. He had poor social skills. He had childhood diabetes and he was not paying attention to his diet or monitoring his blood pressure. When first seen, he denied depression, but it turned out that he had a long-standing history of depression since he was a teenager. The final stressor was the excessive demands from his high-powered job. First, it was essential that he contact his primary care physician about his high blood pressure and have a psychopharmacological check-up. Only after these things were addressed could his sexually compulsive behavior be treated.

Diagnostically, there are no formal categories to address Internet addiction or compulsive Internet use and behavior. More specifically, there are no categories or DSM codes specifically designed to cover compulsive online sexual behavior. Evaluation and ruling out of other preexisting or concomitant problems and disorders should be considered, including but limited to substance abuse and dependence, alcohol abuse and/or dependence, impulse control disorders, obsessive-compulsive disorder (OCD), avoidant personality disorder compulsive personality disorders, depression, and anxiety disorders, especially social anxiety and phobias.

There are numerous *DSM-IV* diagnostic categories that have been utilized in research and that may have applicability in clinical practice. Several that may be adapted to address the clinical issues in Internet-enabled, sexually compulsive behaviors are substance abuse or dependence, and pathological gambling. Impulse-disorder NOS, paraphilic and nonparaphilic sexual problems as well as other categories that include diagnoses that are more specifically related to sexual activity, such as sexual disorder NOS, may be useful.

☐ Conditions That Impact OSA

It is important for the clinician to recognize that patients who are online may have frequent exposure, in addition to instant access to sexual materials, both online and offline. One patient in a group therapy session confessed that he stopped looking at his e-mail because he was consistently bombarded by pornographic sites. Clinicians should include questions in their assessment about what sites their patients view and the effect they have on them. Various forms of Internet advertising for sexual products or materials may serve as a trigger for OSPs. Other forms of advertising may serve as a stimulus for online sexually compulsive behavior.

☐ Online Help

We have reviewed numerous Web sites published by therapists and other health care professionals. Although they are generally informative, in many cases the information presented is not verifiable, and not researched based. Overall, educational and support Web sites can be very useful for patients wanting self-help resources. However, most patients will need to consult an offline therapist. Some Web site publishers have no health care credentials and are really only advertising products or books for sale. It is important to note that all of these Web sites presented unique (however reasonable) definitions of sex or Internet addiction. Most included a quiz to help determine whether a person had a problem or not.

These Web site questionnaires rely entirely on self-report and may ignore many of the other issues in the person's life, which, as we pointed out, may need to be assessed and treated first. Overall, there is probably as good deal of valuable information on all areas of medicine and psychology online, but the user should be wary. It is always better to get some verification from several sources before performing a self-diagnosis.

☐ Conclusions

The special features of OSA have been discussed in this chapter. These diagnostic designations equally apply to the paraphilic and nonparaphilic patterns of sexual behavior that psychologists increasingly encounter in clinical practice. As more and more facets of daily living come to depend extensively on the use of computers, psychologists can expect to face the challenge of computer use and abuse involving sexual behavior more frequently.

Psychologists should strive to reach consensus about how to deal with the diverse manifestations of these phenomena. Computer and Internet abuse has come to the fore as a common thread in many behavioral problems, especially sexual issues. The assessment of OSPs presents a new and challenging addition to the clinical treatment of sexual problems and disorders.

Proper diagnosis requires evaluation of the full scope of events in the patient's life. It is always important to note that each person's behavior is the sum of their total experience, including learned experiences, family history, psychiatric history, and environmental influences. Some patients' behaviors during compulsive sexual situations may resemble OCD, while others may be closer to depression; and still others may appear similar to addictions to drugs, alcohol, or gambling. Diverse diagnoses can include impulse control disorder, NOS, and other comorbid behaviors such as OCD, bipolar disorder, and anxiety spectrum illnesses. As previously noted, it seems that several categories in *DSM-IV* may initially appear applicable. Trying to fit the variety and complexity of these behaviors into such current diagnostic guidelines is a difficult task. A new and comprehensive separate diagnostic disorder labeled OSP would more accurately reflect this new form of sexual behavior. Such a clear diagnostic category would provide clinicians the freedom to do expanded research and to refine assessment processes and procedures. Researchers need to evaluate assessment and treatment procedures as well as methods for training clinicians to assess and treat the OSPs.

☐ References

American Psychiatric Association. (1994). *Diagnostic and statistical manual of mental disorders* (4th ed.). Washington, DC: Author.

Anderson, N., & Coleman, E. (1991). Childhood abuse and family sexual attitudes in sexually compulsive males: A comparison of three clinical groups. *American Journal of Preventive Psychiatry and Neurology, 3,* 8–15.

Barak, A. (1999). Psychological applications on the Internet: A discipline on the threshold of a new millennium. *Applied and Preventive Psychology, 8,* 231–246.

Becker, R. E., & Heimberg, R. G. (1988). Assessment of social skills. In A. S. Bellack & M. Hersen (Eds.), *Behavioral assessment: A practical handbook* (3rd ed., pp. 365–395). New York: Pergamon Books.

Bingham, J. E., & Piotrowski, C. (1996). On-line sexual addiction: A contemporary enigma. *Psychological Reports, 79,* 257–258.

Bradford, J. (1997). Medical interventions in sexual deviance. In D. R. Laws & W. O'Donohue (Eds.), *Sexual deviance: Theory, assessment, and treatment* (pp. 449–464). New York: The Guilford Press.

Brenner, V. (1997). Psychology of computer use: XLVII. Parameters of Internet use, abuse and addiction: The first 90 days of the Internet use survey. *Psychological Reports, 80,* 879–882.

Carnes, P. (1991). *Don't call it love: Recovery from sexual addiction.* New York: Bantam Books.

Carnes, P. (1993). Addiction and post-traumatic stress: The convergence of victims' realities. *Treating Abuse Today, 3*(13), 5–11.

Coleman, E. (1992). Is your patient suffering from compulsive sexual behavior. *Psychiatric Annals, 22*(6), 320–325.

Cooper, A. (1998). Sexuality and the Internet: Surfing into the new millennium. *CyberPsychology & Behavior, 1,* 187–193.

Cooper, A., Boies, S., Maheu, M., & Greenfield, D. (2000) Sexuality and the Internet: The next sexual revolution. In F. Muscarella & L. Szuchman. (Eds.), *Psychological perspectives on human sexuality: A research based approach* (pp. 519–545). New York: Wiley.

Cooper, A., Delmonico, D., & Burg, R. (2000). Cybersex users and abusers: New findings and implications. *Sexual Addiction & Compulsivity: The Journal of Treatment and Prevention, 7,* 1–25.

Cooper A., Putnam, D. E., Planchon, L. A., & Boies, S. C. (1999). Online sexual compulsivity: Getting tangled in the net. *Sexual Addiction & Compulsivity: The Journal of Treatment and Prevention, 6,* 79–104.

Cooper, A., Scherer, C. R., Boies, S. C., & Gordon, B. L. (1999). Sexuality on the Internet: From sexual exploration to pathological expression. *Professional Psychology, 30*(2), 154–164.

Delmonico, D. L. (1997). Cybersex: High tech sex addiction. *Sexual Addiction and Compulsivity: The Journal of Treatment and Prevention, 4*(2), 159–167.

Earle, R. H., & Earle, M. R. (1995). *Sex addiction: Case studies and management.* New York: Brunner/Mazel.

Goldberg, A. (1998, April). *Monthly users report on adult sexually oriented sites.* Washington, DC: Relevant Knowledge.

Greenfield (1999a). Psychological characteristics of compulsive Internet use: A preliminary analysis. *CyberPsychology and Behavior, 2*(5), 403–412.

Greenfield, D. N. (1999b). Virtual addiction: Help for netheads, cyberfreaks, and those who love them. Oakland, CA: New Harbinger Publications.

Greenfield, D. N. (2000). *Cybersex and Cyber-affairs: Digital dating and the electronic bedroom.* Paper presented at the 2000 Annual Meeting of the American Psychological Association, Washington, DC.

Greenfield, D. N. (2001a). Presentation to the Oregon Psychological Association, Portland, OR, April.

Greenfield, D. N. (2001b). Sexuality and the internet. *Counselor, 2,* 62–63.

Griffiths, M. (1997, August). *Does internet and computer "addiction" exist?: Some case study evidence.* Paper presented at the Annual Conference of American Psychological Association.

Grubin, D., & Mason, D. (1997). Medical models of sexual deviance. In D. R. Laws & W. O'Donohue (Eds.), *Sexual deviance: Theory, assessment, and treatment* (pp. 434–448). New York: Guilford.

Hapgood, F. (1996). Sex Sells, Inc. *Technology, 4,* 45–51.

Junginger, J. (1997). Fetishism: Assessment and treatment. In D. R. Laws & W. O'Donohue (Ed.), *Sexual deviance: Theory, assessment, and treatment* (pp. 92–110). New York: Guilford.

Kafka, M. (2000). The paraphilia-related disorders: Nonparaphilic hypersexuality and sexual compulsivity. In S. A. Liebman & R. C. Rosen (eds.), *Principles and practice of sex therapy* (3rd ed.). New York: Guilford.

Kafka, M., & Prentky, R. (1992). Fluoxetine treatment of nonparaphilic sexual addictions and paraphilias in men. *Journal of Clinical Psychiatry, 53,* 351–358.

Kraut, R., Patterson, M., Lundmark, V., Kiesler, S., Mukopadhyay, T., & Schewrlis, W. 1999. Internet paradox: A social technology that reduces social involvement and psychological well being. *American Psychologist, 53*(9), 1031.

King, S. A. (1999). Internet gambling and pornography: Illustrative examples of the psychological consequences of communication anarchy. *CyberPsychology & Behavior, 2*(3), 175–194.

King, S. A., & Barak, A. (1999). Compulsive Internet gambling: A new form of an old clinical pathology. *CyberPsychology & Behavior, 2*(5), 441–456.

King, S. A., & Moreggi, D. (1998). Internet therapy and self help groups—the pros and cons. In J. Gackenbach (Ed.), *Psychology and the Internet: Intrapersonal, interpersonal and transpersonal implications* (pp. 77–109). San Diego, CA: Academic Press.

King, S. A., Poulos, S. T., & Engi, S. (1998). Using the Internet to assist family therapy. *British Journal of Guidance and Counseling, 26,*(1), 43–52.

Leiblum, S. R. (1997). Sex and the net: Clinical implications. *Journal of Sex Education and Therapy, 22*(1), 21–27.

Madara, E. J. (1997) The mutual aid self-help online revolution. *Social Policy, 27*(3), 20–26.

Nietzel, M. T., Bernstein, D. A., & Russell, R. L. (1988). Assessment of anxiety and fear. In A. S. Bellack & M. Hersen (Eds.), *Behavioral assessment: A practical handbook* (3rd ed., pp. 279–312). New York: Pergamon Books.

Orzack, M. H., & Ross, C. (2000). Should virtual sex addiction be treated like ordinary sex addiction? *Sexual Addiction and Compulsivity, 7,* 113–125.

Pavlov, I. (1927). *Conditioned reflexes.* Oxford, England: Oxford University Press.

Putnam, D. E. (1998, March). *Advances in distance learning.* In B. L. Gordon (Chair), Issues and Opportunities in Behavioral Telehealth, Symposium presented at the annual meeting of the California Psychological Association, Pasadena.

Putnam, D. E. (1999, March). *Assessment and treatment of online sexual addiction.* In D. E. Putnam (Chair), Cybersex: Psychological Assessment, Treatment, and Ethical Issues, Symposium presented at the annual meeting of the California Psychological Association, San Diego.

Putnam, D. E. (1997a). *Module 1: What is online sexual addiction?* Online sexual addiction course. Retrieved from http://onlinesexaddict.org/course/module4.html

Putnam, D. E. (1997b). *Module 4: Behavioral theory and the cycle of addiction.* Online sexual addiction course. Retrieved from http://onlinesexaddict.org/course/module4.html

Putnam, D. E. (1997). Online Sexual Addiction Questionnaire. Online document: http://onlinesexaddict.org/osaq.html

Rickards, S., & Laaser, M. (1999). Sexual acting-out in borderline women: Impulsive self-destructiveness or sexual addiction/compulsivity. *Sexual Addiction & Compulsivity: The Journal of Treatment and Prevention, 6*(1), 31–46.

Robinson, D. W. (1999). Sexual addiction as an adaptive response to post-traumatic stress disorder in the African American community. *Sexual Addiction & Compulsivity: The Journal of Treatment and Prevention, 6,* 11–22.

Sampson, J., Kolodinsky, R. W., & Greeno, B. P. (1997). Counseling on the information Highway: Future possibilities and potential problems. *Journal of Counseling and Development, 75,* 203–211.

Schwartz, B. (1984). *Psychology of learning and behavior* (2nd ed.). New York: Norton.

Schwartz, M. (1992). Sexual compulsivity as post-traumatic stress disorder: Treatment perspectives. *Psychiatric Annals, 22,* 333–338.

Sealy, J. R. (1999). Dual and triple diagnoses: Addictions, mental illness, and HIV infection guidelines for outpatient therapists. *Sexual Addiction & Compulsivity: The Journal of Treatment and Prevention, 6*(3), 195–220.

Sexual Recovery Institute. *Cybersex addiction checklist.* Retrieved from http://www.sexual recovery.com/sri_docs/cyber.htm

Tedesco, A., & Bola, J. R. (1997). A pilot study of the relationship between childhood sexual abuse and compulsive sexual behavior in adults. *Sexual Addiction and Compulsivity, 4*(2), 147–157.

Walther, J. B. (1996). Computer-mediated communication: Impersonal, interpersonal, and hyper-personal interaction. *Communication Research, 23,* 1, pp. 3–4.

Whitfield, C. L. (1998). Internal evidence and corroboration of traumatic memories of child sexual abuse with addictive disorders. *Sexual Addiction & Compulsivity: The Journal of Treatment and Prevention, 6,* 79–104.

Young, K. S. (1996, August). *Internet addiction: The emergence of a new clinical disorder.* Paper presented at the 104th Annual Convention of the American Psychological Association, Toronto, ON, Canada.

Young, K. (1999). Internet addiction: Symptoms, evaluation, and treatment. In L. VandeCreek & T. Jackson (Eds.), *Innovations in clinical practice: A source book* (Vol. 17, pp. 1–13). Sarasota, FL: Professional Resource Press.

Young, K. S. *Cybersexual addiction quiz.* Retrieved from http://netaddiction.com/resources/cybersexual_addiction_quiz.htm

8

CHAPTER

David L. Delmonico
Elizabeth Griffin
Patrick J. Carnes

Treating Online Compulsive Sexual Behavior: When Cybersex Is the Drug of Choice

☐ Introduction

An estimated 90 million people use the Internet each month, a number that has rapidly increased and continues to rise. In addition to the more than 100 billion homepages, there are innumerable chatrooms, newsgroups, and e-mails. What was once used by the U.S. Department of Defense, has become a medium for research, communication, and, for some, a venue for online sexual activity.

Just as the use of the Internet has increased dramatically over the past 10 years, so has the interest in studying the phenomena associated with this microcosm of the world. Research regarding sexual behavior has also been of great interest in Western culture. Perhaps it is not serendipitous, then, that these two fields have come together to form a new area of research and treatment: cybersex. Cybersex creates a virtual world in which participants can be whomever they wish, engage in erotic behaviors, and live out fantasies that could never before be realized. Although not everyone is negatively impacted by cybersex, researchers such as Carnes, Cooper, Delmonico, Griffin, Putnam, and Young study individuals who have jeopardized everything so that they may engage in cybersex.

Cybersex users continue to perplex researchers and clinicians with the depth and breadth of their online behavior. This chapter explores and explains how some individuals become obsessed with sexuality on the Internet and the treatment strategies that may be employed to help them with their compulsive behavior. The focus of this chapter is on helping those who appear to be sexually lost in cyberspace: the cybersex compulsive.

☐ Understanding Cybersex Compulsivity

Schneider (1994) set forth three necessary and rudimentary criteria to screen a behavior as addictive/compulsive: (a) loss of freedom to choose whether or not to engage in a behavior (compulsivity); (b) continuation of the behavior despite adverse consequences related to the behavior (consequences); and (c) obsession with the behavior. Although Schneider's criteria are broad, they help define the basic aspects of a process addiction, a compulsive behavior that does not include the ingestion of substances. Schneider also suggested that the criteria for pathological gambling (American Psychiatric Association [APA], 1994) serves as an analogy for other process addictions, pointing to the fact that even substance abuse criteria are primarily behaviorally based. If certain behaviors such as gambling can be considered pathological, could it not also be true that other behaviors, such as cybersex, may be considered pathological if they meet specific diagnostic criteria?

The Internet: An Attractive Medium

It is important that clinicians understand the psychological components that permit and/or promote addictive processes on the Internet. The "triple-A engine" (Cooper, 1998) suggested that there are three basic components that attract individuals to the Internet: accessibility, anonymity, and affordability. The combination of these three factors explains why the Internet is a powerful medium that attracts millions of users, including the cybersex compulsive.

Not all cybersex users report problems with Internet sexual behavior. Research by Cooper, Delmonico, and Burg (2000) found that nearly 83% of all users of cybersex did not report any difficulties in their life as a result of their Internet sex. However, they also found that 17% of their sample were either at-risk users or actively engaging in cybersex-compulsive behaviors.

Compulsive cybersex involves more than simply engaging in online sexual activity, it involves components of escape and self-medication. Some cybersex compulsives describe experiences of tolerance and psychological/physiological withdrawal related to their use of cybersex. For some, Internet sex has become their "drug of choice," to which all other aspects of their life become secondary.

Types of Cybersex Users

Carnes, Delmonico, and Griffin (2001) proposed a model for conceptualizing cybersex users and defined each of the categories (see Figure 8.1).

Appropriate recreational users: These users engage in cybersex without any report of consequence or life difficulties.

Inappropriate recreational users: Although these users are not compulsive with cybersex, they often use sexual information gathered from the Internet at inappropriate times (e.g., jokes at work, sexual screen savers, inappropriate stories) or with inappropriate people (e.g., sharing inappropriate sexual jokes with coworkers, the opposite sex, or children). It seems they are unaware of or ignore social etiquette, boundaries, and the norms of their culture. Their behavior is intrusive, sometimes in an attempt to gain attention or be humorous.

Discovery group: Individuals in this group begin using the Internet compulsively with no prior inappropriate sexual fantasies or behaviors. For this group, the Internet serves as the "trigger" for problematic or compulsive sexual use of the Internet.

Predisposed group: Individuals within this group have indicators of problematic sexual behavior in other areas of their lives. For example, they may have had minor sexual behavioral problems and struggled with inappropriate sexual fantasies for some years, but the Internet serves as the "fuel" that encourages the problematic sexual behavior to accelerate.

Lifelong sexual compulsives: These individuals have had lifelong struggles with problematic or compulsive sexual behavior. The Internet can (a) be an extension of their behavior and simply one more way to act out; (b) become a less risky way of acting out their sexually problematic behaviors; or (c) become a way to heighten arousal and add new risk to their already existing pattern of sexually problematic behaviors.

Cooper, Putnam, Planchon, and Boies (1999) suggested that these groups may be further divided into two subtypes. The first is the *stress-reactive* user who uses sex on the Internet as a way to relieve high levels of stress. Second was the *depressive* subtype, for whom sex on the Net becomes an escape from the depression in their daily lives. New research by Cooper,

Griffin-Shelly, Delmonico, and Mathy (2001) showed initial support for these subtypes, as well as introducing a third subtype known as *fantasy*. The fantasy user acknowledges that Internet sex allows for an escape from the daily routine of life into a world of fiction and fantasy that fulfills one's sexual desires. Researchers are only starting to understand the types of cybersex users, the reasons they use Internet sex, and how treatment may be applied to these various groups.

☐ Assessment and Treatment

Assessment

As with all forms of assessment, clinicians must operate only within their scope of practice. Clinicians who anticipate working with cybersex compulsives must familiarize themselves with the terminology and technologies used by cybersex compulsives in order to conduct a comprehensive and accurate assessment.

The process of cybersex assessment remains in its formative stages. There is no comprehensive, reliable, and valid instrument available to clinicians. However, several screening instruments have been developed for the screening of cybersex problems. Examples of these include the Internet Sex Screening Test (ISST; Delmonico, 1999), the Online Sexual Addiction Questionnaire (OSA-Q) developed by Putnam (1997), the Cyber-Addiction Checklist developed by Weiss (2000), and the Cybersexual Addiction Quiz composed by Young (1998). It is cautioned that all of these instruments are for initial screening. The information gathered should be considered preliminary and followed up with other forms of assessment. Further validity and reliability studies are needed on all mentioned instruments.

In addition, as with any complex psychological issue, no single instrument should be used for diagnosing online sexual compulsivity. The use of collateral informants (e.g., partner, parents, boss, etc.) helps increase the validity of the assessment. Clinician knowledge about cybersex and the Internet also increases the likelihood of a valid clinical interview.

An in-depth interview is necessary to understand the complexities involved with cybersex compulsivity (e.g., reasons for use, collateral issues, etc.). Assessment instruments cannot replace the personal interaction and clinical judgment of a trained therapist.

Cybersex compulsives begin at different intensity levels and escalate at different rates. Progression to higher risk and more unhealthy behaviors is often seen. As an example, some cybersex users will engage in sexually compulsive behaviors on the Internet only to become bored with online sex and increase the risk by arranging to meet individuals offline. Research has demonstrated that one such risk for those who meet sexual partners online is the increased likelihood of contracting a sexually transmitted disease (McFarlane, Vull, & Rietmeijer, 2000), including HIV (Toomey & Rothenberg, 2000).

An additional form of risk for some cybersex compulsives is engaging in behaviors that target vulnerable individuals for offline exploitation or online harassment. It is critical that a risk assessment be completed as part of a comprehensive evaluation to determine the level of risk to the client or others. Critical areas that should be considered in a risk assessment include the history of other offline sexual exploitation, psychiatric comorbidity, history of poor impulse control, and a pattern of escalation in either frequency or intensity.

Users of online sexual activity (i.e., any form of online sexual exploration) are not all the same, as was previously discussed in the user categories (Figure 8.1). Assessment and evaluation must take this into account in order to prescribe the most appropriate treatment methods. Clinicians must use their assessment skills to determine the type of user and to develop appropriate treatment plans. For example, an individual who has been caught sending sexually suggestive e-mails from work dictates a much different type of intervention than the individual who is a lifelong sexual compulsive and has been caught with child pornography.

A Multifaceted Treatment Approach

Mental health professionals serve their clients best when they acknowledge that there are a variety of approaches in the treatment of cybersex behavior. In fact, treatment is most effective when clinicians consider utilizing a multifaceted approach that includes various modalities (e.g., individual, group, family, support groups, medication, etc.), and various theoretical orientations (e.g., cognitive–behavioral, reality therapy, psychodynamic, etc.). Treatment plans will differ for each patient based on the assessment of the user category in which they fall, the types of cybersex behaviors, and related underlying issues. The following sections discuss interventions for the cybersex compulsive based on this multifaceted approach.

Promoting Change in the Cybersex Compulsive

There are a variety of ways to be creative in the treatment of cybersex compulsivity. Many therapists take already-existing treatment techniques

Recreational Users

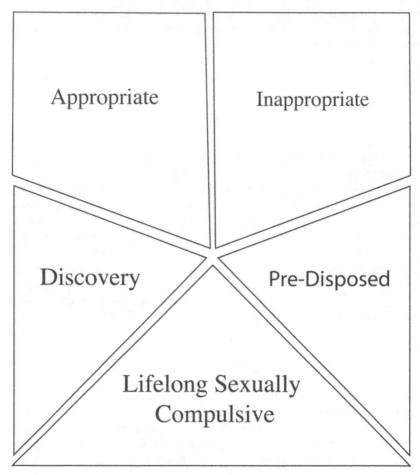

FIGURE 8.1. Cybersex user groups.

and exercises and adapt them for use with the cybersex compulsive. Exercises that deal with such issues as grief and loss are often helpful in assisting clients to overcome unresolved grief related either to their compulsive use of the Internet or to other unresolved issues. Other topics that can be addressed through various exercises include assertiveness training, stress reduction, relapse prevention, addiction cycle awareness, coping strategies, social skills, and exploration of underlying psychological issues (e.g., depression, anxiety, etc.).

Various theoretical approaches are appropriate for the treatment of cybersex addicts. The process one follows in working on issues is one of preference for both the client and therapist. As with all treatment techniques and approaches, the involvement of the client in a collaborative atmosphere is predictive of getting them to institute change.

Watzlawick, Weakland, and Fisch (1988) introduced the concepts of first- and second-order change. Carnes et al. (2001) suggested that these concepts could be modified to assist in the treatment of compulsive cybersex behaviors.

First-Order Changes

First-order-changes are concrete actions taken to quickly stop a problem and address or avoid certain consequences. These changes can be referred to as the crisis management of cybersex treatment. When treating compulsive cybersex behavior, several immediate types of crisis intervention strategies can be employed. They are used to help stabilize obsessive thinking and compulsive behavior in order to generate and implement a long-term recovery plan. Delmonico (in press) suggested focusing on the following two areas of first-order change.

> *Reducing access:* Concrete steps include moving the computer to a different location in the house, installing cyber screening software (e.g., CyberPatrol, NetNanny, SafeSurf, SurfWatch, etc.), packing up the computer, directing the computer monitor where others can see the screen, self-limiting the time online and time of day online, disclosing to one trustworthy person the nature of your problem, and/or changing to an Internet service provider that prefilters its content (e.g., family.net, Cleansurf, Kwyknet, etc.). Reducing access is most often needed with a "problematic user"; it is rare that this type of change is necessary for the "recreational user."
>
> *Raising awareness:* Clinicians should assign tasks that will help raise a client's awareness that he or she may have a problem with sexually compulsive behaviors on the Internet. For example, provide tasks that help break through denial (e.g., taking the ISST), make cybersex a primary therapy issue, engage in support groups for sexually compulsive behavior, obtain a sponsor (or another individual to maintain accountability), conduct a sexual/cybersexual history, examine the cycle of cybersex use, and/or make a list of consequences as a result of his or her cybersex behaviors.
>
> Raising awareness can be a critical task for the "inappropriate rec-

reational user." Often, inappropriate recreational users are unaware of the impact of their behavior on others. Education that raises awareness of such impact, informs them of social etiquette and sexual harassment policies in the workplace, and addresses other topics will often resolve issues associated with this group. However, raising awareness is a critical task for the problematic user as well.

Second-Order Changes

Second-order changes are the actions taken to produce long-term effects at a deeper level. After spending some time diffusing the crisis and raising awareness, second-order change begins. Delmonico (in press) suggested the following areas to consider during second-order change.

Attacking the appeal: Remember the attraction of the Internet and plan interventions to short-circuit the cycle that has been ritualized around cybersex use (i.e., triple-A engine, Cyberhex of the Internet). The cybersex use has often become ritualized and cyclical in nature. Finding a critical point to intervene with the ritual can help reduce the frequency and intensity of online sex.

Include psychiatric evaluation: In some cases, psychiatric evaluation may be necessary to address collateral issues such as depression, anxiety, other addictions, or obsessive/compulsive behaviors. Medications such as the selective serotonin reuptake inhibitors (SSRIs) may be helpful in reducing the obsession with cybersex and assist the client to progress further and more rapidly in their recovery. Medications may also be helpful in dealing with depression, anxiety disorders, or other related issues that contribute to the tendency to want to engage in online sexual activities. Recent data has emerged suggesting that there may be underlying reasons why individuals use the Internet for sex, including stress reduction, depression, and escape from daily life (Cooper, Griffin-Shelly, Delmonico, & Mathy, 2001). A psychiatric evaluation would address some of these possible comorbid conditions.

Include the family: The family is often overlooked as a component of cybersex treatment; however, in treatment for sexually compulsive behavior, the family can be one of the critical elements in predicting successful recovery. Schneider (2000) addressed some of the complex issues involved in the treatment of cybersex within the family and further elaborated on those issues elsewhere in this text. Difficult treatment issues such as disclosure to partners, children, and other family members must be considered and addressed in the therapeutic setting. Several common goals for couple/family treatment include appropriate disclosure of past and current behaviors, reestablishing open lines of communication, building trust in the coupleship and family, and creating methods of accountability for the cybersex compulsive.

Couples therapy may be most effective after both partners have had a chance to process their emotions on an individual basis. Therefore, it is suggested that both partners have separate, individual therapists prior to the commencement of couples counseling. It is also important to advise families/couples to not make any major decision in the first couple of months of treatment, since they may be responding in "crisis mode" rather than making informed decisions.

A final potential negative result of these types of activities is that these behaviors often occur on the lone home computer. The computer used to gain access to cybersex materials may be the same computer on which children complete homework assignments or e-mail their friends. This greatly increases the chances of a child's exposure to inappropriate sexual material that may be stored in bookmarks or on the computer's hard drive. In treatment, the cybersex compulsive will benefit from examining how their cybersex behaviors do or could adversely impact their family.

Social isolation: One of the most common consequences of cybersex is isolation from others. Carnes (2001) referred to it as *relational regression*. Cybersex allows virtual relationships to replace real-life relationships. Those who are close to the cybersex compulsive are greatly aware of the impact of the isolation. In most cases, not only do clients physically withdraw from others, they begin to significantly neglect the relationships that they once valued.

Address collateral issues: A number of critical issues must be addressed to help the cybersex compulsive manage their online sexual activity. These issues include unresolved grief/loss, stress management, shame/guilt, anger management, childhood trauma issues, victim empathy, and so forth. Although cybersex may be the primary focus in therapy sessions, these collateral issues must be addressed to move a client forward in his or her second-order recovery.

Promote healthy sexuality: One issue that must be addressed is the client's examination of what constitutes healthy sexuality. Although this definition may vary by individual, it is important to address in treatment so that the client has an understanding of his or her goals in recovery, as well as to help find ways to make offline sexual relations more fulfilling.

Explore spirituality: An essential part of treatment includes the incorporation of spirituality as a dimension of one's sexuality. This may include how one's religion influences an individual's sexual practices.

However, it also addresses how an individual's sense of spirituality and/or "higher power" may be beneficial during long-term recovery.

Treatment Planning

Developing a treatment plan that addresses cybersex compulsivity can be complex and time-consuming. Figure 8.2 presents common issues that should be addressed as part of a comprehensive cybersex treatment plan. This treatment plan provides a template that will need to be modified based on a particular client's problems and goals. The treatment plan was developed with first- and second-order changes in mind and is therefore organized into two phases: first-order phase and second-order phase. The first-order phase is relatively brief and straightforward but can be difficult for the client to implement. This phase occurs early in treatment to stabilize the patient and prevent further deterioration. The second-order phase is more complex and lengthy and requires more emotional investment from the client. For this reason, as well as that the proximal crisis may have passed, clients often embrace the first-order changes but terminate therapy once the second-order phase begins. Strategies for helping individuals remain in treatment beyond first-order change should be developed early in treatment. For example, discussing ways to handle the discomfort both in therapy and outside of therapy provides tools that will assist the client in working through these difficult issues, as well as helping prepare them for the discomfort they are likely to experience.

Case Example

Robert is a 32-year-old single male. He sought counseling several years ago that focused on his concern about frequent masturbation and the use of pornography. Although he terminated therapy, he remains distressed by his fantasies of teenage females during masturbation. He has been sexual with only one woman in his life, and that was nearly 8 years ago. Robert discovered Internet sex about 2 years ago. Since that time, he has increased his frequency of masturbation, and his fantasies have become more intense as a result of the teenage female pornography he finds online. He has tried to set limits with his online behavior, but these attempts have only lasted a few days at most. He feels drawn back into pornography on the Internet, which he views while he masturbates. Robert finds himself thinking about pornography on the Net constantly and becomes anxious if he knows he will be without Internet access for more than a day or two. He believes his sexual fantasies and masturbation are out of control.

Sample Cybersex Treatment Plan

First-Order Phase

Goals:
Stop inappropriate behavior

Action Steps
1. Move computer to high traffic area in house
2. Face computer monitor at home and at work so people can see the screen if walking by the computer
3. Have client tape a picture of significant people on the computer both at home and at work
4. Have client put a picture of self and family as computer's background both at home and at work
5. Have client switch to a family-oriented service provider at home
6. Have client disclose the problem to at least one person

Note: If above steps do not assist client with stopping the cybersex behavior, then consider the more drastic step of eliminating Internet access.

Second-Order Phase

Goals	Action Steps
1. Look honestly at denial and minimizations	a. Completes a description of the offense b. Reads/discuss victim statement c. Completes therapeutic polygraph
2. Accept responsibility for cybersex behavior	a. Completes statement of responsibility
4. Assess psychological health and needs	a. Completes psychological testing: MMPI 2, Millon, MSI, BDI, BAI Sexual Card Sort, Gender Attitudes b. Completes substance abuse screening c. Completes assessment for medication
6. Develop a support system	a. Finds a sponsor b. Attends and participates in group therapy c. Attends and participates in support group d. Discloses to appropriate people in their life
7. Understand the dynamics and decision process of the sexually intrusive behavior	a. Completes addiction cycle exercise b. Completes behavior chain exercise c. Understands dynamics underlying offense

(Continued)

FIGURE 8.2. Sample cybersex treatment plan.

8. Understand the distorted thinking involved in the sexually intrusive behavior

   a. Adds distorted thoughts to behavior chain
   c. Completes distorted thinking exercise
   d. Adds new thoughts to behavior chain

9. Develop a healthy lifestyle maintenance plan

   a. Completes a healthy lifestyle cycle
   b. Completes living your life differently
   c. Completes relapse prevention plan
   d. Develops an plan for stress/anxiety
   e. Monitor stress and overcommittment
   f. Understands first-order vs. second-order recovery

10. Understand the nature of your sexuality and develop a sexual health plan

   a. Arousal template exercise
   b. Implements techniques to manage inappropriate arousal
   c. Develops a sexual health plan

11. Understand family of origin/childhood trauma issues

   a. Completes genogram
   b. Completes family dynamics exercise
   c. Completes childhood survival strategies

12. Demonstrate victim empathy

   a. Writes narrative from victim point of view
   b. Adds victim empathy statements to behavior chain
   c. Writes letter to victim/s

13. Develop healthy communication skills

   a. Becomes familiar with healthy communication
   b. Completes communication exercise identifies style of communication/impact on others
   c. Attends couple therapy when partnered

14. Develop healthy personal relationships

   a. Attends couples therapy when partnered
   b. Becomes familiar with healthy courtship

15. Develop a spiritual life

   a. Joins a spiritual community
   b. Develops a spiritual passion

FIGURE 8.2. Sample cybersex treatment plan (*continued*).

Robert appears ready and willing to discuss his concerns about his fantasies and his Internet usage. The assessment begins with an interview and gathering of relevant historical data, including a detailed sexual history and cybersex history. Robert is given several screening tests for

Internet-, sexual-, and cybersex-compulsive behavior to determine if one aspect is more powerful than another. Robert is instructed to keep a log of his sexual and Internet behavior for one week and bring the log to the next therapy session. A Minnesota Multiphasic Personality Inventory (MMPI-2) is administered to determine if there are underlying comorbid psychological issues that should be addressed, including depression or anxiety. A Beck Depression Inventory (BDI) and Beck Anxiety Inventory (BAI) were also administered to detect depression and anxiety and also to establish a baseline prior to the onset of treatment. An examination of past and present behaviors was conducted to screen for other compulsive or addictive behaviors. A risk assessment was completed based on the content of his fantasies to determine if Robert poses any threat to teenage females. Robert's arousal patterns were also assessed with an Abel Screen to determine gender and age preferences.

Robert was compliant throughout the evaluation and completed the behavioral log, sexual history, and cybersex history. Based on the clinical interview and his history, it was determined that Robert is a "predisposed user," an individual who has a history of struggling with sexual thoughts and fantasies that are exacerbated by the Internet. There was no evident history of compulsive behaviors or addiction for Robert or his family. The screening tests administered indicated he was a problematic user of the Internet and cybersex, with no evidence of other compulsive sexual behaviors. The MMPI-2 and BDI results indicated that Robert was significantly depressed. This, paired with his self-report of ongoing depression, was indicative of a referral to a psychiatrist for further evaluation and possible medication. Given the level of depression, a suicide risk interview was conducted, and Robert was determined to be a low-level risk for suicide. The arousal assessment indicated his overall gender preference was for females, with no arousal to prepubescent females. These results indicated that his preferential arousal was to adult females. During the clinical interview, Robert indicated that he was more socially comfortable with younger females than with adult females. However, because of his attraction to and fantasies of younger females, he was asked to remove himself from any regular contact with teen females at this time.

Based on the results of the assessment, Robert's treatment plan consists of "first-order changes" which should take place in the first week of treatment. These include:

- Locating and subscribing to a family-oriented Internet service provider. This will help screen out any pornography over the Internet.
- Finding one person who he can trust and share with on an ongoing basis his difficulties with Internet pornography.
- Setting self-limits: Not going on the computer after 10:00 p.m., and not using the computer for more than 60 minutes at a time.

- Beginning a personal journal that records not only behaviors but also thoughts and feelings at the time of the behavior.

Based on the assessment, the critical issues for this client appears to be the development of appropriate social skills and communication skills that would foster his ability to develop relationships with age-appropriate females. Below are the second order changes that will initially be considered for treatment:

- Continue to monitor psychological health and needs with specific emphasis on depression and medication compliance if medications were prescribed.
- Help Robert accept responsibility for his cybersex behavior by developing a "Statement of Responsibility" that would include a description of the specific behaviors, the method for engaging in the behavior, how Robert violated himself and others, and his plan for addressing the problem.
- Assist Robert in the development of healthy support systems. This would include mixed-gender group therapy and/or support groups, social skills training, and communication training to help develop other relationships.
- Facilitate a sponsor-type relationship to share difficulties and triumphs. Part of this support system may include focus on a spiritual relationship with a higher power. This may be developed into an additional treatment priority if necessary.
- Develop healthy communication skills by having Robert attend a basic class on communication or assertiveness training. A mixed-gender group would be an appropriate place to practice developing this skill.
- Develop healthy personal relationships by encouraging a reconnection with family and prior friends if appropriate. Basic education regarding dating skills and development of intimate and romantic relationships with others.
- Develop a healthy sex plan by starting with basic sexual education to fill in any gaps in knowledge about males, females, and sexual relationships. The plan would include how Robert will define healthy sexuality for himself, the role of Internet sex in his future, and signs that would indicate he is developing healthy sexual habits.

The above items represent some of the initial second-order issues to be addressed after first-order changes have commenced. This list is not meant to be exhaustive, but rather to represent the clinical prioritization of issues from Figure 8.2. Other issues may need to be addressed as therapy progresses.

Common Challenges of Treatment

Distorted Thinking

Although your cybersex clients will have periods of success, relapse is a normal part of the change process (Prochaska, Norcross, & DiClemente, 1995). Delmonico, Griffin, and Moriarty (2001) discussed some common distorted thinking patterns that clients face during treatment.

1. *"Now that the crisis is over, there's no longer a problem."* Clients who say or think this believe that the problem is short-lived and not symptomatic of other underlying issues. Once the immediate crisis is resolved (e.g., the client is able to stop using cybersex for a short time), the client feels he or she is "cured" and has no need to continue treatment. One possible intervention is a variation of a technique borrowed from family therapy called "prediction." The therapist would tell the client early in therapy that once the crisis is resolved, chances are he or she will want to quit therapy entirely. The client is then asked to describe the indicators (behavior and thoughts) that the therapist could observe and challenge should they surface. The client is instructed to dispute these thoughts and behaviors that are leading toward terminating treatment.

2. *"Chaos helps me remember I'm alive."* For some users of cybersex, they embrace the chaos that is generated in their lives. This may be chaos within their family, work, or other settings. The need for chaos may be present for a variety of reasons, but it is important not to attempt to reduce the chaos too quickly. More importantly, the clinician should facilitate the client in determining the "function" of the chaos rather than treating it directly. Otherwise, clinicians spend more time "putting out fires" than engaging in therapy.

3. *"I'll start feeling better immediately."* Desire for instant gratification is common among those who use behaviors compulsively. Normalizing the fact that we all want to feel better quickly is important to the treatment process. Warning clients early that they may feel worse before they feel better can be a way of ensuring more long-term successes.

4. *"I'll be able to handle or manage sex on the Internet."* Once clients feel some control over their behavior, they may lapse into thinking patterns that they can "manage" their cybersex. Reminding clients about the triple-A engine and the powerful lure of the Internet is one way to prevent this ambivalence.

5. *"I can do this on my own."* Whether you believe in the addiction model of treatment or not is irrelevant when this thinking distortion appears. Twelve-step support groups help cybersex compulsives embrace the

power of a group. The groups are free and provide a built-in support system and accountability mechanism. These groups can be a powerful way to help clients break through the denial that they can't do this on their own. These groups can also be helpful in dealing with other cognitive distortions such as those mentioned above. Professionally led therapy groups can also be helpful in this regard.

Entitlement

Cybersex compulsives often experience a great deal of self-pity as they discover they are different than others when it comes to sex on the Internet. These feelings of self-pity may make them feel that they are entitled to special considerations (e.g., they should not be expected to stop using sex on the Net) or that they should be rewarded in some way after a period of health (e.g., I can visit this X-rated site after 2 weeks of no cybersex). These feelings of entitlement often lead to a cybersex relapse.

Deprivation

Carnes (1997) introduced the concept of sexual anorexia. He described a phenomenon that can be as problematic as sexually compulsive behavior. Since addicts often live in extremes, some may deprive themselves of any sexual or physical contact with others, including healthy contact. This type of severely restricted behavior may ultimately place the individual at a higher risk for bingeing. This also may be the case for the cybersex compulsive who simply eliminates sexual behavior and does not develop healthy sexual habits. Although treatment may involve a period of abstinence from sex, complete denial of any sexual activity forever is not the goal. Even in 12-step programs for sexual recovery, healthy sexuality is the ultimate goal, not abstinence from all forms of sexual behavior. Individuals must learn the differences between healthy and unhealthy sexuality and begin to replace unhealthy sexual practices with healthy ones.

One goal for many clinicians (and clients) is to integrate sexuality and intimacy and avoid seeing sexual behaviors as either "good" or "bad." Deprivation of sexual behavior is a short-sighted solution, but both extremes represent different ends of the same unhealthy sexual continuum. Clearly clients will have anxiety about being sexual after a period of abstinence. Clinicians should reassure clients that this response is normal and healthy and may, in fact, produce unexpected progress in treatment.

The "lifelong sexually compulsive" user group may be at greatest risk to experience sexual anorexia. This may result from the anxiety they feel from their years of out-of-control sexual behavior. Their anxiety is based in the thinking that sexual behavior cannot be healthy, and they fear harming themselves or others with their behaviors as they may have in the past. This anxiety may result in long-term abstinence from sexual behavior and possibly sexual anorexia.

Stress

Higher than normal stress levels can quickly increase the risk of relapse. Clinicians should monitor and teach stress reduction strategies to prevent relapse into old coping behaviors such as cybersex. Cooper, Griffin-Shelly, Delmonico, and Mathy (2001) found that more than half (56%) of individuals with online sexual problems used cybersex as a way of coping with stress, while only 30% of the general population reported doing the same. This finding supports that stress management and healthy coping strategies would be beneficial in reducing cybersex compulsivity.

Teaching clients to dispute irrational statements and counter the attitudes that lead to relapse will help troubleshoot difficult times in their recovery and ultimately lead to long-term second-order changes.

Common Treatment Mistakes

Cybersex is a complex and new phenomenon. Clinicians have little to guide them in the assessment and treatment process. No single method of treatment has been established for cybersex compulsivity, however, clinical work with this population has found that several critical issues can be counterproductive to the therapy process.

Moving Too Fast or Too Slow

Timing is an important consideration in the application of any treatment or technique. For example, first-order changes should be firmly in place and practiced regularly and successfully prior to introduction of most second-order changes. Just as the client is interested in moving forward quickly, so too are many clinicians. However, pushing too hard or too fast puts unrealistic expectations on client and therapist and might paradoxically contribute to the client feeling overwhelmed, ineffectual, and inadequate. Implementing second-order changes is not a sign of success if the first-order changes are not solidly in place. In fact, without first-order change, relapse is more likely to occur. Most clinicians agree that a slow but steady pace leads to the most lasting progress in the treatment of cybersex compulsives. The balance is not letting clients stay too long at one level. A client who has successfully instituted first-order changes but is reluctant to move beyond those changes will not maintain gains over the long term and may be at risk for returning to a compulsive behavior. Accurate timing is a skill that requires a high degree of clinical acumen and the ability to be "in tune" with clients.

Overlooking Pharmacological Interventions

Considering a referral for a psychiatric evaluation for medication should be a routine part of a comprehensive cybersex evaluation. Each day more information is available about the relationship between brain chemistry/ activity and addictive behaviors and the medications that are helpful with these issues. Cutting-edge research is examining brain chemistry and brain functioning as possible explanations for how individuals become dependent on a compulsive behavior (Maas et al., 1998). It is only a matter of time before researchers make similar discoveries about the relationship between brain chemistry and other potentially compulsive behaviors (e.g., sex, gambling, cybersex, etc.). Clinicians who have a personal or philosophical bias against the use of medications may be denying themselves and their clients a powerful treatment adjunct.

Encouraging Online Activities

There are instances when certain types of online sexual activities can be healthy and educational for an individual or couple. There are also many couples where one partner has unrealistic expectations about sexual desire. In these cases the therapist may be inclined to encourage the use of certain sexual aides to enhance the relationship, including the prescription of cybersex for its educational value (Cooper, Scherer, & Marcus, chapter 11 of this book). It should be cautioned, however, that these options are not appropriate in the case of cybersex compulsivity. Other sources of information should be used to educate cybersex compulsives and their partners about healthy sexual behavior.

In addition, some clients, partners, or parents may have unfounded concerns about a loved one's cybersex behavior based on their fear, inadequacy, or lack of knowledge. In these cases, it may be tempting to normalize cybersex behaviors (e.g., "many people masturbate to online pornography"). However, it is not helpful to normalize cybersex for individuals who are compulsive cybersex users. In the majority of the population, cybersex can be a healthy, nonproblematic behavior; however, for the cybersex addict, the normalization of the behavior provides the justification and minimization needed to continue their compulsive use of the

Internet. Appropriate screening and interviewing will help to determine whether normalizing or behavior reduction is more appropriate.

Encouraging Partner to Serve as Enforcer

If a client has an intimate partner in his or her life, it is tempting to utilize the resources of that partner to assist in the monitoring and reporting of the client's cybersex behavior. Clinicians should resist the urge to allow partners to function in the role of "monitor." Most partners have their own issues to address (e.g., codependency, power, control, etc.). Assigning the task of "monitor" or "keeper of the password" puts the partner in a position of authority to decide whether or not the cybersex compulsive is allowed to access certain areas of the Internet. This arrangement sets up an unhealthy dynamic in the relationship by placing the responsibility and accountability for cybersex behavior on the partner. As a result, the partner may feel responsible for the addict's successes and failures. If possible, use friends, other relatives, or a 12-step sponsor to support the cybersex compulsive in recovery.

Failing to Acknowledge Own Limitations

It is imperative that clinicians understand their role and limitations in working with cybersex compulsives. Ethical codes clearly dictate that clinicians practice within their scope of competency. In order to be effective in treating cybersex compulsivity, it is critical that practitioners have an understanding of cybersex terminology, the technology involved, and the various forms of cybersex. Knowledge in these areas allows the clinician to ask relevant questions and understand important aspects of a client's cybersex compulsivity. Clinicians should engage in workshops and read articles that would enhance their general knowledge about the Internet, technology, and cybersex.

The above list is not exhaustive, but represents some of the common challenges treating the cybersex compulsive.

☐ Future Directions

The field of cybersex is young. Internet growth over the past 10 years has required researchers and clinicians to examine paradigms that never before existed. The helping professions have been slow to respond to the phenomenon of sex on the Internet, an issue of increasing prevalence and importance (Cooper, 1998). Continued research will provide the necessary information to fully understand, evaluate, and treat the cybersex compulsive. Understanding who uses cybersex and how it may be similar and dissimilar from other disorders is a critical first step. Differentiating between the various subtypes of cybersex users will also prove useful in the development of effective treatment plans. As technology continues to advance, helping professionals will face far more complex issues regarding sex on the Internet. Issues such as virtual reality, video/audio streaming, and transmission of touch, smell, and other senses will increase the attraction to Internet sex and challenge the assessment and treatment skills of clinicians.

Once cybersex is better understood, future research must focus on the development of valid and reliable protocols to assist with accurate evaluation and treatment of problematic online behaviors. The lack of appropriate instrumentation makes scientific investigation of cybersex compulsivity difficult. This inability to empirically study cybersex poses a challenge in securing funding to further understand the cybersex phenomenon. Effective clinical interventions must be developed, documented, and tested to determine which techniques produce the most effective outcomes for the various permutations of cybersex users.

The future of the Internet is an open landscape. The Department of Defense could never have predicted the course of the Internet, nor can we predict its future. The Internet will continue to change and shape the way we communicate and exchange information. Clinicians must learn about the multitude of mental health issues that are certain to emerge as a result of these technological advancements.

Technology will never replace empathy, understanding, and the human connection; for that, our clients seek us, and we must be prepared to respond.

☐ References

American Psychiatric Association. (1994). *Diagnostic and statistical manual of mental disorders* (4th ed.). Washington, DC: Author.

Carnes, P. J. (1997). *Sexual anorexia: Overcoming sexual self-hatred.* Center City, MN: Hazelden Foundation Press.

Carnes, P. J. (2001). Escalating arousal: Factors in addictive sexual desire. *Sexual Addiction & Compulsivity: Journal of Treatment and Prevention, 8*(1), 45–78.

Carnes, P. J., Delmonico, D. L., & Griffin, E. J. (2001). *In the shadows of the net: Breaking free from compulsive online sexual behavior.* Center City, MH: Hazelden Foundation Press.

Cooper, A. (1998). Sexuality and the internet: Surfing into a new millennium. *Cyberpsychology & Behavior, 1*(2), 187–193.

Cooper, A., Delmonico, D. L., & Burg, R. (2000). Cybersex users, abusers, and compulsives: New findings and implications. *Sexual Addiction & Compulsivity: The Journal of Treatment and Prevention, 7*(1–2), 5–29.

Cooper, A., Griffin-Shelly, E., Delmonico, D. L., & Mathy, R. (2001). Online sexual problems: Assessment and predictive variables. *Sexual Addiction & Compulsivity: The Journal of Treatment and Prevention, 8*(3-4), 267–285.

Cooper, A., Putnam, D. E., Planchon, L. A., & Boies, S. C. (1999). Online sexual compulsivity: Getting tangled in the net. *Sexual Addiction & Compulsivity: Journal of Treatment and Prevention, 6*(2), 79–104.

Delmonico, D. L. (1999). *Internet sex screening test* [Online]. Available at http://www.sexhelp.com/internet_screening_test.cfm

Delmonico, D. L. (in press). Sex on the superhighway: Understanding and treating cybersex addiction. In P. J. Carnes & K. Adams (Eds.), *Treatment of sexual addiction.* Philadelphia: Taylor & Francis Publishing.

Delmonico, D. L., Griffin, E. J., & Moriarty, J. (2001). *Unhooking from cybersex: A workbook for breaking free from compulsive online sexual behavior.* Wickenburg, AZ: Gentle Press.

Maas, L. C., Lukas, S. E., Kaufman, M. J., Weiss, R. D., Daniels, S. L., Rogers, V. W., Kukes, T. J., & Renshaw, P. F. (1998). Functional magnetic resonance imaging of human brain activation during cue-induced cocaine craving. *American Journal of Psychiatry, 155*(1), 124–126.

McFarlane, M., Vull, S. S., & Rietmeijer, C. A. (2000). The internet as a newly emerging risk environment for sexually transmitted diseases. *Journal of the American Medical Association, 284*(4), 443–446.

Prochaska, J. O., Norcross, J. C., & DiClemente, C. C. (1995). *Changing for good.* New York: Avon Books.

Putnam, D. E. (1997). *Online sexual addiction questionnaire* [Online]. Available at http://onlinesexaddict.com/osaq.html

Schneider, J. P. (1994). Sex addiction: Controversy within mainstream addiction medicine, diagnosis based on the DSV-III-R and physician case histories. *Sexual Addiction & Compulsivity: Journal of Treatment and Prevention, 1*(1), 19–44.

Schneider, J. P. (2000). Effects of cybersex on the family: Results of a survey. *Sexual Addiction & Compulsivity, 7*(1-2), 91–112.

Toomey, K. E., & Rothenberg, R. B. (2000). Sex and cyberspace: Virtual networks leading to high-risk sex. *Journal of the American Medical Association, 284*(4), 485–487.

Watzlawick, P., Weakland, J. H., & Fisch, R. (1988). *Change: Principles of problematic forma ilon and problem resolution.* New York: Norton.

Weiss, R. (2000). *Cyber addiction checklist* [Online]. Available at http://www.sexualrecovery.com/sri_docs/cyber.htm

Young, K. (1998). *Cybersexual addiction quiz* [Online]. Available at http://www.netaddiction.com/resources/cybersexual_addiction_quiz.htm

9

CHAPTER Jennifer P. Schneider

The New "Elephant in the Living Room": Effects of Compulsive Cybersex Behaviors on the Spouse

In addiction treatment, the "elephant in the living room" refers to a situation in which the addictive use of alcohol (or other drug) by a family member significantly impacts the remainder of the family, yet no one talks about it. The apparent blindness to the presence of a behavior that adversely affects the user and the family results from a variable combination of true unawareness by the spouse and/or children, along with some element of denial, disbelief, and/or covering up by the family. Effective family treatment of addictive disorders includes bringing to light the dysfunctional behaviors of both the addict and family members, addressing the associated shame, and developing strategies (a) for the addict to stop addictive use of the substance (alcohol, cocaine, etc.) or behavior (gambling, sex, risk-taking, etc.), and (b) for spouses or partners to focus on their own needs rather than on the addict's behavior and to become empowered to set boundaries for what is acceptable in the home and in the relationship.

With the increasing presence of computers in the home, a growing number of users neglect family, social, and work obligations, as well as their own health and well-being, in order to spend many hours per week viewing the computer screen in search of sexual gratification. As Cooper and his colleagues (Cooper, Putnam, Planchon, & Boies, 1999; Cooper, Delmonico, & Burg, 2000) have shown, most people who access the

169

Internet for sex are "recreational users," analogous to recreational drinkers or gamblers, yet a significant proportion have preexisting sexual compulsions and addictions that are now finding a new outlet. For others with no such history, cybersex is the first expression of an addictive sexual disorder, one that lends itself to rapid progression, similar to the effect of crack cocaine on the previously occasional cocaine user. Regardless of the user's diagnosis, when cybersex begins to take precedence over a committed relationship, the partner suffers.

The Internet has several characteristics that make it the ideal medium for sexual involvement (Cooper et al., 1999). It is widely accessible, inexpensive, legal, available in the privacy of one's own home, anonymous, and does not put the user at direct risk of contracting a sexually transmitted disease. It is also particularly well suited for hiding the activities from others because it does not leave obvious evidence of the sexual encounter. It often takes some computer knowledge on the part of the spouse to retrace the user's online adventures.

There is still some disagreement in the fields of psychiatry and addiction medicine about appropriate terminology for this disorder (Schnieder, 1994). Carnes (1983) was the first to apply the addiction paradigm to out-of-control sexual disorders. In this chapter, the terms *sexual addiction* and *compulsive sexual behaviors* will be used interchangeably. However, I prefer the term *sexual addiction* because compulsive cybersex use fits the criteria formulated by Schneider and Irons (1996) for all addictions: The compulsive cybersex user experiences (a) loss of control, (b) continuation despite adverse consequences, and (c) preoccupation or obsession with obtaining and using the substance or behavior. These criteria were adapted from the *Diagnostic and Statistical Manual of Mental Disorders*, 4th Edition (1994). Although some clients who are compulsively sexual have been successfully treated with a developmental and psychotherapeutic approach, in the author's experience and research, many persons have not been able to stop their behaviors until they approached the problem from an addiction paradigm. Addiction-model treatment, which includes cognitive-behavioral relapse prevention strategies along with attendance at self-help groups modeled after Alcoholics Anonymous (AA) and its offshoot, Al-Anon, is also helpful for cybersex addicts and their partners (Carnes, Delmonico, & Griffin, 2001; Hecht-Orzack & Ross, 2000; Schneider, 2000a; Schneider & Weiss, 2001).

Compulsive cybersex use, like all addictive sexual disorders, significantly impacts the couple relationship (Schneider, 2000a, 2000b; Schneider & Schneider, 1996). Children may also be adversely affected (Freeman-Longo, 2000). Early involvement of the family in treatment of compulsive sexual behavior is an important ingredient to a successful treatment outcome (Carnes, personal communication, 1990). Unfortunately, in the treatment of cybersex-related problems, the effect on the spouse or partner is all too often ignored, as attention is focused solely on the user.

To summarize the types of behaviors involved, the viewing of pornography while masturbating is nearly universal among male cybersex addicts and also found among some female cybersex users, although women often prefer relational activities such as chatrooms to strictly visual activities (Cooper et al., 2000; Schneider, 2000b). Other behaviors are reading and writing sexually explicit letters and stories, e-mailing to set up personal meetings with someone, placing ads to meet sexual partners, visiting sexually oriented chatrooms, and engaging in interactive online affairs with same- or opposite-sex people, which may include real-time viewing of each other's bodies using electronic cameras connected to the computer. Related activities include phone sex with people met online and online affairs that progress to skin-to-skin sex. A preliminary study suggests that a higher percentage of women cybersex addicts (80%, vs. 30% of men) progress to offline sexual encounters (Schneider, 2000b). Some cybersex users participate in illegal or paraphilic online activities such as sadomasochism and domination/bondage, bestiality, viewing child pornography and pornographic pictures of teenagers, and having sex with underage persons.

To assist the clinician in formulating a treatment approach that includes the significant other, this chapter will describe the reactions of the partner to discovery of the compulsive cybersex use, the stages of "prerecovery" of the partner, and elements of an effective therapeutic plan.

☐ One Woman's Story

When no offline sexual interactions have occurred, therapists may underestimate the impact on the partner, likening it to having a spouse who enjoys perusing *Playboy* or *Penthouse*. The following description may make the distinction clearer. A 38-year-old woman, now in the process of ending her 15-year marriage, wrote:

> I knew my husband was masturbating all the time, but I thought it was my fault. He would blame me when I would catch him masturbating at the computer. He would not do any chores when I was out. When I returned, he would quickly clear the computer screen. He'd keep looking at his pants to see if I could tell he had an erection. He would run out of the bedroom like he was just changing. At other times he would call me and say he was coming right home at 4 o'clock, and not show up until 3 hours later. He'd say he was working really hard and not to give him a hard time.
>
> I knew he'd be masturbating if I left the house. I never said no to sex unless I was not feeling well or I was working. I believed if I had sex more

often, or if I were better at sex, he would not masturbate as much. I surveyed my friends to see if they'd caught their husbands masturbating, to see how often they thought it was normal to masturbate, to see what kind of sex they had with their husbands and how often.

I thought I was not good enough because I did not look like the girls in the pictures. I thought if I dressed and looked good it would keep him interested. I gave up competing with his masturbating and chose not to have sex with him

If the kids and I were coming home from somewhere and his car was there, I would run into the house first and be loud so the kids wouldn't walk in on him. I found semen on my office chair and lubricant next to the keyboard. I stopped making dinner because I would not know when he'd be coming home. I tried to talk with him about masturbation and how often he wanted to have sex.

My husband does not believe he has an addiction. He doesn't think it's a big deal because he says he was never with anyone else. He thinks all he needs is a more loving wife.

☐ One Man's Story

A 44-year-old man had been married for 24 years when his wife became hooked on the Internet (Schneider, 2000a). He explained that she wrote and read erotic stories and e-mails, participated in sexually oriented chatrooms, became involved in a bondage/dominance/submission, sadomasochism (BDSM) online community, and participated in both online and real-life sexual encounters with various men. She spent thousands of dollars on airplane tickets and phone calls and eventually lost her job because of her online activities. She stopped paying bills or doing housework. She stopped going on family outings, locked the kids out of her room, and ignored them.

> The whole family is still suffering the consequences of my wife's sex addiction. The kids are still hurting, and one of them is being treated for depression. I've been depressed too, and am still on medication. She exposed me to sexually transmitted diseases.
>
> I began to doubt my masculinity. At first we had sex more than ever as I desperately tried to prove myself. Then the sex with her made me sick—I'd get strong pictures in my head of what she did and lusted after, and I'd feel repelled and bad. When we were making love, she was thinking of her online partners. She reported all our personal sexual activities to her online partners. I used to see sex as a very intimate, loving thing. Now I can't be intimate or vulnerable—sex now is more recreational or just out of need.
>
> Why am I still with her? I feel if I divorce her she will end up dead in a hotel room somewhere or bring perverted people into my children's lives. I'm still very codependent and I feel I have to protect her. I also don't want anyone to find out about her.

With this introduction to the feelings of the partner, we will turn to a broad overview of the stages partners go through when living with "the elephant in the living room." This will be followed by discussion of specific aspects of the relationship that are of interest to therapists: the effects of cybersex on the partner and the relationship, and specifically on the couple's sexual relationship; partners' perceptions of what constitutes adultery; specific issues for male partners of female cybersex addicts; gay relationships; and, finally, various implications for therapists.

☐ The Stages of Prerecovery of the Cybersex User's Partner

Addictionists speak of *recovery* as the process of healing from addictive disorders, both for users and for family members. Recovery begins with recognition that one needs help for oneself. Partners of cybersex addicts, go through a sequence of responses to the user's ongoing involvement with online sex (Schneider, 2000a)

Stage 1: Ignorance/Denial

In contrast to the more traditional forms of sexual acting out, cybersex use happens in the user's own home. Paradoxically, it is therefore easier to conceal. There are no telltale receipts, lipstick stains, or unaccounted-for absences. Instead, the user is simply "working at the computer" in the home office or study. When the user withdraws emotionally and/or physically from the marriage, the partner recognizes there is a problem in the relationship but is unaware of the contribution of cybersex to the problem. The partner believes the user's denials, explanations, and promises. She (or he—we will use the female pronoun for simplicity) tends to ignore and explain away her own concerns and may blame herself for sexual problems that are commonly present. The compulsive cybersex user is often uninterested in marital sex; in response the partner may try to enhance her own attractiveness to her partner.

Stage 2: Shock/Discovery of the Cybersex Activities

At some point the partner learns of the cybersex user's activities, either accidentally (because the partner comes upon the activities in progress or turns on the computer and discovers a cache of pornographic pictures) or as a result of deliberate investigations. In either case, the partner's ignorance and denial are over. Discovery often results in shock, betrayal, anger, pain, hopelessness, confusion, and shame. Because the pull of the computer is so strong and its availability in the home and at work is so great, there is a great tendency for the user to return to cybersex activities even after discovery by the spouse, no matter how sincere the initial intention to quit. A common result is a cycle of discoveries, promises made and broken, and additional discoveries and promises.

Feelings of shame, self-blame, and embarrassment often accompany the early days of dealing with a partner's cybersex addiction. The cybersex user often minimizes the significance of the behavior ("What's the big deal—I'm not cheating, after all") and may even suggest that the real problem is the partner's antipornography attitude ("All men like to look at pictures—you're just too uptight about these things"). The partner may wonder if indeed *she* might be the only problem. These feelings may prevent the partner from talking with others and appealing for help, and the resultant isolation worsens the situation.

Covering up for the user is part of this stage, as these comments from a 25-year-old woman, married for 2 years, who recently discovered her husband's cybersex addiction demonstrate.

> We have only told our therapists about this problem. It's so hard to go to family events where everyone thinks we're doing great. I don't want to tell them because I don't want this to be all that they think of when they think of my husband. And we don't feel like we can trust any of our friends with our "secret." So we're dealing with this alone and that hurts.

Stage 3: Problem-Solving Attempts

The partner now begins to take action to resolve the problem, which is perceived as the cybersex behaviors. If real-life sexual activities have in fact occurred in addition to online sex, then the spouse's feelings and behaviors will be familiar to therapists who have counseled couples regarding a traditional affair. However, when the behaviors have been limited to the computer, the reaction is likely to be somewhat different: The computer has become such a staple in many homes that the partner is more likely to try to control the addict's use rather than eliminate it. This would be analogous to the alcoholic's wife who believes that if the alcoholic drinks only under her direct supervision at home, the problem would disappear.

At this stage, behaviors typical of "codependency" peak: snooping, bargaining, controlling access to the computer, giving ultimatums, asking for full disclosure after every episode, obtaining information for the user on sex addiction and addiction recovery, and (early in this stage) increasing the frequency and repertory of sexual activities with the user in hopes of decreasing his desire for cybersex.

A sexual solution to the sexual problem seems to make sense in this stage. Partners may agree to sexual practices with which they are not comfortable, have sex even when tired, and think about improving their appearance by undergoing breast enhancement surgery or liposuction. For the cybersex user, none of these methods are likely to diminish the lure of the Internet.

The partner at this stage believes that additional information will enhance her or his ability to manage the situation. This leads to snooping or "detective" behaviors. Partners who are computer-savvy learn how to trace the user's activities, and in some cases may even try to entice him by logging into the same chatrooms themselves under false names.

The couple often comes to some agreement to try to limit the addict's use of the computer. This may consist simply of promises not to use it or to restrict usage to legitimate needs. The partner or the couple may purchase filtering software (e.g., CyberPatrol or Net Nanny) that prevents access to sexually oriented sites. Often, the partner, with the user's agreement or at least knowledge, assumes control of the access. This type of agreement rarely works for long. It provides a measure of comfort for the wife to know what is going on and gives her the illusion of control. But the result is to establish a parent–child dynamic between the couple and to engender resentment in the cybersex user The user will begin or increase cybersex activities on the work computer or find ways to defeat blocking software at home, and will simply become more skilled at deception. Until the user is motivated to stop the cybersex activities, relying on external controls via the spouse or partner is effective temporarily at best.

In describing the phases of prerecovery of partners of sex addicts (coaddicts) in the precybersex era, Milrad (1999) found the end of the prerecovery phase and the beginning of recovery to be an awareness that they are in crisis and need help. Similarly, partners of cybersex addicts enter the crisis stage when they realize that their problem-solving efforts have been unsuccessful and when the costs of remaining in the status quo become intolerable: depressive symptoms, isolation, loss of libido, a "dead" marriage, their own dysfunctional behaviors in some cases (affairs, excessive drinking, violence), as well as awareness of the effects on the children of the family dysfunction. This is the stage when the partner seeks help for herself/himself rather than in order to "fix" the cybersex user. Once the partner is in therapy and getting help, the equilibrium of the system is disrupted, forcing some type of real change. Either the problematic behavior will change as the cybersex user also becomes engaged in treatment, or the relationship will end.

☐ Effect of Cybersex on the Partner and the Relationship

Some of the most troubling effects of a person's compulsive cybersex involvement result from the large amount of time spent on the computer. Cooper et al. (1999) reported that compulsive sex use on the Internet occupies an average of 11 hours per week, time that clearly decreases the user's availability to the family. Partners of compulsive cybersex users feel lonely, ignored, unimportant, neglected, or angry as a result of the users' spending so much time on the Net.

However, there are additional consequences for the partner that result specifically from the sexual content of the user's Internet addiction. When the partner perceives that the user prefers a computer construct to the real-life committed partner, her self-esteem often suffers and she feels she cannot compete with the fantasy person on the computer. Most partners experience some combination of devastation, hurt, betrayal, loss of self-esteem, abandonment, mistrust, suspicion, fear, and a decreased level of intimacy in their primary relationship. Some partners, including females, become physically abusive to their spouses. Some men and women engage in extramarital affairs or encounters, either to shore up their own self-esteem or to get revenge on their cybersex-using spouses. Other reactions include feeling sexually inadequate and unattractive, doubting one's judgment and even sanity, severe depression, and in extreme cases attempting suicide. The loss of trust felt by most partners is at least as harmful to the relationship as the sexual activities themselves. Despite the user's promises, the behaviors and the lies often continue, which leads to further erosion of trust.

Compulsive cybersex use elicits partners' deepest insecurities about their ability to measure up to the fantasy men and women online. The need to compete with interactive online sex pressures them into unwanted sexual activities. A 34-year-old woman, married 14 years to a minister, said:

> He's never been physically unfaithful, but nonetheless I feel cheated. I never know who or what he is thinking of when we are intimate. How can I compete with hundreds of anonymous others who are now in our bed, in his head? When he says something sexual to me in bed, I wonder if he has said it to others, or if it is even his original thought. Now our bed is crowded with countless faceless strangers, where once we were intimate. With all this deception, how do I know he has quit or isn't moving into other behaviors?

On the Internet it is possible to find groups of people who are interested in all kinds of unusual, paraphilic, and/or degrading sexual practices. Interacting with these people online desensitizes the cybersex user to such activities and "normalizes" them. Some cybersex users eventually come to blame their partners for being unwilling to engage in these behaviors.

The therapist who treats a cybersex user's spouse can validate the client's sense of betrayal resulting from her spouse's cybersex activities and can support her feelings as typical of others who have had similar experiences. In working with such couples, the therapist can help cybersex users become more empathetic to their spouse's feelings by reviewing with the users how they felt about the same activities before beginning to view them online. Another useful approach is to consider unusual or deviant sexual practices which the cybersex user has not viewed and normalized to himself and ask him to imagine his reaction if his spouse were to pressure him to engage in these activities.

The significant consequences of cybersex on the partner and the relationship can be summarized as follows:

- Many users lie repeatedly about the sexual activities; in response, their partners feel distrust and betrayal.
- The devastating emotional impact of a cybersex affair is described by many partners as similar if not the same as that of a real affair. The partner's self-esteem may be damaged; strong feelings of hurt, betrayal, abandonment, devastation, loneliness, shame, isolation, humiliation, and jealousy are evoked.
- The couple's sexual relationship suffers, not only generally because the user spends so much time alone on the computer, but specifically because the spouse (and often the user) compares her body and her sexual performance to that of the online women and believes she can't measure up.
- Online sexual activities may be followed by physical contact with others; rather than confronting the behavior directly, withdrawing, or becoming depressed, the partner may retaliate or seek solace in extramarital affairs.

☐ Effect on the Sexual Relationship

Compulsive cybersex use by one member of a couple usually has significant adverse effects on the conjugal sexual relationship. Sexual and other energies taken away from the relationship cheat both partners of addressing issues of self-development and deepening their sexual and relational connection. In the author's study of partners of cybersex addicts (Schneider, 2000a), two-thirds of the 94 respondents (68%) described sexual problems in the couple relationship, usually coinciding with the beginning of the cybersex activities. Fifty-two percent of the cybersex users had decreased interest in relational sex, as had one-third of the spouses. In some of these cases (18%), both partners had decreased interest. In only 32% of the couples were both partners still interested in sex with each other.

Spouses who lose interest in sex with the cybersex user report being repulsed by the user's sexual activities with cybersex, phone sex, live encounters, and other activities. This generally does not cause a problem for the cybersex user, who has already substituted cybersex for sex with spouse. On the other hand, when it is the user who loses interest in sex with the spouse, this is definitely a problem for the spouse, who feels angry, hurt, rejected, and often sexually unfulfilled.

Recurrent themes among such couples are:

- The user makes excuses to avoid sex with the partner (not in the mood, too tired, working too hard, has already climaxed and doesn't want sex, the children might hear, his back hurts too much).
- The partner feels hurt, angry, sexually rejected, inadequate, and unable to compete with computer images and sexy online women (or men) who are willing to do "anything."
- During relational sex, the cybersex user appears distant, emotionally detached, and interested only in his/her own pleasure
- The partner ends up doing most or all of the initiating, either to get her/his own needs met or else in an attempt to get the user to decrease the online activities.
- The user blames the partner for their sexual problems.
- The user wants the partner to participate in sexual activities that she or he finds objectionable.

A 33-year-old man, partner of a male cybersex user wrote:

> Currently we have sex once every 3 months, usually only after I blow my stack and I suppose he feels obligated. Although I know that I am bright and attractive, emotionally I feel ugly, worthless, and unwanted by him or anybody else. For me the issue has not been the difference between him having e-mail sex or actual physical contact, it is that someone else is receiving his attention and I am not. I do many mental gymnastics in order to cope with this. In order to prevent becoming irritated with my partner because he rejects my sexual advances, I masturbate daily with the hope that it will prevent me from becoming "horny." Sometimes it works. I would not care at all if he masturbated online with a host of others, as long as I was an active part of his sex life.

In a small minority of cases (16% in Schneider's, 2000a, study), the cybersex user maintains his or her desire for sex with the partner, but the partner is less interested. In some cases the partner refuses to have sex; in others, the partner doesn't want to, but continues out of fear of driving the user further into online activities. Major themes in such relationships are:

- The partner initially increases the sexual activities in order to "win back" the addict. This early response is only temporary.
- The partner feels repelled and disgusted by the addict's online or real sexual activities and no longer wants to have relationship sex.
- The partner can no longer tolerate the addict's detachment and lack of emotional connection during sex.
- The partner's anger over the addict's denial of the problem interferes with her or his sexual interest.
- In reply to pressure or requests by the addict to dress in certain ways or perform new sexual acts, the partner feels angry, repelled, used, objectified, or like a prostitute.
- The partner fears catching a disease from the user, or already caught one.

The knowledge that the addict's head is full of cybersex images inevitably produces in the partner a comparison between herself and the fantasy woman in terms of appearance, desirability, and repertory of sexual behaviors. The partner feels she is competing with the computer images and people. ("If only I was perfect like his porn, then he would want the real thing and love me.") The result is often confusion between, on the one hand, the desire to emulate and better the computer woman (or man) and, on the other, revulsion at the lack of intimacy and the mechanical nature of sex. Some people vacillate between these two polarities, as does the 48-year-old women, married for 4 years, quoted here:

> His cybersex activities made me angry. They made me want to be more sexy and desirable, then at other times made me not want to have anything to do with him. It made me feel that when we were having sex and he closed his eyes, he was viewing some other person's body and therefore was not really "with" me.

☐ What Constitutes Adultery?

When one partner has some sexual involvement outside the marriage, there is often disagreement by the couple on what constitutes adultery. The reason is that there is still disagreement about what constitutes sexual relations. For example, in a study reported in 1999 (Sanders & Reinisch, 1999), 59% of college students surveyed believed that oral sex does not constitute "having sex," and 19% believed that even penile penetration of the anus did not constitutes "having sex." There is now a similar disagreement about the meaning of the varieties of computer sex. When the cybersex user engages in real-time online sex with another person, most partners react as though skin-to-skin adultery has taken place. According to one distraught woman,

> My husband is using sexual energy that should be used with me. The person on the other end of that computer is live and is participating in a sexual activity with him. They are doing it together and are responding to each other. It is one thing to masturbate to a two-dimensional screen image. But to engage in an interactive sexual encounter means that you are being sexual with another person, and that is cheating.

To effectively counsel partners of cybersex addicts, therapists must understand and be able to validate the intensity of their feelings that this is indeed a significant betrayal of the relationship. The main reasons reported by partners include:

- Having interactive sex with another person is adultery, whether or not they have skin-to-skin contact.
- Cybersex results in lying, hiding one's activities, and covering up, and the lies are often the most painful part of an affair.
- The spouse feels betrayed, devalued, deceived, "less than," abandoned, same as with a real affair.
- Cybersex takes away from the sexual relationship of the couple. As one woman wrote, "I may not be getting a disease from him, but I'm not getting anything else either!"
- A real-life person cannot compete with fantasy. The cybersex addict loses interest in his spouse because he has "ideal" relationships where there is no hassle.
- Cybersex takes the addict away from his partner in terms of time and emotions. It results in emotional detachment from the marriage.

☐ Implications for Therapists

Online Addiction in General versus Cybersex Addiction

Although some of the most troubling effects of a person's compulsive cybersex involvement result from the large amount of time spent on the computer, the sexual content of the material can have an huge impact on the person and the partner. Accordingly, it would be a mistake to focus in therapy primarily on the time element of computer use without specifically considering the sexual content of the activities. It is crucial to spend enough time getting a thorough sexual history of the client and of the couple's sexual relationship, as well as details of the computer user's activities online (and, by extension, offline).

Sexual Anorexia and Cybersex Addiction/Compulsivity

Some compulsive cybersex users and/or their partners have erroneously been labeled by their therapists as suffering "sexual anorexia" or a sexual aversion disorder (APA, 1994, p. 499). It is a mistake to apply this label to a person simply because he or she is uninterested in sex in one particular context (e.g., within the couple relationship). Cybersex addicts do not avoid sex; on the contrary, they engage in sex compulsively. However, they often redirect their sexual interest away from the spouse and toward the computer. It is crucial for the therapist to get a thorough sexual history and, especially, to inquire at length about the presence of online sexual activity in the life of a client who appears not to be interested in sex with the partner. Similarly, the cybersex user's partner who feels unconnected, ignored, and betrayed and who therefore loses sexual interest in the cybersex addict is not suffering from sexual anorexia, but rather may be reacting with integrity and autonomy to a situation in which (s)he does not feel valued. As Schnarch (1996, p. 127) wrote, "Healthy people don't want sex when it's not worth wanting."

Understanding Sexual Compulsivity

Schneider (2000a, 2000b) reported that several people in her study consulted counselors or psychotherapists who apparently failed to obtain an adequate history and therefore missed the diagnosis of sexual compulsivity. Some counselors urged the partner to initiate sex more frequently. Some had never heard of sexual addiction/compulsivity or failed to understand how a person could be threatened by the use of a computer or other inanimate object. Others were so committed to being nonjudgmental that they missed the big picture: One young woman reported that her pastor had dismissed her concerns about her fiance's online preference for young girls, telling her that "once we were married, my husband's curiosity would be filled by me. Now that we *are* married, and I find that he has continued his acting out and lied to me so much, I am afraid of what could happen if we have children and one is a girl."

A client's complaints about her spouse's cybersex use may simply reflect her own discomfort with pornography, but it also may be a sign of a significant cybersex problem in the family; each of these requires a different treatment approach. Therapists who wish to treat cybersex problems effectively need a basic understanding of addictive sexual disorders so that they can determine if this problem exists in the client and, if so, institute appropriate treatment or refer out. Compulsive behavior is by definition out of control. Suggesting to the client that he access cybersex only 1 hour per day instead of 4 is likely to be as effective as suggesting to an alcoholic to cut down his consumption of alcoholic beverages from 15 to 4 per day.

Mistakes to Avoid

Where compulsive cybersex use is in fact present, potential mistakes by the uninformed counselor are:

- to underestimate the adverse consequences of the behavior, for both the user and the family;
- to fail to make it a priority for the cybersex addict to stop illegal or dangerous behaviors;
- to omit the partner or spouse, if one exists, from the treatment process;
- to diagnose the couple's problem as poor communication, the partner's frigidity, or a need by the partner of greater acceptance of the Internet user's activities;
- to diagnose the compulsive user's problem or that of his partner as sexual anorexia; and
- to recommend that the cybersex user limit the time devoted to cybersex activities to some predetermined number of hours, or to have the partner join in the addict's cybersex activities.

How to Avoid Mistakes: Begin With a Thorough Assessment

The first step for the counselor is to gather information, preferably from both partners. Ask specific questions: What is a typical day in the life of each partner, hour by hour? Are there large chunks of time that are unaccounted for? Have there been changes in the couple's sexual relationship? In the amount of time the family spends together? In the time spent with children? Is there evidence of cybersex involvement? Is there a history of other compulsive sexual behaviors? Ask about the partner's beliefs regarding sex, pornography, and masturbation. Obtain a thorough sexual history from both partners and a history of their sexual relationship with each other.

   If cybersex addiction is indeed present, some psychotherapists report success using cognitive–behavioral and developmental approaches. Many patients are best helped using the same principles of treatment as for any other form of sex addiction or compulsivity: Initially, the user needs to be helped to break through the denial that a problem exists and to recognize the impact of the behaviors on the partner and family; to stop the behaviors and associated lying; to stop blaming the partner; to learn problem solving in ways other than escape through cybersex activities; to develop strategies for dealing with sexual urges. Support through membership in 12-step programs such as Sex Addicts Anonymous (SAA), Sexaholics Anonymous (SA), or Sex and Love Addicts Anonymous (SLAA) is as useful as with any other addiction. Strategies specific to the computer are discussed in other chapters in this book and include limitations on use of the computer, acquisition of blocking software, and avoidance of the Internet.

Treating the Cybersex User's Partner: Begin With Validation

For the spouse or partner, the negative consequences detailed in this chapter constitute a lengthy list of issues to explore in therapy. Early on, partners need validation of their belief that a real problem does exist and of their perception that cybersex addiction can be as damaging to the relationship as more traditional sexual affairs. They need to feel "heard" by the counselor and encouraged to state their needs. Other early goals of therapy are to help clients accept that they did not cause the problem, cannot control it, and cannot cure it, and that the belief that having enough information will allow control of the situation is an illusion. The focus needs to be moved from fixing the other person to working on oneself, especially one's damaged self-esteem, and learning to pay attention to one's own needs and desires. Education about appropriate boundaries is useful, along with development of appropriate boundaries regarding the presence of the computer in the home and conditions for its use. Except perhaps very temporarily, however, it is not useful to have the partner be the "keeper" of the computer or to control the cybersex user's involvement with it; this is better left to the user's therapist or 12-step sponsor. Like the cybersex addict, the partner can be greatly helped and supported by membership in a 12-step program such as S-Anon, COSA, or Al-Anon.

Male Partners of Cybersex Addicts

There is very little written thus far in the professional literature about male partners of cybersex addicts. Gay men often have sexually inclusive relationships, and monogamy is less of an issue than in heterosexual relationships. However, isolated first-person accounts (Schneider, 2000a, 2000b) suggest that themes of loss of esteem and feelings of abandonment and betrayal are common to both male and female partners. Like most women, one gay man felt very hurt by his partner's loss of interest in relational sex with him, but unlike most women, he claimed not to be bothered by his partner's involvement with other men online. Whether the relationship is heterosexual or homosexual, compulsive energy takes away from one's relationship with oneself and would be a relational problem as well.

An earlier study of husbands of women sex addicts, written before cybersex existed (Schneider & Schneider, 1990), found that husbands who were not themselves recovering from chemical or behavioral addictions had difficulty accepting that their wives' behavior was an addiction, were more likely than women to react with rage and wishes to dispatch the "other man," experienced more shame than did women, and were less willing to get involved in treatment or self-help groups which focused on themselves rather than on "fixing" their spouses. They tended to excuse the wife's behavior as a symptom of illness or stress and were very ready to believe that the problem had solved itself at the first sign of progress.

Research in the marriage and family therapy literature (Glass, 1992) about extramarital affairs shows that men are more upset than women when there has been actual sexual contact without loving feelings, whereas women are more upset than men when there has been a strong emotional connection but no sexual contact. One may hypothesize that in the case of cybersex activities where there has not been offline sexual contact, men would be more likely than women to minimize the significance of the activities. More research is clearly needed in this area.

☐ Conclusions

When recreational cybersex use becomes compulsive, therapists need to consider the impact on the partner. Rather than simply encouraging the partner to be more understanding and more supportive of the user's enjoyment of the Internet, therapists need to understand and validate the partner's distress and the impact of the compulsive cybersex use on the partner's emotions and self-esteem, as well as on the couple's sexual relationship, level of emotional intimacy, and family time together. Therapy with the partner includes

1. validating the partner's feelings;
2. helping the partner understand that it is futile to try to compete with fantasy online sex partners;

3. empowering the partner so that he or she is in a position to make real choices regarding the relationship;
4. helping the partner to set appropriate boundaries for herself or himself regarding the user's sexual behavior online and off (for example, "I can't control what you do all day, but it is too painful for me to have this going on in my home; the computer has got to go," or "I am not comfortable having sexual relations with you if you are having real-time sex with women online"); and
5. informing the partner about the availability of support groups where (he or she can share experiences, feelings, and solutions with others who have lived through similar situations.

As with other issues affecting couples, the prognosis is better if both members of the couple recognize that there is a problem and are willing to work to resolve it.

☐ References

American Psychiatric Association. (1994). *Diagnostic and Statistical Manual of Mental Disorders* (4th ed.). Washington, DC: Author.

Carnes, P. J. (1983). *Out of the shadows: Understanding sexual addiction.* Center City, MN: Hazelden.

Carnes, P. J., Delmonico, D., & Griffin, E. (2001). *In the shadow of the Net.* Center City, MN: Hazelden.

Cooper, A., Putnam, D. A., Planchon, L. A., & Boies, S. C. (1999). Online sexual compulsivity: Getting tangled in the net. *Sexual Addiction & Compulsivity, 6,* 79–104.

Cooper, A., Delmonico, D. L., & Burg, R. (2000). Cybersex users, abusers, and compulsives: New findings and implications. *Sexual Addiction & Compulsivity, 7,* 1–25.

Freeman-Longo, R. E. (2000). Children, teens, and sex on the Internet. *Sexual Addiction & Compulsivity, 7,* 75–90.

Glass, S. P., & Wright, T. L. (1992). Justification for extramarital relationships: The associations between attitudes, behaviors, and gender. *Journal of Sex Research, 29,* 361–387.

Hecht-Orzack, M., & Ross, C. J. (2000) Should virtual sex be treated like other sex addictions? *Sexual Addiction & Compulsivity, 7,* 113–126.

Milrad, R. (1999). Coaddictive recovery: Early recovery issues for spouses of sex addicts. *Sexual Addiction & Compulsivity, 6,* 125–136.

Sanders, S. A., & Reinisch, J. M. (1999). Would you say you "had sex" if. . .? *Journal of the American Medical Association, 281,* 275–277.

Schnarch, D. (1996). *Passionate marriage.* New York, Henry Holt & Co.

Schneider, J. P. (1994). Sex addiction: Controversy within mainstream addiction medicine, diagnosis based on the DSM-III-R and physician case histories. *Sexual Addiction and Compulsivity, 1,* 19–44.

Schneider, J. P. (2000a). Effect of cybersex addiction on the family. *Sexual Addiction and Compulsivity 7,* 31–58.

Schneider, J. P. (2000b). A qualitative study of cybersex participants, gender differences, recovery issues, and implications for therapists. *Sexual Addiction and Compulsivity, 7,* 250–278.

Schneider, J. P., Corley, M. D., & Irons, R. R., (1998). Surviving disclosure of infidelity: Results of an international survey of 164 recovering sex addicts and partners. *Sexual Addiction & Compulsivity, 5,* 189–218.

Schneider, J. P., & Irons, R. R. (1996). Differential diagnosis of addictive sexual disorders using the DSM-IV. *Sexual Addiction & Compulsivity, 3,* 7–21.

Schneider, J. P., & Schneider, B. H. (1990). *Sex, lies, and forgiveness: Couples speaking on healing from sex addiction.* Center City, MN: Hazelden.

Schneider, J. P., & Schneider, B. H. (1996). Couple recovery from sexual addiction/ coaddiction: Results of a survey of 88 marriages. *Sexual Addiction & Compulsivity, 3,* 111–126.

Schneider, J. P., & Weiss, R. (2001). *Cybersex exposed: From fantasy to obsession.* Center City, MN: Hazelden.

Nathan W. Galbreath
Fred S. Berlin
Denise Sawyer

10
CHAPTER

Paraphilias and the Internet

☐ Introduction

At the time of the last major revision of the *Diagnostic and Statistical Manual of Mental Disorders* (*DSM-IV*; American Psychiatric Association, 1994), public use of the Internet had been quite limited. During subsequent years, its rapid development and expansion has fundamentally changed how the world communicates and accesses information. Those with unpopular viewpoints or interests, heretofore excluded either by publication cost or societal repercussion, have found the World Wide Web a relatively inexpensive and expedient medium for both expression and interaction. People with atypical and/or paraphilic sexual interests and practices are included in this collective.

According to the *DSM-IV*, the primary characteristic of a paraphilic disorder is that the afflicted individual experiences intense, recurrent erotically arousing fantasies and urges of an aberrant nature. In the case of the paraphilic disorder of pedophilia, those sexualized urges are about children; in exhibitionism, about public genital exposure; in transvestitic fetishism, about dressing in clothing of the opposite gender; and in paraphilic coercive disorder, about raping others. The Internet's "triple-A engine" of accessibility, affordability, and assumed anonymity (Cooper, 1998) allows for exploration of many sorts of paraphilic desires with little sense of embarrassment and often with the illusion of personal security.

In some instances, the exploration of paraphilic interests via the Internet does not come without risk. For example, the pursuit of pedophilic involvements can be particularly risky, as most countries prohibit adult sexual interactions with minors. Those persons who either solicit children via the Internet for sex or who electronically send or receive sexualized images of them risk apprehension by a variety of national and international law enforcement agencies. Other criminal and civil sanctions are risked by voyeurs who transmit either nude or sexualized images of nonconsenting individuals from hidden cameras. Additional personal risk is often reflected in the time and productivity that such online pursuits can take away from work, family, and other societal obligations. Finally, there are the emotional risks associated with the possibility of being victimized by paraphilic practices. Due to the pervasive nature of the Internet and its impact upon the lives of those who use and abuse it, clinicians are more and more likely to encounter individuals with paraphilic disorders who have "gotten caught up in the Web."

☐ Sexual Differences and the Internet

People differ from one another sexually in at least four ways: (a) the kinds of partners whom they find to be sexually attractive (e.g., adults, children, animals), (b) the kinds of behaviors that they find to be erotically stimulating (e.g., cross-dressing, bondage, public genital exposure), (c) the intensity of their sexual desires (and hence their sense of feeling pressured to act sexually), and (d) their attitudes about whether or not they should try to resist doing so (Berlin & Krout, 1986). Without arguing the moral and legal implications, it is safe to say that not all of these differences are equally accepted by society. In fact, the sexual differences that our society has judged to be outside of the mainstream are often labeled "deviant." Sexual practices that involve the unwilling, or those incapable of giving consent, are ordinarily illegal. In the psychiatric community, sexual interests that are categorized as paraphilias are a cause of concern because they can either interfere with the individual's optimal functioning or cause harm or psychological distress. Paraphilias can impair full volitional capabilities in the same way that appetite can impair the capacity to successfully lose weight.

Sexual orientation and interests are generally thought to be discovered rather than decided. That is, a person does not wake up one morning and decide what will arouse him or her sexually. Rather, finding out about one's own sexual interests is a process of discovery that starts in childhood (Berlin, 1988). As an individual matures, possibly discovering new or novel sources of sexual stimulation, these novel stimuli may become incorporated into his or her repertoire of sexual interests. However, in most cases sexual interests appear to be known to oneself (though perhaps not yet enacted) rather early in life. The Internet can afford a readily available means for exploring such differences and interests.

☐ Cruising Society's New Red-Light District

Two decades ago, sexually explicit "stimuli" had largely been the domain of adult bookstores and strip clubs relegated to "the seedier side of town." With the advent of home video and the Internet, virtually all forms of erotica and pornography have now become readily accessible from one's own living room. For those with Internet capabilities, this ease of accessibility has streamlined the ongoing discovery, and potential enactment of one's sexuality, into a "point and click" process. Technology-assisted sexual discovery has reportedly been liberating and fulfilling for some. However, others have found it to be cumbersome, debilitating, and in a few extreme cases, such as those involving sexual masochism, even life threatening. In that sense, cybersex has been seen as both adaptive and pathological (Cooper, Scherer, Boies, & Gordon, 1999).

Just like other sexual behaviors, Internet sexuality involves the expression of a powerful biological drive. When a person's sex drive becomes pathological (for example, directed toward children), no amount of punishment or legislation can make it go away. Nor can punishment enhance one's capacity to successfully resist succumbing to unacceptable sexual urges. Sexual drive that has become "aimed" in the wrong direction (e.g., toward children), like all basic biological drives, such as hunger, thirst, and sleep, will recurrently crave satiation. For the person with a paraphilic disorder who is driven toward sexual exploration involving illegal or socially prohibited activities, surfing the Internet's red-light districts can be problematic.

☐ Seducing the Internet User

Electronic commerce rather quickly recognized that there was a desire by many to explore sexual interests via the Internet. Seeking to attract potential customers, some companies specializing in the production of sexually explicit materials have developed a number of ways to expose as many Internet users as possible to their products. Hence, many Internet users have found themselves to be the recipients of unsolicited e-mails advertising sexually explicit Web sites, including paraphilic Web sites. Once included on an e-mail address list, recipients may find it difficult to avoid these unwanted solicitations, also known as *spam*.

In an attempt to trick consumers into accessing their sexually explicit sites, some companies have capitalized on the fact that not everybody can remember Web site addresses perfectly. Consequently, they have registered Web site names that either are common misspellings or can be mistaken as addresses for other sites. Still other companies have copied government, or private sector Web addresses in full, substituting the ".com" suffix for ".gov" or ".org." The most notorious instance of this recruitment ploy took place when a sexually explicit Web site successfully mimicked the U.S. presidential Web site. In that instance, teachers and parents became alarmed when their children accessed sexual materials instead of the White House, as a consequence of having typed in a ".com" instead of a ".gov" at the end of the Web site address. Transmitting certain forms of sexually explicit materials to a child, or to a vulnerable person with a paraphilic disorder may be analogous to sending whiskey to an alcoholic.

☐ Searching for Paraphilias

For those interested in purposely finding a paraphilia-containing Web site, as opposed to having been unintentionally drawn in, one merely needs to go to any Internet search engine (e.g., Yahoo, Infoseek, Altavista), type in the desired name, and execute the search. While many adult sites limit access (and generate profits) by charging people to view their sexually explicit materials, there are also a number of free sites as well. Subsequently, for those wanting to then exit a site, their departure may be purposely impeded by the presence of an "exit loop." Sites often use this marketing ploy to automatically propel a user to additional Web sites, thereby opening several new browser windows at once. In such instances, each window closure can spawn the opening of an additional two or three windows, each containing unsolicited offers of additional sexually explicit materials. For vulnerable persons with paraphilic disorders, this method of delaying their intended exit from a sexually explicit Web site can prove to be particularly problematic.

For most persons, Internet sites containing paraphilic materials are usually dismissed as either humorous, bizarre, or even repulsive. However, such Web sites can become riveting for those discovering that their sexual appetites are whetted by such exposure. Some patients have found the process of seeking out, and then collecting, paraphilic images and stories to be akin to an illicit scavenger hunt. Some have spent literally hours on the Internet, compulsively looking for the types of materials that excite and arouse them. Such Web sites and newsgroups are often explored for hours in painstaking detail. Individual electronic collections of a sexually explicit nature can sometimes contain tens of thousands of photographic images and video clips. Such behavior often comes to clinical attention only after a concerned family member or employer has discovered its existence.

Presumably, the Internet may have led to the discovery of new paraphilic interests in some; it has certainly served to facilitate seeking out paraphilic experiences among those with a preexisting predilection to do so. Once an individual has discovered that there are others on the Internet with similar interests, he or she may then begin to rationalize that paraphilic behavior (e.g., masochistic or pedophilic conduct) is acceptable. Chatrooms can provide the opportunity to discuss shared sexual interests, or they can even be used to teach the novice how to become an active practitioner. They can also act as a forum through which liaisons can be arranged. Some newsgroups and Web sites offer detailed guides for the practice of specific paraphilias such as voyeurism, transvestitic fetishism, sadism, or masochism. Such sites may innocuously describe favored fashions for the cross-dresser or, alarmingly they may checklist steps in the abduction, sexual exploitation, and rape of a child. However, thankfully, the latter is extremely rare. Thus, whereas for some individuals with medical and psychological disorders, such as diabetes or depression, the Internet may serve as a kind of technological support system, for those with a paraphilic disorder, it can sometimes reinforce problematic behaviors instead.

Information and photographs relating to various paraphilias is widely available on the Internet. A recent cursory review of all of the newsgroups available through a U.S. Internet service provider (ISP) disclosed over 36,000 different entities. While the vast majority of these discussion groups were not of a sexual nature, groups highlighting such paraphilias as pedophilia, bestiality, sadism, masochism, and necrophilia (sex with corpses) were rather easily located. Durkin (1997) has noted that one newsgroup (with ".boy-lovers" in the address) has been utilized as a source of validation and information for those with pedophilic interests. At the time of this writing, that newsgroup had been receiving between 150 to 200 postings per month. Although some persons with pedophilia may receive positive support and feel less socially ostracized by interacting with others via such a site, for many, access to it may simply make it more difficult to appreciate the need to resist succumbing to potentially harmful sexual cravings.

Both cybersex (Internet activities intended to enhance sexual excitement) and chatting have elevated the paraphilia of voyeurism to a new level with the availability of inexpensive Internet cameras and videoconferencing software. Many adult Web sites use this technology to offer ongoing video depictions of live sexual performances. Individual users of this technology can link up for an interactive erotic interchange featuring both sight and sound. One highly publicized case in the late

1990s featuring videoconferencing technology involved Web site operators who had allegedly abducted and then sexually exploited child victims live on camera for the benefit of their voyeuristic (and presumably
pedophilic) Internet subscribers. Fortunately, cases such as this are extremely rare.

While popular on a daily basis with hundreds of persons who seem to
care little for their own modesty, voyeuristic/exhibitionistic sex through
two-way videoconferencing takes away the "triple A" element of anonymity (Cooper, 1998) so much desired by many Internet users. Nevertheless, we have seen paraphilic patients who have transmitted nude pictures of their own genitalia to others via the Internet. A recent review of
video chatrooms available through the "iVisit videoconferencing program"
disclosed adult content rooms with titles such as "SadoMaso," "Be My
Slave," "Boi [sic] punishment," and "Daddys [sic] wanted." Clearly these
are sites meant to appeal to persons with the paraphilic disorders of sadism, masochism, and pedophilia.

☐ When Self-Control Fails and Treatment Is Necessary: A Case Example

The behaviors of persons afflicted with paraphilias are energized by sexual
drive, which is a powerful biological force. Thus, for persons with paraphilic
disorders such as pedophilia or voyeurism, their behaviors can represent
acts that are biologically driven, in the same sense that drug addiction is
biologically driven. Although the average man is clearly quite capable of
viewing pornography over the Internet, he does not have to repeatedly
fight off recurrent and intrusive urges to do so, as would be the case for
the individual with the paraphilic disorder of voyeurism. The power of a
biological appetite can be such that many decent individuals, in spite of
their best efforts, may fail to successfully resist unacceptable sexual temptations.

The ease of access to paraphilic materials on the Internet has serious
implications for a subset of individuals whom, but for its advent, might
not normally have been inclined to seek them out. Cooper, Putman,
Planchon, and Boies (1999) described this group as "at-risk users." This
type of user may not have had a prior history of having acted in a sexually improper fashion. Cooper et al. suggested that these users may have
had sufficient control to resist acting upon sexually driven impulses until
confronted with the "triple-A engine" of the Internet. In that sense, having the Internet in one's home for such individuals may be analogous to a
person who has successfully resisted the temptations of alcohol suddenly

being confronted with the presence of a great deal of liquor in his or her own house.

Some persons who have accessed paraphilic materials over the Internet appear to have done so in association with either depression, anxiety, or stress. Downloading sexually explicit materials, including paraphilic images, may have helped to temporarily palliate their discomfort. Such persons, sometimes troubled and confused by ongoing life events, ordinarily do not manifest a malicious disregard for the wellbeing of others. The following case example demonstrates how, absent proper treatment, self-control can give way to one's paraphilic interests with deleterious results.

> Doctor Z is a 45-year-old, Caucasian physician previously employed at a major metropolitan teaching hospital. He had had no prior criminal or psychiatric history, and his childhood had been essentially unremarkable. Though his early adult years had been occupied with the rigors of medical school, he had found time to marry and eventually to have a family. Reportedly, he had never looked at pornography until reading a newspaper account describing its presence on the Internet. Using his computer at work, Dr. Z had then begun to explore a wide variety of pornographic Web sites, downloading many different types of sexually explicit images. Eventually, he had happened to come across explicit images of children, which he had then included in his quest to view and to collect as many kinds of sexually explicit materials as possible. Periodically, he would delete all of the sexually explicit files that he had collected, attempting to refrain from any further such behavior, considering it to be a "major waste of time." However, after a few days he would feel driven to resume his collecting.
>
> Collecting files had eventually become a virtual obsession, and by the time of his apprehension, he had gathered nearly 9,000 computer files containing pornographic images. There had been no evidence that he had ever attempted to meet a child via the Internet, or in any other fashion. He seemed to have had a very good value system, and he indicated that he would never have acted in a fashion whereby children might have been harmed. However, he acknowledged that he had not previously considered the possibility of children being victimized through the production of such materials. Doctor Z had never imagined that simply downloading such pictures could have resulted in his becoming a convicted felon with all of its associated ramifications.
>
> Following the discovery of the images on his work-based computer and subsequent arrest, he had become extremely fearful about how he would be able to continue to support his family in the future. He had recognized that there was a high probability that he would lose his medical license and that his two children might be harmed by the likely adverse publicity. There was no evidence that he had ever attempted to be sexually improper with either of them, or with any other children, for that matter. Lacking a criminal history, he was also fearful about the implications of possible incarceration. Doctor Z appeared to be both genuinely remorseful and highly moti-

vated for help. There was no evidence that he was generally antisocial or criminal in his makeup. Nor did any evidence emerge to suggest that he had ever posed a danger to any of his patients. Nevertheless, at the time of his initial assessment here, the possibility that he would be allowed to continue practicing medicine seemed very much in doubt. Clearly, he had developed an Internet compulsion, with paraphilic elements of both pedophilia and voyeurism, but without any desire to actually approach a child sexually.

Assessment Considerations

Evaluation and treatment of the Internet user must be based upon a comprehensive psychiatric evaluation (Berlin, Malin, & Thomas, 1996). While the individual's Internet actions may suggest a possible paraphilic diagnosis, a firm and confident arrival at any such conclusion can only follow careful assessment. That assessment should include review of as much collateral information as can be obtained, as well as a careful history and mental status examination of the patient himself.

Before meeting with a patient whose behaviors over the Internet have led to legal consequences, the clinician should insist upon seeing police reports, victim impact statements, a copy of the individual's prior legal history (if any), and copies of any prior psychological treatment records. He should also insist upon seeing an accurate copy (which the police will likely have) of any relevant Internet communications. When possible, family members and others who may have relevant information should also be interviewed. This should not be done to create problems for the person being assessed, but rather to help the clinician become as fully informed as possible.

For understandable reasons, individuals who present for assessment following legal charges ordinarily hope to be seen in a positive light. Although clinicians must have a genuine concern for helping their patients, it is imperative that as much independent data as possible be incorporated into the assessment. Collateral information enhances the clinician's diagnostic reliability and fosters a better conceptualization for treatment purposes. On occasion, a polygraph examination may also be used as a component of an initial overall assessment. However, special care should be used in the interpretation of the polygraph results, as they are not infallible. Finally, although actuarial risk methods may be useful in identifying groups of individuals potentially in need of special scrutiny or services, they have not yet proven themselves to be useful in reliably predicting a particular individual's future behavior. In general, clinicians are well advised to focus on risk management, rather then risk prediction, when developing an individualized treatment plan.

While there are a number of testing methods available to the clinician, two types of paper-and-pencil psychological inventories may be of particular use. One is the Millon Clinical Multiaxial Inventory-III (MCMI-III). The second is the Multiphasic Sex Inventory (MSI). The MCMI-III can aid in the identification of comorbid diagnoses, such as depression. In addition, it can also help to identify various personality vulnerabilities requiring treatment. However, it cannot diagnose a paraphilic disorder. The MSI contains a number of scales that are intended to aid in the diagnosis of a sexual problem. Those scales address issues of sexual knowledge, validity, and the question of a paraphilic diagnosis. Retest reliability studies have documented that the MSI is stable over time (Nichols & Molinder, 1966) and that it has acceptable validity (Day, Miner, Sturgeon, & Murphy, 1989). Once again, the results of these tests should be interpreted in the context of the individual being evaluated. One must always treat the patient, and not his lab tests.

Following psychological testing, each patient should be asked to provide a detailed family, personal, medical, and psychological history, including an in-depth sexual history. Often it is necessary to make frank inquiries, including questions about masturbatory fantasies and about the age of partners towards whom an individual is most attracted. Detailed descriptions of the patient's on-line activities are another important topic area. Clinicians should be careful to note the times of day that the individual had been online and the sites accessed. One should also assess the personal and professional consequences of the patient's Internet use thus far. Clinicians should not be surprised to hear that some patients may have remained on-line for literally days at a time with little sleep, sometimes while masturbating frequently.

Once all such information has been gathered in detail, we recommend, when possible, that the initial clinical evaluator collaborate with a second evaluator, who can also meet with the patient, to discuss relevant diagnostic issues. This two-clinician method can be helpful both in obtaining relevant information from patients and in arriving at a diagnostic formulation. Once assessment and diagnosis (if any) has been completed, specific treatment recommendations should be made and then incorporated into an individualized treatment plan.

Treatment Considerations

Treatment is dependent, in part, upon having made a proper diagnosis. When a person receives a paraphilic diagnosis such as pedophilia, for example, it is important for the clinician to appreciate that it is not his fault that he has such a condition. In growing up, no one would decide to be sexually oriented toward children. Rather, individuals discover that they are so afflicted. However, having in time made such a discovery, it then becomes an individual's responsibility to do something about it so as to ensure that he will not cause problems in the lives of others. As with drug addition and alcoholism, doing something about it may involve considerably more than simply walking away from one's own disorder. Rather, such persons will likely need access to proper treatment. Such treatment will be essentially the same whether paraphilic behavior has been enacted either on or off of the Internet.

Group Therapy

Group therapy can be helpful for those patients with paraphilic disorders who need assistance in learning how to deal with their sexual needs in a healthy and appropriate fashion. One aspect of the group process is therapeutic confrontation (Pithers, 1990). When an individual experiences strong cravings, and when satisfying such cravings is pleasurable, it is often difficult for such an individual to look at the ramifications of his own actions objectively. Such a person may experience difficulty admitting to himself that he should not do that which he craves so strongly and which is pleasurable. Strong emotions can distort and color both perceptions and cognitions. Therapeutic confrontation conducted in the group setting allows rationalizations, denial, and minimizations to be addressed and remedied. In addition to therapeutic confrontation, the group process also allows for therapeutic support. Many individuals are quite embarrassed by the fact that they have experienced abnormal sexual cravings and by the fact that they have succumbed to such temptations, whether via the Internet or otherwise. The support that can be received in such a setting can help to create an esprit de corps that is a useful element in the treatment of a paraphilic disorder.

In following a relapse-prevention model, group therapy can teach methods for achieving better behavioral control. Individuals are taught to identify internal triggers, such as boredom or depression, that might intensify or heighten unacceptable sexual cravings, including cravings for misuse of the Internet. They are also taught to identify external circumstances (such as living too near a schoolyard for a person with pedophilia) that might also intensify unacceptable sexual feelings. This process includes teaching people about the kinds of lifestyle changes that will be needed in order to minimize unnecessary exposure to problematic sexual temptations. For the Internet abuser, this may mean giving up all online activities.

If the patient has victimized others, then he should be helped to appreciate that that was the case. Appropriate feelings of guilt, shame, and remorse should be acknowledged. However, patients should not be expected to remain indefinitely on a nonproductive and debilitating "guilt trip." Comorbid psychiatric conditions such as major depression, drug addition, and/or alcoholism must also be treated. Whenever possible, long-term treatment outcome should be documented. Patient confidentiality should be maintained, but for those on parole or probation, treatment noncompliance should be reported. Should heightened concern develop about maintaining proper control during outpatient treatment, a brief period of inpatient hospitalization may be required.

Since sexually unhealthy Internet use is a relatively recent phenomenon, there have not yet been studies published regarding treatment efficacy. The Johns Hopkins Sexual Disorders Clinic, however, has published a large recidivism study looking at the issue of treating paraphilias in general, most specifically pedophilia, exhibitionism, and paraphilia not otherwise specified (paraphilia NOS). The category of paraphilia NOS included over 100 men with a history of sexual assaults against adult women. That study, which had involved better than a 5-year follow-up period of over 600 men who either had been or still were in treatment documented recidivism rates of less than 10% (Berlin et al., 1991). Over 90% had not recidivated.

Pharmacological Treatments

Some patients may benefit from antiandrogenic (sex-drive-lowering) medications. This may be necessary if the only way in which a person can satisfy his sexual needs interpersonally is either illegally, as in the exclusive form of pedophilia, or by causing harm to others, as in sexual sadism. Thus, a qualitative difference in sexual makeup, such as an exclusive pedophilic orientation, can be an indication for this form of treatment. Other people who may have fairly conventional sorts of sexual interests, but who quantitatively seem to experience a drive that is so intense that, in a sense, it controls them rather than them controlling it, may also be candidates for such pharmacotherapy.

Today there are two drugs in use in the United States that can lower sex drive by lowering testosterone. One is Medroxyprogesterone Acetate (Depo-Provera); the other is Luprolide Acetate (Depo-Lupron). Over the years these medications have gained increasing acceptance as one component of an overall treatment program for persons with paraphilic disorders (Berlin, Malin, & Thomas, 1996). Use of these drugs should always be combined with either group and/or individual psychotherapy. Depo-Provera is ordinarily given at a dosage of 500 mg intramuscularly once per week. Depo-Lupron is given at a dosage of 7.5 mg intramuscularly once per month. At those dosages, each drug will substantially decrease testosterone levels, thereby lowering sexual drive.

The intent in lowering drive is not to prevent the individual in question from having an active sexual life. Rather, the intent is to decrease the intensity of his (or her) drive to the point where he can remain in proper control. Depo-Lupron may be more potent than Depo-Provera, but it is also far more expensive. We have used Depo-Provera with some of our female patients, but we have used Depo-Lupron only with males. Persons receiving Depo-Lupron need to take another medication (Flutamide) for the first 2 weeks following the initial Lupron injection. Flutamide is a testosterone-receptor-blocker that protects the individual from the temporary elevation in testosterone that occurs following the first Lupron injection. Subsequently, testosterone levels will fall, and the Flutamide will no longer be required.

When recommending these drugs, clinicians may find it useful to describe them as "sexual appetite suppressants" intended to enhance self-control. If one could be made less hungry when trying to diet, it would then be easier to resist food but not impossible to eat. The same analogy applies when using medications to lower sexual appetite. Thus, persons on medication should be better able to resist succumbing to unacceptable sexual cravings, but still be capable of performing sexually in situations where it is appropriate to do so. For those who may, nevertheless, still experience difficulties performing due to such medications, it is possible to use sildenafil citrate (Viagra) to enhance performance without increasing the intensity of sexual drive.

The risk of taking antiandrogenic medications is approximately equivalent to the risk assumed by a woman who takes hormones for contraceptive purposes. This is not a zero risk, but it is also not at the high end of the danger spectrum. Such medications should not be overused or forced upon unwilling individuals. On the other hand, an appropriately diagnosed person should not be denied access to the opportunity to find out whether or not such treatment can be helpful.

Persons on medication should undergo a yearly physical examination with appropriate laboratory testing. Such testing should include CBC, SMA, testosterone, FSH and LH levels, along with x-rays to determine bone density. The latter is necessary because thinning of bone can be a treatable side effect of antiandrogenic medication. The patient's blood pressure and weight should be monitored regularly.

☐ Internet Use During Treatment

Continued Internet use is ordinarily not recommended for most patients at the outset of treatment. This may be a moot point for some, as conditions of either parole or probation may forbid any kind of personal online activity. However, should computer use be required for employment or school, patients are encouraged to accept monitoring by their employer, probation officer, or a responsible family member. Commercial Internet blocking software, such as CyberPatrol or CyberSitter 2000, can be a useful tool to impede access to adult-themed Web sites. Other software can be installed on a computer that monitors the user's online viewing habits. Snapshots of the computer screen can be taken at random intervals while online, and automatically forwarded to a preselected e-mail address, usually the individual's parole or probation officer. These programs can serve to remind the patient that he or she is at high risk for lapse or relapse whenever online. However, clinicians should be aware that such programs can often be easily defeated. In fact, a recent review of Web site blocking applications disclosed that they failed to limit access to between 22 and 90% of a sample of explicit sites (Consumers Union, 2001). While these technologies can be a useful adjunct to treatment, they do not constitute an independent method for addressing Internet misuse.

☐ Impact of Current Public Policy on Treatment

Since most countries have public policies and laws prohibiting the sexual exploitation of minors, pedophilic behaviors are usually those most frequently targeted for interdiction. Consequently, clinicians may find that an inordinate number of Internet users referred for evaluation or treatment have been apprehended for involvement with children. Today, most Internet investigations by law enforcement begin in an Internet chatroom. Persons who wish to meet for sex find a chatroom with a label that fits their interest and enter the area. People using the Internet to approach children for sexual conversation or contact will usually choose a chat area that youngsters are likely to enter. However, some individuals may also use adult-oriented chatrooms to make contact with the occasional child who happens to be there. By and large, the "conversations" taking place in these areas are explicitly sexual. Undercover agents posing as both male and female children of differing ages usually first make contact with potential offenders in such chatrooms. The "courting" process between the agent and the potential offender may take several days or several weeks. During the interchange with the undercover agent, it is not uncommon for the offender to transmit pornography to the "child." Once an individual has expressed sexual interest and has solicited a meeting, law enforcement typically plans an apprehension. Some persons travel considerable distances to meet with their "child," many times crossing state or country borders, thereby invoking potential federal or international penalties. Even before such a person arrives at the predetermined meeting location, he or she is first surveilled, then photographed, and then, upon arrival, subsequently arrested.

Since no one likes to be played for a fool, patients who enter treatment following a "sting" operation often feel as though they have been en-trapped. Many have a hard time accepting that what they did violated the law. Some may try to rationalize or justify their conduct. Some patients have a tendency to become very legalistic in reviewing their behavior. Rather than paying attention to the larger issue of their sexual problem, this subset of patients tends to focus on technicalities, or possible errors in their legal cases. While police conduct may sometimes be questionable, it is important to try to encourage the patient to look at his or her own problems. Many times, the group process (as described above) used in treatment helps to confront such issues, since a large portion of group members may already previously have been through the legal system.

A number of those arrested may have had no history of prior criminal involvement. Some patients may only have had problems because the Internet has made access to sexually explicit materials so easy. Others may have mistakenly believed that their actions were legal because their service provider allowed them access to the prohibited materials. In many instances, criminal arrest has had a devastating impact. Many patients find themselves terminated from successful careers and thus incapable of continuing to provide for their families. Still other patients had never considered that even a "first offense" could lead to a felony conviction with a mandatory prison sentence. Only after arrest do most patients fully appreciate other implications of their conviction, such as losing their vot-ing rights, their jobs, and their reputations. In the United States, some convictions require registration as a convicted sexual offender. Many of these issues may need to be dealt with in treatment.

☐ The Nonadjudicated Internet User: A Case Example

Clinicians may also encounter patients with paraphilic disorders who do not have legal problems, but who may still be struggling with the sexual lures of the Internet. The following is such an example:

> Mr A., a successful screenwriter, has never had any sort of sexual contact with a child. However, for many years the fact that he has experienced recurrent sexual attractions toward boys has plagued him mentally. He had sought therapy for this in the past and had even been advised by his therapist to confide in his wife. Sadly, having confided in her, she had not been able to handle her own feelings regarding his fantasy life, and in spite of the fact that they had two children together (neither of whom he had ever approached sexually), she had elected to divorce him.
>
> With the advent of the Internet, Mr. A has struggled very hard, resolving

not to download sexually explicit pictures involving children. He appears to have very high moral standards, and he has not wanted to harm others in any way whatsoever. However, at times he has found himself weakening, and then giving in, because of both the strength of his paraphilic urges and the ready availability of Internet erotica involving youngsters. As a consequence, at times he has had a block placed onto his computer that denies him access to sexually explicit Web sites. This has not always worked because it slows down his ability to utilize the Internet for work purposes. At times he has given his sister a password and agreed only to go on the Internet when she would turn on his computer and gain access for him. But this, in turn, had led to the temptation to access another computer at a nearby college, which he had then done for a while. Today, he continues to struggle, living with the fear that because he has periods of weakness where he does sometimes download such materials (in spite of his desires not to succumb to such temptations), he may someday be arrested.

In our judgment, this individual is much more a patient than a criminal. However, current public policy would not allow for such a differentiation. As we gain more information about Internet users, clinicians and researchers alike should try to distinguish between those non-ill, dangerous individuals who have a malicious disregard for laws and the well-being of others, and those otherwise decent, struggling individuals who are much in need of therapeutic assistance.

☐ The Compulsive Nature of Internet Use

There have yet to be any well-controlled published studies describing Internet use by individuals diagnosed with a paraphilic disorder. Consequently, an empirically based description of this phenomenon has not yet been possible. However, a few recent studies have begun to describe the patterns of people who engage in cybersex. While most of these studies have relied on self-reports, they have nevertheless still been able to provide some ideas about Internet sexuality. Cooper, Delmonico, and Burg (2000) used an online survey with a measure of compulsivity to better understand the characteristics and usage patterns of individuals who had employed the Internet for sexual purposes. Using a fairly large sample (n = 9,265), the authors were able to identify a small group of users (approximately 1%) for whom Internet sexual activity had become a compulsive behavior. Using the same data set, not surprisingly, Cooper, Scherer, et al. (1999) were able to document a strong correlation between measures of compulsivity and time spent on Internet sex. Those reporting the highest scores on a measure of sexual compulsivity acknowledged spending at least 11 hours per week in online sexual behaviors. Some had spent considerably more time than that. At least some of those who utilize the Internet in a sexually compulsive way may have paraphilic disorders and they may benefit from appropriate paraphilic-specific treatments.

☐ Comorbidity

Comorbidity of other Axis I disorders within paraphilic populations is not uncommon. In a published study that looked at pedophilic sexual offenders, 93% (n = 42) had met the criteria for some other Axis I diagnosis in addition to pedophilia over the course of their lifetime (Raymond, Coleman, Ohlerking, Christenson, & Miner, 1999). Mood and anxiety disorders had been most commonly noted. Conversely, on Axis II, antisocial personality disorder and narcissistic personality disorder were rare. Those with comorbid disorders may find themselves on multiple therapeutic tracks, including group therapy, individual psychotherapy, family therapy, antiandrogenic medications, and antidepressants. In each instance, the risk/benefit ratio of all of these treatments needs to be considered and managed by an attentive clinical team. When drugs are being prescribed, close monitoring by a physician is essential.

Table 10.1 provides demographic information, including data about comorbid psychiatric histories, for a group of 39 Internet users, evaluated and/or treated at the National Institute for the Study, Prevention and Treatment of Sexual Trauma. That table also documents the percentage of cases that had involved the downloading of illegal materials (child pornography) only, as opposed to those cases in which an effort had been made to engage another person (a child) an illegal sexual liaison. Among the group of Internet users who were attracted to children, they did not all try to entice a child into sexual activities.

☐ Conclusions

In historic terms, access to sexually explicit materials via the Internet by persons with paraphilic disorders is a relatively recent phenomenon. There are a wide variety of sexually explicit possibilities available via the Internet. Consequently, an individual struggling with paraphilic behaviors may be easily caught up in the Web. In some instances, persons with paraphilias who are involved in illegal sexual activities over the Internet have a prior criminal history. On the other hand, clinicians may encounter a number of cases where the presence of the Internet itself seems to have been the primary impetus for such conduct.

While some practitioners of paraphilic behaviors over the Internet may

TABLE 10.1. The Internet and Paraphilias: A Snapshot of 39 Internet Outpatients at the National Institute for the Study, Prevention and Treatment of Sexual Trauma (NISPTST), Baltimore, MD.

Sex	%	N	Race	%	N
Male	97	38	Caucasian	92	36
Female[a]	3	1	Hispanic	8	3
Education	**%**	**N**	**Employment**	**%**	**N**
Less than high school	21	8	Attorney	8	3
Diploma/G.E.D.	23	9	Computer Specialist	10	4
College degree	28	11	Physician	10	4
(2 or 4 year)			Sales/retail	10	4
Graduate degree	28	11	Service industry worker	10	4
(M.D., J.D., Ph.D.)			Skilled laborer	21	8
			Student	5	2
			Unemployed/retired	8	3
			Other (radio DJ, gov't, cook, etc.)	18	7
Paraphilic diagnosis	**%**	**N**	**Reported internet behaviors**[c]	**%**	**N**
Paraphilia NOS	49	19	Used sexually explicit Web sites	92	36
Pedophilia[b]	23	9	Used sexually explicit chatrooms	64	25
Voyeurism	8	3	Identified during police "sting"	41	16
Exhibitionism	3	1	Identified due to public complaint	33	13
None	18	7	Identified by spouse or divorce proceedings	10	4
			Reported use of computer at home	85	33
			Reported use of computer at work	21	8
Past psychiatric history	**%**	**N**	**Comorbid disorder**	**%**	**N**
Mood (major depression)	21	8	Mood (major depression)	49	19
Sexual disorder (paraphilia)	10	4	Substance abuse (alcohol)	13	5
None	69	27	None	38	15
				100%	
Criminal history	**%**	**N**	**Nature of instant offense**[c]	**%**	**N**
Prior history (as noted below)	36	4	Attempted to meet a child for sex	33	13
Sexual contact w/minor	5	2	Made no attempt to meet a child for sex	67	26
Indecent exposure	3	1	Sent pornography to a child[d]	28	11
Solicitation	3	1	Downloaded child pornography	54	21
Sexual battery	3	1			
Nonsexual criminal history	23	9			
No known criminal history	64	25			

Note: This data was gathered through a review of cases (*N* = 39) that entered the NISPTST between 1995 and Fall 2000 for sexual problems involving the Internet. Mean age of patients at time of evaluation was 41 (SD = 12.4), ranging from ages 17 to 70. Diagnostic data reflects those disorders identified at time of initial evaluation (Berlin & Galbreath, 2001).
[a] Our sole female patient was accused of Internet abuse by her spouse during divorce proceedings. She was evaluated and found to not be suffering from any sexual disorder.
[b] Includes those attracted to both prepubescent and adolescent children.
[c] Subjects may be included in one or more categories, or not included at all.
[d] Subjects transmitted child pornography to children, or to law enforcement agents whom they believed to be children.

pose a risk to the well-being of others (most often children), in other instances that simply may not be so. Further research will be needed to try to guide both treatment and informed public policy. Hopefully, future approaches can be shaped by a collaborative effort between the scientific-medical community and the criminal justice sector. These policies should enhance community safety while simultaneously ensuring the availability of effective treatments. Many of those whom we have seen have been conflicted and struggling persons whose sexual behaviors seem to be driven more by intense yearnings and cravings than by a lack of conscience or decency. Such persons should be treated fairly, and not demonized.

Criminal justice matters aside, all of us need to find a way to integrate our sexual needs into an overall healthy lifestyle. Some people may find this to be a heightened challenge because of either the nature or intensity of their sexual fantasies and urges. For those who may already be experiencing difficulties, the temptations posed by the Internet may simply prove to be more than they can handle through willpower alone.

The presence of sexually explicit Web sites, newsgroups, and chat rooms can pose special problems for those with paraphilic disorders. In instances where no harm is done by such Internet activity, and where the individual in question feels personally contented, that may not be a concern for either criminal justice or clinicians. The intent is not to require everyone to adhere to a singular lifestyle. However, for many, treatment may be needed.

Treatment possibilities should include individual psychotherapy, group therapy, family therapy, sex-drive-lowering medications, and the development of a social support network. Many individuals who present for treatment will have associated problems, such as major depression and substance abuse, that will also need to be addressed. Finally, the stigma associated with the paraphilias, and with sexual activities over the Internet in general, must somehow be reduced, so that those who want and need help can more easily seek it out.

☐ References

American Psychiatric Association. (1994). *Diagnostic and statistical manual of mental disorders* (4th ed.). Washington, DC: Author.

Berlin, F. S. (1988). Issues in the exploration of biological factors contributing to the etiology of the "sex offender," plus some ethical considerations. *Annals of the New York Academy of Sciences, 528,* 183–192.

Berlin, F. S., & Galbreath, N. W. (2001). [Demographic snapshot of a convenience sample of outpatient Internet offenders]. Unpublished raw data.

Berlin, F. S., Hunt, W. P., Malin, H. M., Dyer, A., Lehne, G. K., & Dean, S. (1991). A five-year plus follow-up survey of criminal recidivism within a treated cohort of 406 pedophiles, 111 exhibitionist and 109 sexual aggressives: Issues and outcome. *American Journal of Forensic Psychiatry, 12*(3), 5–28.

Berlin, F. S., & Krout, E. K. (1986). Pedophilia: Diagnostic concepts, treatment, and ethical considerations. *American Journal of Forensic Psychiatry, 7,* 13–30.

Berlin, F., Malin, H., & Thomas, K. (1996). Treatment of the nonpedophilic and nontransvestic paraphilias. In G. O. Gabbard (Ed.), *Treatment of psychiatric disorders: The DSM-IV edition* (pp. 1941–1958). Washington, DC: American Psychiatric Association Press.

Consumers Union. (2001, March). Filtering software for kids. *Consumer Reports, 66,* 20–23.

Cooper, A. (1998). Sexuality and the Internet: Surfing into the new millennium. *CyberPsychology & Behavior, 1*(2), 181–187.

Cooper, A., Delmonico, D., & Burg, R. (2000). Cybersex users, abusers, and compulsives: New findings and implications. *Sexual Addiction and Compulsivity, 7,* 5–29.

Cooper, A., Putnam, D., Planchon, L., & Boies, S. (1999). On-line sexual compulsivity: Getting tangled in the net. *Sexual Addiction and Compulsivity, 6,* 79–104.

Cooper, A., Scherer, C., Boies, S., & Gordon, B. (1999). Sexuality on the Internet: From Sexual Exploration to Pathological Expression. *Professional Psychology: Research and Practice, 30,* 154–164.

Day, D., Miner, M., Sturgeon, V., & Murphy, J. (1989). Assessment of sexual arousal by means of physiological and self-report measures. In D. R. Laws (Ed.), *Relapse Prevention with sex offenders.* New York: Guilford.

Durkin, K. (1997). Misuse of the Internet by pedophiles: Implications for law enforcement and probation practice. *Federal Probation, 61,* 14–18.

Millon, T. (1992). Millon Multiaxial Inventory: I & II. *Journal of Counseling of Psychotherapy, 38,* 164–179

Money, J. (1984). Paraphilias: Phenomenology and classification. *American Journal of Psychotherapy, 38,* 164–179.

Nichols, H.,& Molinder, I. (1996). *Multiphasic Sex Inventory Manual.* Tacoma, WA: Authors.

Pithers, W. (1990). Relapse prevention with sexual aggressors. In W. L. Marshall, D. R. Laws, & H. E. Barbaree (Eds.), *Handbook of sexual assault: Issues, theories and treatment of the offender* (pp. 343–361). New York: Plenum.

Raymond, N., Coleman, E., Ohlerking, F., Christenson, G., & Miner, M. (1999). Psychiatric comorbidity in pedophilic sex offenders. *American Journal of Psychiatry, 156,* 786–788

OTHER AREAS OF SPECIAL INTEREST

Al Cooper
Coralie Scherer
I. David Marcus

11

CHAPTER

Harnessing the Power of the Internet to Improve Sexual Relationships*

☐ Introduction

The Internet is an increasingly pervasive presence in the global village. Creative minds in every country imaginatively harness cyberspace, while ordinary users (sometimes called "netizens") conjure it up on their computer screens in homes, schools, workplaces, and the palms of their hands. Because of its prevalence, the impact that the Internet has on sexuality is now receiving increased attention in both mainstream and academic media. For example, it is estimated that nearly one-third of Internet users visit an adult Web site (Leone & Beilsmith, 1999) and that *sex* is one of the most commonly searched words on the Web. Increased amounts of time spent at sexually explicit sites have been associated with problematic usage (Cooper, Delmonico, & Burg, 2000), and warnings about compulsive overuse and the addictive potential of the Internet have been widely sounded (Carnes, Delmonico, & Griffin, 2001; Cooper, Griffin-Shelley, Delmonico, & Mathy, 2001).

In contrast, the exciting and laudable outcomes that result from the intersection of the Internet and human sexuality have thus far received

---

*We would like to thank Deb Levine, M.A., sex educator and author of *The Joy of Cybersex* (1998), for her contributions to this chapter.

much less press. As Schwartz and Southern (2000) noted, "the medium of the Internet is essentially neutral or value free" (p. 135); it is the way in which each individual user interfaces with the unique features of internet communication—the triple-A engine of anonymity, accessibility, and affordability (Cooper, 1998)—that makes the Web ripe for facilitating either mayhem or magic. Thus, clinicians need to tread carefully in the realm of sexuality in cyberspace. With more and more helping professionals venturing online to provide treatment, it is clear that there are many ethical, legal, economic, and technical concerns that make Internet counseling an area of uncertainty and controversy that is beyond the scope of this chapter to address (see Plaut & Donahey, chapter 12 of this book). The purpose of this chapter is to accentuate the less well known, yet constructive ways sexuality can be enhanced when Internet-facilitated adjuncts to sex therapy are incorporated into clinical practice.

☐ Internet-Facilitated Adjuncts to Sex Therapy Treatment

The Internet cuts both ways. The lack of face-to-face social cues, the decreased inhibitions, and the experience of losing track of time and one's surroundings while engaged in cyberactivities are as likely to power positive change in some individuals as it is to lead to problematic overuse in others (Cooper, Boies, Maheu & Greenfield, 1999; Cooper, Morahan-Martin, Mathy, & Maheu, 2002; Putnam & Maheu, 2000). This is particularly true in the context of sex and sexuality. The Internet can equally threaten or aid a healthy, sex-positive, emotionally satisfying sex life. Aware and informed therapists may find online interventions a potent adjunct to traditional psychotherapy for some of their clients. When clients' personality traits and learning styles are taken into consideration, online interventions can be an important tool for preventing, ameliorating, and resolving many sexual problems. Thoughtfully designed therapeutic Internet assignments that are tailored to clients' specific needs can maximize their strengths while minimizing the impact of their weaknesses. For those who feel powerless, the Internet can provide a sense of strength (Schwartz & Southern, 2000). For those who feel out of control, the Internet can be used as an anchor. For those who experience emotional paralysis, the Internet can be a bridge to action.

The Internet's triple-A engine provides a counterbalance to the fear, embarrassment, and shame that often accompany sexual concerns. It is this aspect of the Internet that particularly suggests it will be an effective adjunct to more traditional forms of therapy. The anonymity of the Internet (Cooper, Boies, Maheu, & Greenfield, 1999) affords patients the opportunity to increase their comfort with sexual topics without fear of judgment. Knowing that other people with similar problems are available 24 hours a day to discuss them can normalize sexual issues thought to be shameful or embarrassing. The decreased inhibition experienced by many individuals who use the Internet (Turkle, 1995) potentially helps more reserved patients to stretch themselves. Therapists who become familiar with and comfortable navigating cyberspace and its sexual content will be better able to facilitate a similar comfort and skill in their patients.

In general, there are four types of common Internet resources that can be brought into clinical practice: (a) Web sites, (b) bulletin boards and newsgroups, (c) e-mail and listservs, and (d) chatrooms and instant messages. The clinician has the freedom to choose from among these various online forums to customize creative and versatile treatment plans with their patients. A key distinction between these groups of tools is whether they are synchronous interactions (communication that takes place in real time very much like conversations) or asynchronous interactions (text information that is published [posted] on the system and to which other users later post their own reactions and responses).

Web Sites

A Web site exists for just about every sexual subject imaginable. If a Web site for some particular sexual topic does not exist today, simple programs are available for interested parties to easily create one tomorrow. Web sites are particularly appealing to novice Internet users because browser and Web page conventions are simple (i.e., click on back and forward arrows, hyperlinks, etc.) and the learning curve is short. A simple way to introduce the Internet into therapy is to teach patients how to use a search engine so they can embark on information-seeking cyberexcursions to sexual health or lifestyle Web sites that address their specific issues. The multifaceted topic of "positive sexuality" and the ever expanding and contracting world of Web sites make "learning to search"—like "teaching a person to fish"—a preferred choice for both clinicians and their clients.

A word of caution must be offered here. Therapists should be aware, and need to make their patients aware, that assigning random searches of sexual topics may lead the patient to access unwanted sexually explicit material in addition to basic educational information. This can be annoying or shocking depending on the person, and it can place those patients prone to online sexual compulsivity in jeopardy. Depending on the particular issues with which a patient presents, the best option may be for the therapist to search in advance (or use a known source such as this text) and assign prescreened sites rather than encouraging Web-wide searches. In addition, it may be important for the therapist to check the credentials and validity of the Web site before assigning a cyberexcursion. While a great deal of factual, hard-to-find information is available on the Web, both therapists and patients should take into account that the ease of publishing on the Web and inconsistency of editing, monitoring, and fact-checking the sites means considerable misinformation abounds as well. Therefore, excellent material competes with the drivel of crackpots, conspiracy theorists, and self-proclaimed experts. When these cautions are in place, targeted searches can begin. For instance, if a man and his partner are dealing with erection problems, either they or the therapist can type into the blank search bar key words or phrases such as "erection problems" or "erectile dysfunction." Within seconds, lists of hyperlinked Web sites appear, often with brief descriptions. With some guidance, patients can be directed to the Web sites of the foremost medical institutions where the latest and most accurate information in the area is provided. Similarly, if a woman and her partner have questions about resuming sexual activity after mastectomy, Web sites are available to address their physical and psychological concerns. Teenagers who experience confusion and embarrassment around sexual issues can be pointed to teen-oriented Web sites that are available 24 hours a day, 7 days a week to provide them with accurate information without the risks of exposure to the judgment of disapproving adults and peers (Flowers-Coulson et al., 2000). Web sites also furnish information regarding the sexual sequelae of virtually any illness or disease, as well as the latest drugs and remedies, complete with their potential interactions and side effects.

Using cybliotherapy (analogous to bibliotherapy) by assigning patients to seek information through Web sites has several additional benefits. First, patients experience a sense of control as they set the pace for accessing information and learning about their problems. Second, patients who take an active role in the intervention are making an investment in the therapeutic process and have an increased likelihood of better integrating the information into their lives. Those who have fears and perceptions that their sexual predilections are "bad" or "wrong" are likely to be reassured to find written information about their desires and established online social networks and communities of those who share that interest. The downside is that pedophiles and other sexual predators will also find online communities that encourage, even normalize, destructive and criminal behaviors.

Clinical options expand when patients have online resources available to them for the educational pieces of sex therapy. The therapist becomes not only a listener, but also a coach who guides patients to the Web sites most appropriate to their particular sexual concern. He or she encourages them to evaluate and experiment with self-help solutions acquired online and acts as a trouble-shooter who further refines and modifies any exercises or instructions to better fit the individual's or couple's needs. When information is acquired online prior to an office visit (e.g., a description of sensate focus and the details of beginning exercises), time with the clinician can be spent on more complex interpersonal issues that are best addressed in the therapist's office. Sessions become focused on the thoughts and feelings in the room and more complex psychological issues, rather than on information-giving or simple skill-building activities. Acquiring information online also expedites and deepens therapy as sessions center on resistance to the exercises and if relevant, the dynamics of the couple, rather than techniques. The following case example illustrates this.

> Vanessa and Elliot were given the URL to a password-coded Web site with an animation/film clip of the stop-start technique for ejaculatory control. They viewed it a number of times from the privacy of their home. The clarity and specificity of the instructions greatly increased their confidence with the technique. Vanessa blamed less, and Elliot felt less anxious. In session they moved quickly into their interpersonal dynamics and family-of-origin material, which contributed to the individual pressures each felt in sexual situations.

Similar to the proliferating customizable diet and exercise programs available online, interactive sex therapy modules are under development (Ochs & Binik, 2000). Clearly, the technology already exists for patients to electronically submit forms to therapists, educators, and counselors detailing the sexual difficulty they are experiencing, along with some sexual or medical history. In return they could easily receive a set of self-paced remedial exercises complete with illustrations and additional readings. More technically proficient clients could select more complex features, including video and audio clips and interactive programs. These sex-educational tutorials would be particularly useful when assigning specific exercises and instruction for the treatment of sexual dysfunctions. As in any self-help program, clients would receive feedback and track their progress before moving on to the next step of the module.

The Internet is also a means for experimenting with or expanding one's repertoire of sexual stimulation. Like the "feelie" movies predicted in *Brave New World*, the technology already exists for users to wire themselves with special sensors that enable them to have tactile, olfactory, as well as audiovisual experiences over the Internet. With developments such as these, the potential applications to sexual education and entertainment are limited only by human imagination. Technology will make these cybersexual aids as far from the old "blow-up dolls" as the F-16 is from the first biplane. It will allow partners who are separated because of work or other obligations to remotely "stay in touch." One can assume as well that sex workers and sex surrogates will have increased options for expanding their trades.

Some clinicians may not be aware that commercial Web sites, such as online sex shops, are complementary to therapeutic work. Venturing to a "brick and mortar" emporium to look at or purchase sexual education materials, sex aids, toys, erotica, videos, and other related items is not possible for many clients due to lack of access or time or because of feelings of shame and embarrassment. Online sex shops, whether a cyberextension of a physical storefront ("clicks and bricks") or a broadband-only entity ("clicks"), allows immediate access without the uneasiness. From the privacy of a personal computer, patients can comfortably browse the stock of erotica without driving their car, leaving work, or experiencing the discomfort of being seen entering the premises or encountering clerks or other patrons. A judiciously assigned visit to an online sex shop may accomplish several purposes. It can promote communication between sexual partners, ease sexual inhibitions, highlight sexual playfulness, increase intimacy, and help partners discover and expand arousal cues. In the course of cybersexual window-shopping, partners may become aware of unexplored feelings, build familiarity with the paraphernalia of sexuality, expand their sexual fantasies, and see themselves as more sexual beings. As the following case illustrates, therapeutic assignments to peruse online sex shops can lead to great progress, both in and out of session.

> Resentment was building and sexual frequency decreasing as Tomiko became immersed in caring for baby Aki, and Isamu spent long hours getting a new product out at his startup company. Their couples' therapist assigned an online sex shop jaunt. Placing items in and out of their "shopping cart" turned into a fun, in-house, no-babysitter date. While their screen saver flickered, they shared sexual fantasies, adding a new dimension to their arousal repertoire as a result.

Bulletin Boards and Newsgroups

Bulletin Board Systems (BBSs) and newsgroups are announcement and discussion tools that allow individuals to read and post information at any time with and for a group of others who share an interest in the same topic. BBSs, sometimes called message boards, are accessed directly from the Internet and are often part of both private and public Web sites. Discussions via BBSs may be either moderated or unmoderated. Options exist for individuals to be notified by e-mail when a response to their post is received. Newsgroups can be accessed from a browser or the Internet as well, but a user actually gets routed to USENET, a worldwide system of discussion groups spread among hundreds of thousands of computers, only half of which are on the World Wide Web. USENET is completely decentralized, which means that the tens of thousands of discussion groups are not overseen. More often than not, no editorial voice or professional supervision exists on either BBSs or newsgroups. As a result, they are best used as a means of peer support. Whatever information is passed along is typically anecdotal and opinion based rather than authoritative or scientifically based. These cyberforums are asynchronous; that is, contributors post (i.e., publish a text message) without the need for fellow communicants to be online at the same time. Individuals with similar interests or concerns (i.e., living with herpes, foot fetishism, surviving a spouse's affair) share information, resources, and personal stories while offering feedback and support (Putnam & Maheu, 2000). As topics change or subconversations emerge, responses are clustered by themes or "threads." There are usually several threads active at any given moment and a "newbie" (novice) will want to read through past postings to get a sense of the conversations taking place within a particular group.

BBSs and newsgroups are generally a low-tech, low-risk way to venture onto the sexual avenues of the Internet. Clients can choose to simply read postings without making their presence apparent, a practice known as "lurking." There is no expectation or pressure to post, and those who do may take all the time they would like to craft their offering. Discussants generally take each posting seriously, and there is typically a response to most postings. Thus, even small movements toward reaching out and connecting are noticed and reinforced. Individuals who have difficulty approaching shame-based issues themselves can read messages by others who might have had similar experiences. This can diminish the shame and isolation that often accompanies sexual concerns and help to pave the way to greater openness and healing. The feelings these postings evoked can then be brought to therapy for exploration, as the following case example demonstrates.

> Jake, a man who was molested by his mother, could barely even share his experiences with his individual therapist. With great trepidation and after a long delay he followed his therapist's suggestion to find an online discussion group. At first he could only lurk on a mother–son incest bulletin board. With relief at discovering he was not alone, he hesitantly added a post. He received many supportive messages in reply. He felt so encouraged that he eventually joined an Adults Molested as Children (AMACs) therapy group offered on his college campus.

Clinicians need to be aware that there may be times when a client's posting gets no response or a negative response. These clients will more than likely have the same emotional responses they would if socially slighted in real time. They may feel wounded, abandoned, angry, depressed—whatever is typical for them. Despite occasional aberrations, experiences gained from online discussions are generally positive and can provide a wealth of material for exploration in face-to-face therapy sessions.

Participation in newsgroups has been found to increase individuals' acceptance of their social, including sexual, identity (McKenna & Bargh, 1998) and to assist in destigmatizing unconventional sexual desires, such as cross-dressing, and fetishism (Newman, 1997). When patients with sexual compulsivity or other online problems begin to identify their difficulty, BBSs and newsgroups can serve to both challenge one's conception of and help break denial around destructive sexual behaviors (Cooper, Putnam, Planchon, & Boies, 1999). An added benefit of BBSs is that they provide a constantly available pool of compassionate support that is open well past a therapist's normal office hours.

E-Mail and Listservs

E-mail is an electronic means of sending text, graphics, and, very recently, voice data from one computer to another via an Internet service provider (ISP). One message can be simultaneously sent to any number of addresses. Individuals "subscribe" or put their e-mail addresses on a common list called mailists. Listserv, like "kleenex," is a very popular brand of mailist. Subscribers may receive announcements, articles, digests, and other online documents, and also participate in discussions, depending on the nature of the listserv. E-mail is intended to be a specifically targeted and private means of communication like personal "snail mail" or direct mail solicitations, whereas listservs are intended as a more public, mass-audience way to stay up-to-date. Unlike the telephone, which can intrude on one's life at the sender's will, receivers attend to their e-mail messages in a time frame of their choice: minute by minute or days or months later. Readers may choose to ignore or delete messages altogether. Both e-mail messages and listservs are asynchronous forms of communication.

Romance and Dating

E-mail is an effective adjunct to the treatment of sexual issues, especially within the context of a romantic relationship. It is the keystone of present day online dating and introduction services. Persons wishing to find ways to meet potential partners for dating, long-term relationships, marriage, or casual sexual encounters can register at an online dating Web site. Some have become quite specialized, offering databanks that target potential dates by ethnicity, religion, sexual orientation, sexually transmitted disease (STD) status, unconventional sexual practices and other characteristics. At the registration site, participants create a profile of personal data often including name, age, height, weight, interests, and preferences with the intent of locating potential matches. Some sites offer limited access or institute a trial period as an inducement to continuing fee-based use of the site, although often the monthly fees are minimal, with no contractual time commitments. Security measures, such as screen names and numbered accounts, are employed with the purpose of protecting the privacy of those using the service. Most sites have the capacity to post photos along with profiles. Once registered, people begin to search for matches using their preference criteria to narrow the field. The Web site is merely the bridge to where the action really happens: via e-mail. Upon finding an interesting profile, a person sends an e-mail to the potential match's account, indicates his or her interest, and shares some information about himself or herself. E-mail thus becomes the avenue of encounter and attraction, or lack thereof. If one party feels it is not a good match, the correspondence ends there. The e-mail courtship may be brief or quite prolonged. The couple themselves determine the pace, intensity, and progress of their interaction. Many find the emphasis on personal sharing a refreshing relief from the focus on physical attraction. They feel they see others as, and are seen as, people first. Online friendships can blossom into romance for persons who might otherwise have felt unable to compete in the dating and mating game. The following example illustrates just such a case.

> Hunter had never really dated but longed to. He feared that his 300-pound frame and acne-scarred complexion would keep him on the sidelines. He registered with an online dating service and was completely honest about his physical attributes. He responded to a woman whose profile included his shared interests in genealogy and gardening. At first they exchanged emails about their interests and seemed to have a pleasant friendship for over a year. When Dahlia's cat died suddenly, Hunter was there with solace and kindness. Dahlia felt she knew Hunter so well that she suggested they meet for coffee. When they met she was more struck by his gentle and caring demeanor than his physical "package." Many coffee meetings progressed to forays to the library's microfiche room, then concerts and gardening lectures. They became engaged a year later.

Romantic interactions can be emotionally intense for clients whether they occur online or off. Many clients have expressed elation, confusion, and devastation about their online relationships during therapy sessions, even if they had never met their partner face-to-face. Clinicians should not underestimate the power of these online relationships.

Building Intimacy

A different use of e-mail was put forth by Ochs and Binik (2000), who suggested that clinicians can use e-mail to help their clients develop "relationship building skills, and . . . experiment with erotic content in the context of a relationship" (p. 618). Intimacy can be increased when vulnerable feelings are shared via e-mail. The Internet can revive the element of mystery and intrigue in a long-term relationship. For instance, some couples create a private, amorous language of seduction in their correspondence that builds an erotic charge. Sexual playfulness, discovery, and surprise can enliven a relationship that has grown stale, as the following case illustrates.

> Leslie had difficulty disclosing to her partner, Brooke, what things turned her on. Their therapist assigned them to exchange simultaneous e-mails. They were each to list five sexual fantasies in order from least to most difficult to share. They then were given the task of writing a single-paragraph description of each fantasy and e-mailing one fantasy paragraph at a time in ascending order. Leslie then had time to sit with Brooke's fantasies, and vice versa. Leslie worried about Brooke's reactions, and sometimes her own immediate reflex was to recoil in surprise or disgust. She felt pressured at times to please Brooke, even though some of what aroused Brooke did not appeal to her at all. However, given the asynchronous nature of e-mail, as well as the distance (and safety) that the text-based medium provided, Leslie had time to formulate a more considered response. A follow-up discussion at the next therapy session allowed her to voice her reactions and fears. She was relieved that the goal was not necessarily the enactment of the fantasy but a fuller sharing of herself. Eventually she became more comfortable with increased intimacy and developed more acceptance of herself and her fantasies as well as Brooke's. In time, they even picked a few fantasies with which they were comfortable experimenting.

E-mail also provides an avenue for feelings that seem too intense to express when together. E-mail exchanges can be used to help moderate and relieve the anxiety and tension close contact can engender and recalibrate the distance between partners to more comfortable levels. Communicating by e-mail means that interrupting is not possible. This can encourage timid persons to put themselves forward and belligerents to pause and reflect on the progress of hostilities. Paralingual cues of timbre, pitch, and body language are removed. The time lag involved in e-mail exchanges slows emotional reactivity, which gives partners opportunities to practice formulating reasoned, measured responses. That slowdown can help deescalate encounters that might otherwise spiral out of control. E-mail communication used in this way contributes to a better give and take, better understanding, turn-taking, and acceptance. The following case illustrates this.

> Jamal and Kineesha sought therapy because they only had sex once every 6 to 8 weeks 3 years into their relationship. Jamal complained that Kineesha should initiate sex if she loved him, while Kineesha complained that Jamal confused love with sex. During the initial evaluation, the therapist noted that Kineesha lacked details of her childhood and seemed uncomfortable when questioned further about early experiences. As therapy unfolded, Kineesha repeatedly cried when Jamal stated that she must not love him if she didn't want sex. When the therapist noted that communication difficulties are often expressed in the sexual relationship, Kineesha crumpled and whispered that "some things can't be talked about." It was then suggested that they exchange e-mails about what each of them understood as the greatest barrier to sex. The e-mail modality enforced turn-taking. They could not interrupt; they had to wait until a response was composed, sent, and received. They could focus on the content of the issue instead of reacting to facial expressions or decibels. They could respond in haste, but per their instructions they were to focus on the issue and ask for more information and feelings, then read and reread their own responses before replying. Jamal chose to rewrite some of his replies after he recognized he was "off the point." Seeing that Jamal's tone was softer online, Kineesha confessed, "My father touched me." Jamal was able to have his stunned and angry reaction in private, and thus could compose a gentle and loving reply. Kineesha was relieved, and felt that Jamal finally understood her position. The e-mail modality allowed them to express their feelings about this difficult issue without the intensity of face-to-face contact.

E-mail is also a way to maintain connections when couples must be apart from one another. When one member of a couple must travel for business, family matters, leisure, or other reasons, e-mail is a quick and inexpensive way to keep one another informed of events of the day and generally reaffirm that the other is special, important, and in one's thoughts. Intimacy is built and maintained on small gestures as well as large, as is seen in the following example.

> When Gordon was assigned a tour of duty in Istanbul, he and Ramona exchanged daily e-mails. They enjoyed combing the electronic card Web sites for playful and erotic musical and animated e-greeting cards. When Gordon received a miniature digital camera in the mail, they set up simple videoconference calls, some of which became quite long and at times had sexual interludes, which they felt kept them connected.

Cooper and Sportolari (1997) suggested other ways computers facilitate a sense of autonomy, self-efficacy, and good communication patterns.

Chatrooms and Instant Messaging

An Internet relay chat (IRC) is a multiuser live chat facility serviced by a several linked IRC servers. Anyone can create a channel or electronic conduit for establishing two-way text communication. When a message is typed into a particular channel, anyone logged on at that moment will see that message immediately. Private channels are opened for one-on-one messaging that is not shared with a larger group. Instant messaging (IM) is a variation on the private chat. Instead of logging onto an IRC, a person creates a "buddy list" of persons with whom he or she would like to chat. When both the list creator and any of the buddies are online at the same time, a tone is sounded and the buddy's screen name appears. As opposed to BBSs, newsgroups, e-mail, and listservs, chatrooms and instant messaging are synchronous; that is, individuals communicate in real time. While it is possible for individuals to "lurk" in a chatroom by reading exchanges without indicating their presence, it is far more common for one's screen name to become visible to other participants upon entering the room, and for those present to greet or otherwise acknowledge the arrival.

While not as risky as face-to-face interactions, chatroom exchanges are the most social (and potentially the most intense) of the Internet tools. The exchange of text messages in real time makes the online chat experience a virtual laboratory for experimenting with social and sexual behaviors. While the jury is still out on whether social skill building online translates into offline social success, it seems to help some individuals break out of isolation and move toward increased social involvement. As a result, clinicians have at their disposal a valuable instrument for helping to build confidence and social skills in appropriate and interested clients.

Empowerment

The chatroom has a number of inherent features that make it attractive to patients who are developing social control and mastery. For some, just being able to easily enter and exit chatrooms and/or block and accept instant messages is a novel experience. They learn that they can "just say no," in other words, turn the tables on a communicant so as to be on the giving instead of the receiving end of rejection. Going to a chatroom becomes a self-paced progression through the steps of exploring, selecting a chatroom of interest, lurking, joining a conversation, maintaining conversations, and choosing to initiate a romantic dimension to the relation. A person may retreat to a previous step or terminate participation at any time. He or she can practice any step as many times as necessary until reaching a level of comfort. The risks feel smaller because the inhibiting nontext social cues, such as facial expressions, flushing, body language, and tone of voice, are absent. The chance of crossing paths at the water cooler is low and the likelihood of associating Sally Jones with her screen name, "Wildchild55," even less. Thus, the characteristics necessary for skill mastery—discrete steps, opportunity for ample practice, and ability to set one's own pace—are built in to the chat format. The following case shows how even reluctant or ambivalent people can use Internet chat to gain a sense of control over their sexual issues.

> When Andrea began to emerge from grieving the sudden death of her husband of 47 years, she felt embarrassed and guilty for having thoughts of "keeping company" with men. She was certain that she was too old and unattractive and that her grown children would see her as disloyal to Aaron's memory if she were to date after all those years. She found herself gravitating to online dating services, reading profiles and checking the photos of older men. She was still hesitant when she found a chatroom for widows and widowers. At first she "lurked" but found the chat irresistible when others shared their thoughts about dating. One man asked her to chat privately, which she did. However, he became a bit too aggressive for her taste. She dropped out of sight for a while but later rejoined using a new screen name. She's not sure whether she'll actually progress to dating, but she now knows she's not the only one struggling with these issues and feels able to control where and how intense the communications get.

Practice of Sexual-Social Skills

Certain clients will have obvious deficits in their sexual-social skills. For some, this is due to lack of experience; for others, it is because of a long hiatus from the dating and mating game. Some may even be in stable, long-term, committed relationships and still not know how to show interest, flirt, make sexual advances, or build intimacy and romance. Most of these skills can be easily practiced online in chatrooms. There are chatrooms specifically designed for flirting, romance, and cybersex. Patients may be assigned to observe the words and (text-based) behaviors of those participants who can be deemed "popular" and "unpopular," how they approach others and what seems to work and what doesn't. Patients can then apply the lessons they have learned to their own situation in an effort to become more self-observant and confident.

Before incorporating a cybersex chat or observation into an intervention, the cautious therapist will explore the possible meanings and purposes the patient may attach to such an assignment. Clinicians need to be sensitive and aware that such assignments are not appropriate for all clients. Many couples make no distinction between online and offline relationships—both are considered a threat to the couple's fidelity. Similarly, certain vulnerable persons, when given permission to loosen inhibitions, may go too far and indulge in excessive and frightening behavior. In addition, some people may move offline very quickly, which may be fraught with real-world concerns such as personal safety and STDs.

Much of what people seek in sexually explicit chatrooms can be termed cybersex, the exchange of text-based descriptions of arousing sexual acts to which one or both parties masturbate in real time. It has several variants in the online, nonchat world, including cameras trained on live persons who respond to either text or auditory commands. These can be unidirectional or reciprocal interactions. In the former, the viewer requests specific sexual acts and obtains satisfaction from the performance of his or her directives. The latter involves mutual exchanges of requests for erotic acts. These interactions may be a paid-for sexual service, much like phone sex, or they may be amateurs just creating their own good time without any exchange of money. The encounters are interactive in that there is mutual agreement about sexual activity, length of time, taking turns, and so forth. They may be produced in sophisticated studios or arranged by setting inexpensive Web cams on a desktop.

However, cybersex chatting serves different purposes for different clients. It can be a form of light entertainment similar to reading *Playboy* or viewing an X-rated video, or it may serve as practice and a transition to offline sexual activity. It may be an opportunity to explore sexual orientation or try out sexual practices in which one's partner has no interest, or it may be a form of sexual acting out that is destructive to themselves and their relationships. The therapist should explore the possible meanings the client attaches to cybersex and use discretion before deciding to assign these types of activities. A cybersex assignment can have additional therapeutic benefits. It can be an important bonding experience when partners are assigned a cybersex date. As Döring (2000) noted, cybersex has the potential to create "a situation in which people have the ability to share previously hidden or secret aspects of their sexual desires, thus creating especially intimate relationships" (p. 19). When the interaction is between two real-life partners, the feedback that occurs during online sex can help build trust and intimacy that can last long after the computer is turned off.

> Raj and Vreena had difficulty speaking about sex in any manner, and their sex life suffered as a result. Although not acceptable in their culture, Raj thought using some sexually explicit language would help spice things up for them. The assignment was framed as an experiment that could be stopped

at any time by either partner. As a result, Vreena felt assured she was not being coerced, and was willing to try instant messaging some "blue" or sexy invitations to the bedroom from her laptop to his desktop computer. They have had some great fun experimenting with these types of messages. Vreena is still not ready to speak verbally this way, but she and Raj do warm up the keyboards 2–3 times a week.

Creating Personae

Whether outright or by insinuation, some people present themselves online differently than they appear in real life (Turkle, 1995); they present themselves as taller, darker, thinner, younger, or older, having more or less money, education, experience, or hair than they actually do. Some people go so far as to present themselves as a different ethnicity, gender (called "gender-bending"), nationality, or sexual orientation. Masquerading is not new; Shakespeare used it as a device in a number of plays. The capacity to successfully masquerade online adds a dimension of excitement, control, and risk to the experience. It can also lead to anxiety and disappointment if and when the relationship moves offline and the charade can no longer continue. Some persons can lose themselves in the fantasy or lose touch with reality altogether. The press has played up the darker, more lurid uses to which it is put by pedophiles and other sexual predators. Research (Cooper, Delmonico, & Burg, 2000; Roberts & Parks, 1999) indicates that few people consistently change their gender or personalities online. Many of those who do try it once or twice, then lose interest. When a therapist becomes aware of a client's masquerading, it can become data for exploration in session. How long has he or she done it? Is he or she doing it for fun? To trick or trap someone known, like a partner suspected of cheating? Or is he or she doing it to further explore split-off aspects of his or her personality?

Planadri and Green (2000) investigated the nature of the participants in bondage, discipline/domination, submission/sadism, and masochism (BDSM) chatrooms. Like any other group, the persons who participate in BDSM chats are individuals who do so for varying reasons. There are those who only participate in BDSM online and those who use online chatrooms to supplement and support real-life BDSM relationships. While, of course, not all persons who engage in BDSM are masquerading, Planadri and Green's (2000) accounts suggest that one of the most powerful motivating factors for participating in BDSM chats was a psychological excavation of the self. As one of their participants noted, "It's like part of me that has been buried can be free" (p. 634).

☐ Combining Tools in Treatment

Many of the tools discussed provide patients with specific sexual interests or characteristics to find each other and develop online communities: virtual worlds with unique cultures. Whatever the form of the online discussion group, it is fascinating to see that leaders emerge, attachments form and break, and norms for acceptable group behavior develop. The seemingly static or cumbersome mode of text message exchange takes on a life of its own and clients get invested emotionally. With the addition of real-time messaging, the pace quickens. The variety and versatility of these forums, as mentioned above, make them excellent tools to use in practice. By combining several of these applications in therapy, the clinician presents a powerful opportunity to create positive breakthroughs in a client's sexual, emotional, or social needs or issues.

Group Support Online

Support groups abound on the Internet at this time, and the numbers are likely to rise in the future as people become more comfortable with the concept of online therapy. Some health, psychology, and news Web sites have online support groups facilitated by professionals at regular times during the week. Other sites have experts available at specific times of day, on certain days of the week, to answer questions in real time as they are asked. These experts provide information, normalize people's experiences, and provide resources, tips, and techniques to enhance sexual performance or address sexual concerns.

Patients with sexual concerns may have many reasons for not joining an offline support group. For example, they can't find the time, do not have sufficient resources, or are too embarrassed. Online groups challenge these excuses and reduce the barriers to participation. Online support groups also have the clear advantage of overcoming geographical impediments. Individuals anywhere can interact with one another in cyberspace. Gays and lesbians, cross-dressers, fetishists, transsexuals, and others, especially those who live in rural areas or communities in which sexual norms are constricted, may be in special need of accessibility to an understanding and accepting group. This can result in less isolation and greater self-acceptance. Content analyses have shown that the same essential elements (e.g., self-disclosure, provision of information and responding to the concerns of others) that characterize face-to-face groups are also evident in online support groups (Chang & Yeh, 2001; Winzelberg, 1997).

Teaching Online

Just as online support groups have flourished, opportunities for education have also become readily available. Sexual skills that can be learned online include techniques for alleviating many common sexual dysfunctions, such as building ejaculatory control, overcoming anorgasmia, or dealing with erectile dysfunction without or in combination with drugs. Similar to support groups, classes and workshops conducted online by professionals may help diminish the shame and embarrassment associated with these issues by reducing isolation and providing accurate information. Such classes involve the use of Web sites that contain syllabi, didactic materials, homework assignments, and hyperlinks to related sites, e-mail, and live chat. The online medium allows sexual expertise to be conveyed to large numbers of people in diverse geographic areas easily, inexpensively, and without stigma.

☐ Using the Tools of the Internet for Professional Development

Virtual Evaluations and Assessments

The Internet can be used as a tool to streamline practice procedures, respect clients' privacy, and increase time spent in therapeutic interaction. It can be incorporated as a medium for obtaining evaluative information either before or immediately after a first face-to-face meeting between client and therapist. For instance, as part of the initial telephone contact with clients, a clinician might ask if they have access to the Internet and whether they might be willing to complete online forms prior to meeting. Intake information, consent to treatment, practice policies, sexual history, or any other data-gathering instruments typically used at intake or for ongoing research would be e-mailed as an attachment or available on the clinic or clinician's Web site to increase efficiency.

In order to allay client concerns, a short explanatory note should be provided in the e-mail and on the Web site stating that anything needing clarification can be discussed at the next meeting. Any agency or clinic privacy policies can be spelled out on the Web site with a note encouraging clients to read it carefully. Such an arrangement allows clients to set a comfortable pace for completing the forms in the privacy necessary for revealing sensitive sexual information. It reduces time pressure, alleviates embarrassment, and potentially disinhibits responses, especially when the computer is away from the scrutinizing eyes of a partner or other significant person. Clients may download and print copies for themselves and either bring a printed copy to the session or submit it via e-mail to the therapist. Although recent legislation considers electronic signatures as valid and legally binding, it is assumed that the majority of therapists will still feel more secure with signatures executed in their offices, especially regarding financial policies and releases of information. However, when the client arrives in the office with most of the "housekeeping" paperwork completed, therapy can begin much more quickly.

The Internet can expedite formal evaluations as well. Professionals who specialize in testing can find reviews, data, purchase-booklets, and scannable response sheets online. The technology is in place for tests to not only be interactively administered online, but also for responses to be instantly tallied and interpreted. This virtually eliminates delays in having the test data available for interpretation, diagnosis, treatment planning, or time-critical report writing, as is often the case with court dates or other forensic situations.

Professional Networking

One of the most valuable features of the Internet is the easy accessibility it provides to other professionals in the field. Colleagues are able to address one another over the Internet with little effort, whether they are next door or on the next continent. The opportunities are endless. They can place hyperlinks on each other's Web sites or announce meetings on Web sites and via e-mail. They can join newsgroups and listservs and become part of an online community of sexuality professionals. Clinicians who need to locate a sex therapist in another state or country, discover who is doing research on a particular topic, or seek a second opinion or consultation on a difficult case can post to BBSs and listservs or enter online chatrooms filled with qualified professionals. Some counseling-focused Web sites have devoted certain areas to the public and others for professionals. These professional Web pages offer articles of interest to practicing therapists, referral listings, and profiles that include office locations, degree, licensure, and areas of specialization.

Education and Training

Clinicians dealing with sexual issues are always in need of information about the new developments in the field. Do you need to know what are the recent changes in your state's child abuse reporting laws? Visit your state board or local chapter of your professional organization's Web site and look it up. Do you have a client considering gender transition surgery? Run an online search with the terms *Benjamin Guidelines* to find the criteria which must be met in order for surgery to proceed. Visiting health and news organization Web sites can provide easy access to a vast array of sexual topics presented in easy-to-understand language. More technical and scholarly articles may require more highly refined searches for a fee but are still more easily obtained than conventional library searches of a few short years ago.

Internet courses can now satisfy mandatory continuing education requirements for licensure and renewal in some states. Recently, California permitted 8 of 36 hours needed to renew the psychology license to be completed via approved homestudy, including online coursework (http://www.calpsychlink.org/accrediting-agency/ga.htm#7).

Research

Using the Internet to investigate sexual issues is becoming more and more common. Whether online erotic activities or more traditional aspects of sexuality are under scrutiny, the Internet can be invaluable at every step of the process. E-mail connects the primary investigator with his or her coauthors to explore interest in the project and later to incubate ideas; to develop the research design; to exchange leads on related articles or other researchers studying similar topics; to trade drafts for editing and review; to remain in contact with institutions, funding agents, and publishers; and generally to keep in touch. Potential subjects may be contacted by e-mail and receive informed consent instruments, surveys, or other research documents. In instances where the Internet is used as the primary venue for conducting interviews or data-gathering, research teams may wish to build one or more password-protected Web sites where confirmed subjects visit to complete forms and research instruments or where members of the research team post preliminary findings. For more on uses of the Internet to conduct research on sexuality, see chapter 13 of this book by Ochs, Mah, and Binik.

☐ Conclusion

The Internet is here to stay and the profound impact it will have on every dimension of sexuality is just beginning to be recognized. Powered by the triple-A engine, the Net offers knowledge, entertainment, and psychosocial opportunities in ways never before imagined. It allows therapists to reach isolated and underserved groups who otherwise might miss the wealth of sexual information and guidance available. Web sites offer a sense of control in both realistic and fantasy environments, as they allow users to enter into any virtual sexual realm. Chatrooms cater to specific interests and tastes and permit groups of people to relate to each other in complex social interactions. At all hours of the day and night, romantic, erotic, and emotionally intimate encounters are germinating and flowering online—whether a therapist is involved or not.

Clinicians no longer have the choice of deciding whether they are interested in finding out about the Internet. Clients are bringing their virtual encounters into their therapy sessions and therapists need to be prepared to respond. Our collective consciousness has been altered by the online landscape. The options left now involve how fast and in what ways therapists dealing with sexual issues can adjust to and/or incorporate this new technology to facilitate treatment.

Sexual concerns at the turn of the 21st century reflect both the strides and missteps made at the end of the 20th. There remain a number of challenges and concerns for mental health professionals, particularly those who specialize in sexual concerns. Advances in sanitation, hygiene, diet, medication, and health technology have resulted in people living longer than ever before and therefore having the luxury to be more concerned about such quality of life issues as sexuality. In addition, there is an increasing awareness that people do not cease having intimacy needs as they age. Those who cope with chronic illness and disability demand acknowledgment of their unique sexual dimensions, as well as specific help in order to realize their sexual potential. And if the epidemics of STDs (including HIV/AIDS), teen pregnancy, and sexual violence are to be reversed, then voice needs to be given to their psychological and sociological dimensions.

To this end, it is essential that clinicians and those on the frontlines avail themselves of the abundant sexual information and enhancements available through the Internet. Advances in computer and other technologies are already giving sexual health professionals innovative, powerful, and effective methods to intervene therapeutically in order to begin to address these concerns. We currently have the capacity for worldwide wireless, instantaneous communication, three-dimensional facsimile (*Discover*, 2000), robotics, holography, and transmission of long-distance tactile/kinesthetic sensation. It is hard to imagine what marvels technology will make available tomorrow. It is up to us to take leadership roles in harnessing the power of the Internet and using it to enhance sexuality for the people, and in the domains, for which we have responsibility.

☐ References

Carnes, P., Delmonico, D., & Griffin, E. (2001). *In the shadows of the net: Breaking free of compulsive online sexual behavior.* Center City, MN: Hazeldon Information & Educational Services.

Chamberlin, J. (2000, July/August). E-dissertations. *Monitor on Psychology, 31*(2), 78–80.

Chamberlin, J. (2001, January). Digital dissemination. *Monitor on Psychology, 31*(1), 64–66.

Chang, T. & Yeh, C. J., & Krumboltz, J. D. (2001). Process and outcome of an on-line support group for Asian American male college students. *Journal of Counseling Psychology, 48,* 319–329.

Cooper, A. (1998). Sexuality and the Internet: Surfing into the new millennium. *CyberPsychology & Behavior, 1,* 187–193

Cooper, A., Boies, S., Maheu, M., & Greenfield, D. (1999). Sexuality and the Internet: The next sexual revolution. In F. Muscarella & L. Szuchman (Eds.), *The pyschological science of sexuality: A research based approach* (pp. 519–545). New York: Wiley.

Cooper, A., Delmonico, D., & Burg, R. (2000). Cybersex users, abusers, compulsives: New findings and implications. *Sexual Addiction and Compulsivity, 7,* 5–29.

Cooper, A. Griffin-Shelly, E., Delmonico, D., & Mahey, R. (2001). Online sexual problems: Assessment and predictive variables. *Sexual Addiction and Compulsivity, 8,* 265–283.

Cooper, A., Morahan-Martin, J. M., Mathy, R., & Maheu, M. (2002). Toward an increased understanding of user demographics in online sexual activities. *Journal of Sex and Marital Therapy, 28,* 105–129.

Cooper, A., Putnam, D. E., Planchon, L. A., & Boies, S. C. (1999). Online sexual compulsivity: Getting tangled in the net. *Sexual Addiction and Compulsivity, 6,* 79–104.

Cooper, A., & Sportolari, L. (1997). Romance in cyberspace: Understanding online attraction. *Journal of Sex Education and Therapy, 22,* 7–17.

Döring, N. (2000). Feminist views of cybersex: Victimization, liberation, and empowerment. *CyberPsychology & Behavior, 3*(4), 863–885.

Flowers-Coulson, P. A., Mikhel, A. K., & Bankowski, S. (2000). The information is out there, but is anyone getting it? Adolescent misconceptions about sexuality education and reproductive health and the Use of the Internet to get answers. *Journal of Sex Education and Therapy, 25,* 178–188.

Greenfield, D. (1999). *Virtual addiction: Help for netheads, cyberfreaks, and those who love them.* Oakland, CA: New Harbinger Publications.

Huxley, A. (1932). *Brave new world.* New York: Harper & Brothers.

Lemley, B. (2000, February). Future tech: Behold the 3-D tax! *Discover, 21* (2).

Leone, S., & Beilsmith, M. (1999, February). *Monthly report on Internet growth.* Washington, DC: Media Metrix.

McKenna, K. Y. A., & Bargh, J. A. (1998). Coming out in the age of the Internet: Identity "de-marginalization: Through virtual group participation. *Journal of Personality and Social Psychology, 75,* 681–694.

Newman, B. (1997). The use of online services to encourage exploration of ego-dystonic sexual interests. *Journal of Sex Education and Therapy, 22*(1), 45–48.

Ochs, E. P. P., and Binik, Y. M. (2000). A sex-expert system on the Internet: Fact or fantasy. *CyberPsychology & Behavior, 3,* 617–629.

Planadri, M., & Green, L. (2000). Image management in a bondage, discipline, sadomasochist subculture: A cyber-ethnographic study. *CyberPsychology & Behavior, 3,* 631–641.

Putnam, D. E., & Maheu, M. M. (2000). Online sexual addiction and compulsivity: Integrating Web resources and behavioral telehealth in treatment. *Sexual Addiction and Compulsivity, 7,* 91–112.

Roberts, L. D., & Parks, M. R. (1999). The social geography of gender switching in virtual environments on the Internet. *Information, Communication, and Society, 2*(4), p. 28.

Schneider, J. (2000). Effects of cybersex addiction on the family: Results of a survey. *Sexual Addicition and Compulsivity, 7,* 31–58.

Schwartz, M. F., & Southern, S. (2000). Compulsive cybersex: The new tea room. *Sexual Addicition and Compulsivity, 7,* 127–144.

Winzelberg, A. (1997). The analysis of an electronic support group for individuals with eating disorders. *Computers in Human Behavior, 13,* 1–15.

S. Michael Plaut
Karen M. Donahey

Sexuality and the Internet: Ethics and Regulation

☐ Introduction

Computers and the Internet have become a major part of our lives, and it all seems to have happened rather suddenly. Clearly, the Internet has many exciting applications in our professional lives alone. We use it to communicate, both individually and to groups with whom we share professional interests. Through the Web, we can disseminate information about our work and our institutions, and we can easily find resources provided by others. Our teaching and our clinical services can reach people to whom we were once inaccessible.

While some of us have been eager to participate in this innovative technology, others have been dragged into it with considerable reluctance, encouraged and challenged by our children and our students, confused by the jargon, and convinced that this new means of open communication will corrupt us all.

Canadian author Don Tapscott (1998) discussed this new phenomenon in some detail in his recent book, *Growing Up Digital*, and he puts things very nicely into historical perspective: "The first English novels," he says, " were written for the leisure classes, and reading them was considered a sinful waste of time, and it was said that comic books would deaden the ability of youth to think. Newspapers published dire warnings after the arrival of the telephone and telegraph, saying that these devices would make women more susceptible to seduction."

But even if we accept the fact that this is just a new innovation that we have to adjust to, things do seem chaotic at times. Many are concerned about the availability of sex-related material, risks to their safety and privacy, trustworthiness of information provided on the Web, and the often devastating impact of hackers and spammers who can shut down a system thought to be secure or bombard us with useless and undesirable information. Some (e.g., Katsh, 1995; Plaut, 1997) have likened the present state of affairs to the Wild West, where outlaws are everywhere and vigilantes take it upon themselves to enforce self-defined standards of behavior. For example, an organization called peacefire.org "was created in August 1996 to represent the interests of people under 18 in the debate over freedom of speech on the Internet." Among their activities is their claim to create a program "which can execute all popular Windows censorware (Surfwatch, Cyber Patrol, Net Nanny, CYBER sitter, X-Stop, PureSight, and Cyber Snoop) with the click of a button."

Gradually, however, standards of Internet behavior are emerging at different levels. Institutions such as universities and private corporations have developed computer use policies, which are enforced to varying degrees. Internet service providers ask subscribers to agree to what are called terms of service agreements (e.g., America Online, 2001). Our professions are beginning to develop ethical guidelines for computer use in professional work (e.g., www.medem.com), and both local and federal governments have struggled to pass laws that protect vulnerable segments of society, while allowing us the freedom of expression that we value so highly in our culture (e.g., Bray, 2001; Consumers Union, 2001). An excellent example of promising work in this area is a 1999 report from the U. S. Department of Justice (2001) on cyberstalking, which makes a number of recommendations in the areas of law enforcement, the Internet industry, the research community, victim service providers, and consumers.

Of course, even when there are computer use policies and terms of service agreements, how many of us have read them, or did we just click on the little box that says we have, so we can get on with the process of logging in for the first time? We would advocate for mandatory education for anyone using the Internet under the auspices of an institution or through any service provider, however brief it may be, so that we can be better assured that all users have been acquainted with the basic mores, policies and laws regarding Internet use. We are, in effect, buying into a social contract with our fellow users (Rheingold, 1993).

☐ Ethics, Regulation, and Sexuality

Many challenges relate especially to us as sexuality professionals. For purposes of this paper, we have defined four areas of consideration: research and publication, consumer use of the Internet, communication and consultation, and counseling and therapy. We will focus primarily on issues related to clinical practice. In most cases, we will not provide answers as much as we will try to organize the areas of concern and raise questions that need to be addressed. We are still very much in our infancy in the professional use of the Internet.

Sexuality itself may enter into these issues either directly or indirectly. The transmission of or access to sex-related material has been a major public concern, as has the sexual exploitation that can occur as a result of Internet relationships. In addition, almost any ethical issue in clinical practice takes on special significance where sexuality is concerned, because of the sensitivity of the area. Thus, while confidentiality is always of utmost importance when communicating with colleagues about clients (no matter what the mode of communication may be), it may take on an even greater significance when information regarding a patient's sexual functioning is transmitted over the Internet, where more than one person can likely obtain access to this information. The Internet provides a sense of privacy, but that is an illusion, not a reality. Ensuring confidentiality is critical, and therapists need to employ the various methods currently available to mask patients' identities, such as encryption and secure transmission technology (Binik, Mah, & Kiesler, 1999).

☐ Research and Publication

The Internet provides opportunities for relatively low-cost research that minimizes geographic boundaries and provides access to sexual minorities that might not be as readily available in face-to-face settings. However, the same technologies that provide these benefits may also include risks to privacy and security, as well as uncertainties regarding identification of subjects, the validity of informed consent, and the possibility of deception by either researcher or subject. These issues have been discussed more fully by a number of authors (including Ochs, Mah, & Binik in chapter 13).

The idea of publication on the Internet may seem strange to many of us, who grew up with the apparent permanence of the printed word as well as its protection by the copyright process. Anyone can now post anything on the Net, including professional articles, and it is not unusual to see in independent postings frequent inaccuracies, casual language, undocumented references, and an inability to determine when a document was either posted or revised. However, legitimate electronic journals do exist, and the critical characteristic of these journals that provide a bridge to the printed media is the peer review process, which provides both the time and expertise to help ensure that posted articles meet certain professional standards. It is important that our Internet publication standards remain as high as those we have valued in printed journals and books. The American Psychological Association (2001) has provided referencing guidelines for online documents.

☐ Consumer Use of the Internet

The issue of publication on the Internet is relevant also to our patients, who are increasingly using the Internet to seek information about their sexual problems and concerns, to find peer support, to access sexually explicit material, and to pursue sexual needs and desires. In fact, sex has become the number-one searched topic on the Internet (Cooper, 1998; Freeman-Longo & Blanchard, 1998). The easy accessibility and anonymity of the Internet allow clients opportunities they might not otherwise pursue (e.g., to talk to others about their sexual problems, to explore sexual fantasies, to purchase sexually explicit materials, etc.).

There are both positive and potentially negative aspects to these characteristics. On the positive side, clients are better educated because of informational resources and support groups readily available on the Net. Support groups for such problems as vaginismus, herpes sufferers, and rape survivors provide a sense of community and belonging (Cooper, 1998) as well as a level of convenience, and are especially valuable for people with relatively rare conditions who live in rural areas or who have a physical disability or other situation that limits their ability to commute to a face-to-face group (King & Moreggi, 1998). On the negative side, there are those individuals who invest a huge amount of time in Internet interactions to the exclusion of their marital relationship and/or other social activities. It may be a way to avoid the discomfort one might feel in a face-to face interaction or in having a true intimate relationship.

This was true for Mr. J., a 59-year-old married man of 28 years who entered marital therapy with his wife after she discovered he had been corresponding with a girlfriend he had had prior to their marriage. Mrs. J. was shocked to read the very romantic and personal things her husband was writing to this other woman, especially as he had rarely done this with her in the early part of their marriage, and never in the last 20 or so years (much to her consternation). In the marital therapy sessions Mr. J. had considerable difficulty sharing his feelings (other than to complain that Mrs. J. was not very intimate with him) and empathizing with and responding to his wife's feelings or her attempts to have a more emotionally intimate relationship. He often would start the marital session by saying that he was here today to listen to his wife and would stubbornly insist upon not sharing his thoughts in the session. A day or so after the marital therapy session, Mr. J. would sometimes contact the therapist via e-mail to give his side of the story and how this made him feel. In reading these e-mails one would never guess that this was the same man who sat time after time in the therapy sessions offering very little in terms of any emotional expression. The therapist brought these e-mails into the therapy as a way of helping Mr. J. communicate with Mrs. J. Over time the e-mails to the therapist became less frequent. Unfortunately, this is not because Mr. and Mrs. J. had developed a more intimate relationship. Essentially, it appears he is more comfortable keeping a certain amount of distance present in the relationship with Mrs. J.

Another possible negative consequence is that for some people, logging onto sexually oriented sites poses the risk of developing sexually compulsive behavior (Cooper, Scherer, Boies, & Gordon, 1999). In the Cooper, Scherer, et al. (1999) study, men were the largest consumers of sexually explicit material on the Internet. Those who spend 11 hours or more per week on the Internet in sexual pursuits exhibit signs of psychological and interpersonal distress. One couple, in treatment with the second author of this chapter, entered therapy with the presenting problem of low sexual desire on the wife's part. However, it was learned weeks later that the husband was compulsively using the Internet to pursue sexual sites. The husband would actually lock the door to the den so that his wife could not disturb him during this time (3 to 4 hours, several nights a week). The wife attributed her loss of desire to her feelings of rejection and disgust with her husband for engaging in this behavior. She had promised her husband that she would not bring this up in the therapy, but after weeks of nothing changing in their relationship, she decided to tell the therapist. The couple dropped out of treatment 2 weeks later.

Some listservs are designed to serve both consumers and professionals with a common interest in a certain area. For example, confer@advocateweb.org is a closed listserv for people interested in the issue of sexual misconduct by helping professionals. Participants must be nominated by existing members and are accepted if there are no serious objections by current participants.

One of the concerns of both consumers and health professionals about these consumer resources is the credentials of those who sponsor them and the accuracy of information made available. Increasingly, however, rating services are evaluating such sites and reviews are solicited for journals, as with books. In 1996, for example, the *Journal of Sex Education and Therapy* established the position of Computer Resources Editor and has published reviews of sex-related Web sites (e.g., Fagan & Gotlib, 1999). Annotated listings of Web sites in certain areas of interest are also available, for both consumers and professionals (e.g., Gotlib & Fagan, 1997; Semans & Winks, 1999).

Undoubtedly the most controversial and critical aspect of consumer use is the extent to which minor children have access to Internet resources. Few would disagree that children need to be protected from both information for which they may not be ready and exploitation. The most extreme measures toward this end have been legislative efforts that would restrict certain material from being posted on the Internet. However, it is hard to broadly define such material in a way that reliably distinguishes that which may be dangerous to minors from that which serves broader educational purposes, such as information about normal human anatomy (Dyson, 1997; Tapscott, 1998). A number of Internet service provider's (ISPs) have developed blocking software that caregivers can install on their computers, and these have been evaluated by consumer groups such as Consumers Union on a fairly regular basis (Consumers Union, 1997, 2001). As with many similar issues not involving the Internet, many authorities emphasize the critical role of caregivers in educating children and taking responsibility for what they are exposed to and how it is used (Consumer Union, 2001; Dyson, 1997; Tapscott, 1998).

☐ Communication and Consultation

E-mail, whether done one-on-one or through a listserv, has the advantage of being relatively fast, inexpensive, allowing the transmission of entire electronic files, and having virtually no geographic boundaries, thereby enhancing professional relationships at many levels. However, e-mail transmission also raises real and potential problems that the user needs to keep in mind when using this medium. An example follows.

One of us (S.M.P.) received an e-mail some months ago from a young woman in Europe who said that she was romantically involved with her former psychotherapist. She contacted S.M.P. through a publication he had written, which was referenced on a Web site devoted to the area of sexual misconduct by professionals (Fagan & Gotlib, 1999). Although the initial request of the woman was for professional references on the topic, her high level of disclosure in her long, daily postings raised a number of boundary questions for which the recipient sought immediate consultation (from the second author of this paper, as it turned out!). While the importance of setting boundaries is always a factor in therapy relationships, in this case, the individual was not a client and a therapeutic contract had not been established. What, then, are the ethical considerations and constraints for the professional who is consulted by virtually anyone in the world with access to the Internet? What does the sexuality professional do regarding high-risk situations (e.g., if a person e-mails a sexuality professional asking for assistance on his or her attraction to a child, or is having sexually aggressive fantasies about a coworker?). These are issues that require definitive guidelines. Thus far, our stance has been that when a request for information evolves into a request for advice or the therapist's opinion, we inform the individual that we do not engage in personalized e-mail consultation or therapy services. We explain that there are legal and liability issues in providing professional services over the Internet as well as certain limitations in not being able to meet with an individual face-to-face. However, we do want to be helpful, and so will make a referral if we know of a professional who lives in the individual's geographic location, or, if we don't, suggest he or she contact their physician, The American Association of Sex Eduators, Counselors, and Therapists (AASECT), or a university or teaching hospital department of psychiatry or psychology. Certainly, if a person contacts a therapist about potentially harming another person, we would recommend that the therapist notify the appropriate authorities.

☐ Counseling and Therapy

With respect to counseling and therapy, the very nature of the Internet is particularly well suited to dealing with the very sensitive and private nature of sexual concerns (Cooper, Boies, Maheu, & Greenfield, 1999). People who would not be comfortable making an appointment to speak with a professional may instead choose to access a Web site for information and education, enter a chatroom and speak with others who are struggling with similar problems, or participate in an on-line problem-focused treatment with a sex therapy professional. *The Psychotherapy Networker* (Freeny, 2001) reports that to date, 60,000 mental health sessions have been conducted through "telemedicine," the linking of patient and therapist through computers and television. Online therapy sessions consisting of e-mail, private chats, and Web-based teleconferencing range from 5,000 to more than 25,000 per day. Finding a therapist to provide counseling services has become as simple as typing the words "online counseling" into an Internet search engine. Most of the counseling services are text-based. This includes e-mail, online chats, instant messaging, multisubscriber "list serves and bulletin boards" (Freeny, 2001).

Those who have participated in online therapy cite the value of anonymity and the convenience and freedom this type of therapy offers. For online sex therapy services, this may be particularly true. Sexuality is a highly sensitive area of one's life for many people, hence the desire for privacy, and as Ochs and Binik (1998) pointed out, there exist several well-formulated models of treatment for the typical sexual disorders that lend themselves nicely to a computer format. However, there are also a number of factors that limit the use of this medium as well as both ethical and technical challenges yet to be addressed (Rabasca, 2000a).

Perhaps the most obvious of the limitations are those of text-based communication. Most of us depend on nonverbal as well as verbal cues to assess behavior. Facial expressions, eye contact, tears, posture, dress, and grooming are among the many nonverbal cues on which we depend for clinical data. The absence of visual data may also have implications for the ability to positively identify the individual with whom one is interacting and for the ease of doing a fully accurate assessment of mental status, including detection of psychotic behavior. Cooper, Boies, Maheu, & Greenfield (1999) also point to the ease of impersonation (e.g., pretending to be of a different gender or age) and potential liability issues if a therapist is providing sex education or therapy to a teenager posing as an adult. This current deficit in our ability to communicate online will eventually be improved as videoconferencing becomes more accessible (Grohol, 1998).

Other ethical concerns include jurisdictional issues when providers cross state or international lines via computer-mediated communication (CMC) and verification of a therapist's credentials by a client (King & Poulos, 1999). In addition, anyone can set up an e-therapy site at the present time. To address these concerns, therapists can provide the Internet client with information regarding his or her state license or registration, degree and name of school, and/or membership in professional organizations (e.g., AASECT). Some authors have expressed concern that managed care organizations might cover Internet-based therapy more readily than face-to-face therapy simply because of the cost saving, ignoring the cautions expressed above (Grohol, 1998). On the other hand, we need to be mindful of the so-called "digital divide" in helping to ensure that all segments of society have access to the benefits of CMC in their own health care (Grohol, 1998).

These concerns need to be addressed by professional associations and credentialing bodies, so that providers have some guidance in this new and rapidly growing area and so that consumer needs are best served (King & Poulos, 1999; Ochs & Binik, 2000). One effort at meeting these needs has been the formation of the International Society for Mental Health Online (ISMHO) in 1997 "to promote the understanding, use, and development of on-line information and technology for the international mental health community" (King & Moreggi, 1998). Additional information about this group may be found at www.ismho.org. The American Medical Association (AMA) has published extensive guidelines for Internet use in clinical settings (Winker et al., 2000). The Web site www.medem.com is coordinated by a group of health professional societies and liability insurance carriers and has published joint guidelines for physician–patient online communications. The American Psychological Association (2001) has published some guidelines as well, although these are not as extensive as those promulgated by the AMA, and have apparently not been revised since 1997. However, a search of their website (www.apa.org) using the word "Internet" yielded at least 25 documents related to implications of the Internet for various aspects of professional activity such as research, publication, support groups, and clinical services. The National Board for Certified Counselors (2001) has published a set of standards for the ethical practice of Internet counseling. The authors are not aware of any professional society that focuses on sexual issues that has developed guidelines for the ethical practice of sex therapy or counseling on the Internet.

Internet relationships have presented a particular challenge for those providers who specialize in sexual and relationship issues. As with the extent of computer use, Internet relationships cover a wide range of experience. Some people have taken advantage of Web-based dating services and found long-term relationships that have moved successfully into their real world with all of its trappings (Cooper & Sportolari, 1997). Others have gotten into online relationships that have become seriously abusive (Barrett, 1996).

The important issue here is an understanding of what is characteristic of online relationships and why these characteristics are important to a given individual. Perhaps the anonymity and disinhibition (Joinson, 1998) of the Internet allow a person to overcome a shyness they have experienced all their lives in the "real" world. For others, that same anonymity allows them to be dishonest and even abusive. Still others may deceive themselves to the point of believing that a relationship that exists only on the Net can be as fulfilling as a real-world relationship, despite the limitations inherent in online communication. Schnarch (1997), while finding certain value in online communication, sees severe limitations in the extent to which an online relationship can approximate real-life, face-to-face intimate relationships. Even when supporting the use of the Internet to seek potential partners, therapists can educate clients about the potential abuse of such relationships and provide guidelines for reducing risk of abuse (Barrett, 1996; Plaut, 1997).

☐ Guidelines for Health Professionals Working with Sexual Issues

The following guidelines are proposed for health professionals working with sex-related issues in CMC. Some of these guidelines are appropriate for all health professionals, while others may deserve increased attention because of the sensitive nature of sex-related issues.

- Be informed about laws, standards, policies, and guidelines regarding CMC for professional use.
- Be aware of the extent to which your own biases about the values and limitations of CMC may color your assessments of resources available for professional or consumer use.
- In doing research on the Internet, be cognizant of the limitations of such research as well as risks to privacy and confidentiality.
- Be aware of both professional and consumer resources available on the Internet in order to be better informed about these resources and sensitive to consumer activities and expectations.
- Be cautious in responding to requests for online information, counseling, and therapy.
- Be sure that the use of CMC for the transmission and recording of confidential information by you or by staff members includes appropriate precautions for protection of client privacy.
- Include direct questions about sex-related CMC in doing psychosexual evaluations.
- Be aware of characteristics of CMC that may make clients more vulnerable to sexual exploitation and other forms of abuse. These characteristics may include disinhibition, deception, absence of sensory information, or impulsive, poorly considered communication. In addition, a lack of social skills or confidence may lead clients to depend disproportionately on CMC for interpersonal relationships.
- As necessary, counsel clients about professional and consumer resources or behaviors that may put them at risk for exploitation on the Internet.
- Because of the immediacy and accessibility of CMC, remain cognizant of the value of deliberation and peer review in the posting of any communications or documents.
- Ensure that students and supervisees are aware of CMC-related resources, problems, and ethical guidelines.

☐ Future Directions

However one might feel about the impact of CMC on our lives and work, there is no doubt that this major technological innovation is becoming as much a part of our lives as did the telegraph and then the telephone in their own day. For young people today, computers and all the benefits of Internet communication are a natural part of their lives, and they will expect these capabilities to be a part of virtually everything they do (Tapscott, 1998). Whether or not we utilize CMC in our own practices, clients are bringing problems to us that involve Internet use, and we need to be prepared to address these issues.

As with any other technological innovation, our role as health professionals will be to experiment with these new capabilities, to learn how they can be used to advantage and what their limitations are, and to overcome some of the limitations. Counseling and therapy are rapidly reaching beyond the limits of written verbal communication and will increasingly include video and possibly other sensory modalities as well (Grohol, 1998; Rabasca, 2000b). Research efforts to assess the effectiveness of computer-based applications need to be enhanced (Maheu, 1999; Ochs & Binik, 2000). We must continue to develop techniques to ensure the security and confidentiality of our clients' data (Alpert, 1998). We must continue to monitor the appropriate use of these technological innovations to ensure that they are used for the benefit of our clients and not only as cost-saving measures by managed care organizations. We must continue to develop guidelines and professional ethics that govern Internet communication so that access can be as unrestricted as possible, while still protecting clients from abuse (Dyson, 1997; Foxhall, 2000; King & Poulos, 1999; Plaut, 1997). Finally, the technology, methodology, and ethics of CMC need to be a part of the educational process for all health professionals, so that these techniques are systematically taught and can be applied in an appropriate and comfortable manner, no matter what one's background in this area. Ultimately, our goal should be an enhancement of the services we provide, while maintaining the humanness of the provider–client relationship.

☐ References

Alpert, S. A. (1998). Health care information: Access, confidentiality, and good practice. In K. W. Goodman (Ed.), *Ethics, computing, and medicine* (pp. 75–101). New York: Cambridge University Press.

America Online. *Terms of service.* Retrieved March 7, 2001, from http://aolhclp.web.aol.com/ /SS/AT/221001.html

American Psychological Association. (2001). *Services by telephone, teleconferencing, and Internet: A statement by the ethics committee of the American Psychological Association.* Retrieved March 6, 2001, from http://www.apa.org/ethics/stmt01.html

American Psychological Association. (2001). *Publication manual of the American Psychological Association* (5th ed.). Washington, DC: Author.

Barrett, D. J. (1996). *Bandits on the information superhighway.* Sebastopol, CA: O'Reilly and Associates.

Binik, Y. M., Mah, K. M., & Kiesler, S. (1999). Ethical issues in conducting sex research on the Internet. *The Journal of Sex Research, 36,* 82–90.

Bray, H. (2001, January 22). Internet privacy debate brewing. *Baltimore Sun,* pp. C1–C2.

Consumers Union. (1997). Is your kid caught up in the web? How to find the best parts and avoid the others. *Consumer Reports, 27–31.*

Consumers Union. (2001, March). Digital chaperones for kids. *Consumer Reports, 20–23.*

Cooper, A. (1998). Sexuality and the Internet: Surfing into the new millennium. *Cyberpsychology and Behavior, 1*(2), 181–187.

Cooper, A., Boies, S., Maheu, M., & Greenfield, D. (1999). Sexuality and the Internet: The next sexual revolution. In F. Muscarella & L. Szuchman (Eds.) *The psychological science of sexuality: A research-based approach,* (pp. 519–545). New York: Wiley.

Cooper, A., Delmonico, D., & Burg, R. (2000). Cybersex users and abusers: New findings and implications. *Sexual Addiction and Compulsivity: The Journal of Treatment and Prevention, 7,* 5–29.

Cooper, A., Scherer, C., Boies, S., & Gordon, B. (1999). Sexuality on the Internet: From sexual exploration to the pathological expression. *Professional Psychology, 30*(2), 154–164.

Cooper, A., & Sportolari, L. (1997). Romance in cyberspace: Understanding online attraction. *Journal of Sex Education and Therapy, 22*(1), 7–14.

Dyson, E. (1997). *Release 2.0: A design for living in the digital age.* New York: Broadway Books.

Fagan, P., & Gotlib, D. (1999). Website review: Advocateweb HOPE (Help Overcome Professional Exploitation) Website Address: www.advocateweb.org/hope. *Journal of Sex Education and Therapy, 24,* 294–295.

Fink, J. (Ed.). (1999). *How to use computers and cyberspace in the clinical practice of psychotherapy.* Northvale, NJ: Jason Aronson, Inc.

Fink, J., & Allman, D. (1999). In J. Fink (Ed.), *How to use computers and cyberspace in the clinical practice of psychotherapy* (pp. 107–119). Northvale, NJ: Jason Aronson.

Foxhall, K. (2000). How will the rules on telehealth be written? *Monitor on Psychology, 31*(4), 38.

Freeman-Longo, R. E., & Blanchard, G. T. (1998). *Sexual abuse in America: Epidemic of the 21st century.* Brandon, VT: Safer Society Press.

Freeny, M. (2001, March/April). Better than being there. *Psychotherapy Networker, 70,* 31–39.

Goodman, K. W. (1998). Bioethics and health informatics: An introduction. In K. W. Goodman (Ed.), *Ethics, computing, and medicine* (pp. 1–31). New York: Cambridge University Press.

Gotlib, D. A., & Fagan, P. (1997). Mean streets of cyberspace: Sex education resources on the Internet's World Wide Web. *Journal of Sex Education and Therapy, 22*(1), 79–83.

Grohol, J. M. (1998). Future clinical directions: Professional development, pathology, and psychotherapy on-line. In J. Gackenbach (Ed.), *Psychology and the Internet: Intrapersonal, interpersonal, and transpersonal implications* (pp. 111–140). San Diego: Academic Press.

Joinson, A. (1998). Causes and implications of disinhibited behavior on the Internet. In J. Gackenbach (Ed.), *Psychology and the Internet: Intrapersonal, interpersonal, and transpersonal implications* (pp. 43–60). San Diego: Academic Press.

Katsh, M. E. (1995). *Law in a digital world.* New York: Oxford University Press.

King, S. A., & Moreggi, D. (1998). Internet therapy and self-help groups: The pros and cons. In J. Gackenbach (Ed.), *Psychology and the Internet: Intrapersonal, interpersonal, and transpersonal implications* (pp. 77–109). San Diego: Academic Press.

King, S. A., & Poulos, S. T. (1999). Propriety on the online couch: A discussion of guidelines for virtual therapy. In J. Fink (Ed.), *How to use computers and cyberspace in the clinical practice of psychotherapy* (pp. 121–132). Northvale, NJ: Jason Aronson.

Maheu, M. (1999). What can we do? A call to action. In J. Fink (Ed.), *How to use computers and cyberspace in the clinical practice of psychotherapy* (pp. 261–268). Northvale, NJ: Jason Aronson.

National Board for Certified Counselors. (2001). *The practice of Internet counseling.* Updated November 3, 2001. www.nbcc.org/ethics/wcstandards.htm

Ochs, E. P. P., & Binik, Y. M. (1998). A sex-expert computer system helps couples learn more about their sexual relationship. *Journal of Sex Education and Therapy, 23*(2), 145–155.

Ochs, E. P. P., & Binik, Y. M. (2000). A sex-expert system on the Internet: Fact or fantasy. *Cyber-Psychology and Behavior, 3,* 617–629.

Ochs, E. P. P., Mah, K. M., & Binik, Y. M. (2002). Obtaining data about human sexual functioning from the Internet. In A Cooper (Ed.), *Sex and the Internet*. New York: Taylor and Francis.

Plaut, S. M. (1997). Online ethics: Social contracts in the virtual community. *Journal of Sex Education and Therapy, 22*(1), 84–91.

Rabasca, L. (2000a). Self-help sites: A blessing or a bane? *Monitor on Psychology, 31*(4), 28–30.

Rabasca, L. (2000b). Taking telehealth to the next step. *Monitor on Psychology, 31*(4), 36–37.

Rheingold, H. (1993). *The virtual community*. Reading, MA: Addison-Wesley.

Schnarch, D. (1997). Sex, intimacy, and the Internet. *Journal of Sex Education and Therapy, 22*(1), 15–20.

Semans, A., & Winks, C. (1999). *A woman's guide to sex on the web*. San Francisco: HarperCollins.

Tapscott, D. (1998). *Growing up digital*. New York: McGraw-Hill.

U. S. Department of Justice. (2001). *1999 Report on cyberstalking: A new challenge for law enforcement and industry*. Retrieved March 7, 2001, from http://usdoj.gov/criminal/cybercrime/cyberstalking.html

Wallace, P. (1999). *The psychology of the Internet*. New York: Cambridge University Press.

Winker, M. A., Flanagin, A., Chi-Lum, B., White, J., Andrews, K., Kennett, R. L., DeAngelis, C. D., & Musacchio, R. A. (2000). Guidelines for medical and health information sites on the Internet: Principles governing AMA web sites. *Journal of the American Medical Association, 283,* 1600–1606. Retrieved from http://jama.ama-assn.org/issues/v283n12/full/#aainfo

13

CHAPTER

Eric P. Ochs
Kenneth Mah
Yitzchak M. Binik

Obtaining Data About Human Sexual Functioning From the Internet

The growing proportion of the population using the Internet presents a unique research opportunity for the scientific study of human sexuality. Whereas most of the other chapters in this book focus on the influence of the Internet on human sexuality and sexual practices, we will present the relatively less explored domain of the Internet as a tool to obtain data about human sexuality and sexual functioning in general. There are two key issues that sex researchers need to address: (a) methodological considerations that will insure the integrity and credibility of the data obtained, and (b) the adherence to appropriate ethical guidelines that will protect study participants and researchers. Thus, the chapter includes a review of relevant findings along with a brief description of a computerized sex therapy program, Sexpert, as a potential model for guiding the development of online therapy programs. Discussions of the methodological advantages of the Internet for research on human sexuality and ethical considerations of Internet-based research are then provided.

☐ Literature Review

Because the field of online research necessarily draws on diverse and complex areas of study, such as computer science, clinical intervention research, and studies of human–computer interactions, an integrated body of scientific literature is only gradually taking shape. A number of journals are now devoted solely or partly to human–computer interactions, for example, *Behavior Research Methods Instrumentation and Computers, Computers in Human Behavior, Computers in Human Services, CyberPsychology & Behavior, Human-computer Studies, Interacting With Computers,* and *International Journal of Human-Computer Interactions.* There are also recently established online journals (e.g., *Journal of Online Behavior, Journal of Computer Mediated Communication, Internet and Society*). In addition, special issues of mainstream journals have dealt with the topic (Carnes, 2000; Whiteley, 1983), as have a number of specialty books (e.g., Birnbaum, 2000; Lieff, 1987; Miller, Hammond, & Hile, 1996; Riva, 1997; Schwartz, 1984; Sidowski, Johnson, & Williams, 1980; Wagman, 1988) and symposia (e.g., Annual Symposium on Computer Applications in Medical Care; Annual Meeting of the Society for Computers in Psychology; International Conference on Computational Medicine, Computers and the Delivery of Services in Health Psychology: Symposium of the American Psychological Association, 1994). There are as yet no journals devoted solely to online sexual behavior research (cf. Carnes, 2000). Nevertheless, there is a growing body of research relating to dysfunctional sexuality on the Internet (e.g., Cooper, Boies, Maheu, & Greenfield, 2000; Cooper, Griffin-Shelley, Delmonico & Mathy, 2001 (see chapter 1); Goodson, McCormick, Evans, 2000; Szuchman & Muscarella, 2000), but little else has addressed the uses of the Internet for conducting basic and clinical research on human sexuality.

☐ Behavioral Psychotherapies Online

Much of the available Internet-based research has focused on examining the efficacy of online behavioral psychotherapies. Therapeutic interventions involving e-mail interactions have shown some promise. White and her colleagues (White, McConnell, Clipp, Bynum, Teague, Navas, Craven, Halbrecht, 1999) reported an intervention that utilized Internet access and e-mail to improve the psychosocial well-being of older adults. Although not, strictly speaking, about therapy, a study by McKenna and Bargh (1998) of newsgroups' social processes described how group membership helped persons with marginalized sexual identities develop greater self-acceptance. Thus, there appears to be a potential to use purely text-based communications online for therapeutic purposes.

More sophisticated programs have also been evaluated. In an early example of online research, Schneider and his colleagues (Schneider, 1986; Schneider, Walter, & O'Donnell, 1990) investigated a computerized smoking cessation program that was made available on the Internet. They compared two versions of the computer program: one version with and the other without an online talk forum. To compare the effects of a pure computer program with one utilizing human-to-human communications, one version of the computer program was interactive and tailored the therapy to the individual, whereas the other version was more rudimentary. The abstinence rates obtained by participants in the experimental conditions were comparable to face-to-face treatment programs (Curry, McBride, Grothaus, Louie, & Wagner, 1995). The more interactive version of the computer program was more effective, and the groups that had access to the talk forum also did better than those without. By demonstrating the feasibility of conducting research on the treatment of addictive behavior online, this study serves as a possible model for similar treatment approaches in sexual addictions.

More recently, computer programs that treat anxiety spectrum disorders (agoraphobia, anxiety, simple phobias, obsessive-compulsive disorder [OCD], and panic) appear to be an active sector of research (M. G. Newman, Consoli, & Taylor, 1997). These automated treatment programs employ techniques such as relaxation exercises, cognitive modeling, in-vivo exposure, and systematic desensitization. A number of recent studies have demonstrated the efficacy of automated psychotherapy for phobias (Coldwell et al., 1998) and virtual-reality-based graded exposure in the treatment of acrophobia (North, North, & Coble, 1997; Rothbaum et al., 1995) and agoraphobia (Harcourt, Kirkby, Daniels, & Montgomery, 1998). Treatments for sexual dysfunctions involving phobic elements (e.g. sexual aversions, inhibited desire, sexual traumas) could be modeled after these paradigms.

Of particular interest is the ongoing effort to demonstrate the efficacy of automated psychotherapy for OCD (e.g., Clark, Kirkby, Daniels, & Marks, 1998; Marks et al., 1998). One computer program, BT Steps, provided exposure and response-prevention via a telephone-based audio interface (Baer & Greist, 1997; Baer, Minicheillo, Jenike, & Holland, 1988). Participants in the program reported improvements and also found the program easy to use. The study, however, did not include a control group, and so the program requires further controlled validation. In any case, although not Internet administered, it would be straightforward to adapt this program to online use as a practical and effective means of providing cost-effective therapy to large numbers of patients.

To the extent that the techniques used in this study (exposure and response prevention) could be applied towards the treatment of sexual dysfunctions (e.g., compulsive use of the Internet for sexual pursuits; see Cooper, Scherer, Gordon, & Boies, 1999), they may encourage sex therapists and researchers to develop their own programs for online use. Another computerized OCD program developed by Clark et al. (Clark et al., 1998) incorporated an interactive graphical element within a vicarious exposure and ritual prevention approach. Results showed post-treatment declines in Beck Depression Inventory scores and in one of two measures of OCD symptomatology. The use of graphics could also be adapted to the treatment of psychosexual issues.

☐ Methodological Shortcomings

Overall, these studies suggest that automated behavioral psychotherapies on the Internet may be an effective means of targeting individuals with various sexual dysfunctions. However, few outcome studies are well controlled (cf. Ghosh, Marks, & Carr, 1984). A serious deficiency in this literature has been the frequent use of inappropriate control groups (e.g., Baer & Greist, 1997; Marks et al., 1998; Newman et al., 1997), insufficiently large control groups (e.g. Noell, Biglan, Hood, & Britz, 1994), or a total lack of control groups (e.g., Marks et al., 1998). The reliance on a limited number of case studies (e.g., Wilson, Omeltschenko, & Yager, 1991) and the lack of sufficiently long-term follow-up assessment (e.g., Selmi, Klein, Greist, Sorrell, & Erdman, 1990; Smith, 1987) also raise serious questions about the validity of these studies. Overall, the field is still dominated by discussions of potential rather than empirical demonstrations of the efficacy of computer- and Internet-based psychotherapies.

Furthermore, there are almost no studies directly examining the efficacy of online therapies for sexual difficulties. B. Newman (1997) presented a case study of the use of the Internet to assist in sex therapy for a couple with divergent sexual preferences. The couple was referred to newsgroups that dealt with the sexual practices in question. This strategy allowed each member of the couple to become more educated concerning issues of what constitutes "normal" sexuality. Unfortunately, unsystematic case studies do not provide sufficient evidence for the efficacy of interventions.

☐ Automated Online Interventions

The treatment of sexual dysfunction online would be ideal for an automated computer program that could assess problems and provide information and cognitive therapy in a private manner to those who would otherwise not seek treatment (Aradi, 1985; Reitman, 1984). For example, Kann (1987) found that a computer-assisted instruction (CAI) program was able to influence adolescent attitudes and behaviors concerning sexuality. Sex therapy lends itself to a learning-based approach to deal with the well-specified cognitive distortions underlying many sexual dysfunctions, such as spectatoring, performance anxiety, fear of failure and rejection, and the mislabeling of arousal. The relative anonymity of the computer program also has the potential to facilitate disclosure of sensitive information relating to sexual problems (Erdman, Klein, & Greist, 1985).

Cognitive psychologists have applied rule-based techniques to the design of CAI programs that can "diagnose" the difficulties experienced by users and then customize an intervention to facilitate learning (Binik, Servan-Schreiber, Freiwald, & Hall, 1988). This approach is generally congruent and compatible with the techniques of cognitive–behavior therapy and can be applied to the specific domain of sexual dysfunction (Neigigh & Kinder, 1987). These computerized instruction programs that simulate real-life experts' knowledge and behaviors (i.e., expert systems) include a reasoning component and a separate dialogue-control structure. These two elements make it possible for the program to carefully tailor its delivery of domain information and the conclusions it draws from client data (Binik, Ochs, & Meana, 1996). The hierarchical design of the dialogue control structure insures that all topics are dealt with logically and in keeping with the overall plan of an assessment and therapeutic interview.

☐ Sexpert

In this regard, the development and evaluation of Sexpert to treat sexual dysfunctions can provide an instructive model. Sexpert is a computer program that combines the characteristics of a rule-based expert system with a sophisticated model of therapeutic interactions. As a stand-alone program, Sexpert may be an ideal candidate for exploring the efficacy of online sex therapy interventions.

The early-published Sexpert studies showed that Sexpert could positively influence the attitudes of naive users towards computerized psychotherapy and also provided preliminary retrospective self-report evidence of sexual behavior changes (Binik, Meana, & Sand, 1994; Binik, Westbury, & Servan-Schreiber, 1989). In subsequently published papers comparing the use of a self-help video and self-help book with the Sexpert program, all were shown to have positive effects on couples' sexual behavior and communication. Sexpert was shown to be the most engaging of all the experimental manipulations. While initial attitudes towards computerized psychotherapy were quite negative, participants exposed to Sexpert dramatically improved their attitudes towards computerized psychotherapy, replicating earlier findings. A subsequent study used a therapist as a control condition. Participants who interacted with the therapist, video, and Sexpert retrospectively reported significant changes in the areas of communication, sexuality, feelings, and attitudes and also indicated significant learning about their relationships and the couples' sexuality compared with a control group. The highest ratings of reported change occurred in a therapist group, followed by the Sexpert and video groups (Ochs & Binik, 1998).

In all, these studies provided sufficient evidence of Sexpert's capabilities to justify a controlled clinical trial of Sexpert's efficacy as a network-based therapy. To date, a pilot study was conducted on a pre-Internet regional network called ALEX. In this pilot study, we installed Sexpert on ALEX in 1991. Sexpert was made available to members of the general public who had access to Bell Canada's ALEX terminal services. Potential Sexpert users were provided with basic information concerning the service and its experimental nature. If they wished to continue with a Sexpert consultation, they were required to indicate their consent by making a keystroke. We were interested in determining if Sexpert would be engaging enough to maintain user interest in the face of a 10 cents per minute charge. Engagement with Sexpert was thus assessed in strictly behavioral terms as duration of the log-on to Sexpert. Findings suggested that Sexpert was able to maintain the interest of almost one-third of an unsolicited sample of paying ALEX subscribers who had made an initial connection to find out what Sexpert was (Ochs & Binik, 2000).

An equivalent trial of Sexpert on the current Internet could be expected to attract large numbers of users, especially since the existence of search engines makes it possible to bring Sexpert to the attention of a large number of potential clients. A limited-term pilot study of Sexpert online to establish its therapeutic efficacy is recommended prior to running the program on the Internet. This trial would also allow a number of other issues to be addressed, such as the design of the interface and informed consent. An augmented version of Sexpert could benefit from the incorporation of recent advances in voice recognition technology to reduce its reliance on text-driven information exchanges, as well as the inclusion of graphical and video displays to enhance communication.

☐ Methodological Issues in Online Research

The Internet is a venue for conducting research on human sexuality that allows for a number of interesting issues to be considered. These include (a) efficiency gains in online research, (b) experimental control online, and (b) the participant's online experience. We will discuss how these factors are relevant to carrying out sexual behavior studies online.

Efficiency Gains

When properly conducted, online research can lower costs and increase the speed with which information may be obtained (Schmidt, 1997). Study designs that are suitable for Internet application include those with large-scale samples (i.e., high-power designs), that involve large data sets or complex polling strategies to insure valid data inputs, and that lend themselves to automation in service delivery (e.g., most educational approaches). For example, many of the surveys, questionnaires, and experiments previously developed for traditional studies are easily adapted to Internet use (Birnbaum, 2000; Buchanan & Smith, 1999; Stern & Faber, 1997; R. J. White & Hammer, 2000). Automated data entry, data checking, and feedback generation make Internet-based surveying much less expensive than traditional means (Cooper et. al., 2001; Pettit, 1999). In addition, the ability to avoid mailing questionnaires or other printed materials brings huge cost savings (Pettit, 1999; Schmidt, 1997). The software tools already available make it possible to obtain larger samples at far less cost (Birnbaum, 2000; Buchanan & Smith, 1999). A recent survey conducted in the United States sampled 3,432 cases at a cost of 1.6 million dollars (Lauman, Gagnon, Michael, & Michaels, 1994).

Internet-based surveys are also well suited to both broad and targeted topic domains (Schmidt, 1997). As Internet use evolves into a basic communications tool in society, it will become easier to obtain more representative samples. On the other hand, by targeting specific populations through newsgroups concerned with specific sexual interests, valid research data may be collected on specific subgroups such as men with low-frequency sexual dysfunctions (e.g., retarded ejaculation) or transsexuals. These participants will become more accessible through their use of online support and chat groups; in fact, the triple-A conceptualization of the internet (affordability, access, and anonymity) will eventually make many groups accessible to researchers (Cooper et al., 2000). An efficient way to recruit these participants is to publicize the researcher's survey site information to various Internet search engines. Internet search engines then direct potential respondents to the information about the surveys as well as the surveys themselves.

Cross-cultural research could also be conducted on an unprecedented scale. Researchers may use an online protocol to gather information about behavior from geographically distant locales in a way that would be logistically or economically impractical using any other modality. The use of the Internet makes it feasible to obtain large-scale surveys of sexual behaviors and attitudes from diverse cultures using a consistent methodology. A recent study (Krantz, Ballard, & Scher, 1997) demonstrated that the determinants of female attractiveness were driven by the same psychological variables as determined in both an online and a laboratory-based study. This study could, in principle, be extended to sample diverse cultural or subcultural groups to determine if these psychological processes are universal.

Experimental Control

While the population using the Internet is gradually beginning to approximate the general population (Schmidt, 1997), the current demographics of the Web may still result in biased samples if appropriate measures are not taken. For example, there is still a demographic bias in favor of young males of above-average socioeconomic status. This demographic sample is likely to exhibit biases in sexual interests and beliefs when compared to other samples. Thus, survey administrators may choose to screen respondents via the use of questionnaires (to determine age and gender) or by insuring that their access to the Internet is from a specific geographic locale (e.g., for cross-cultural comparisons).

One of the most common methods of obtaining data about sexual behavior is and will likely remain the survey. Traditional means of conducting surveys in this area include interviewer-administered and self-administered questionnaires. The limitations of these modalities include overreporting of normative behaviors, underreporting of sensitive behaviors, the assumption of high levels of respondent literacy, and the ability of respondents to follow sometimes complicated skip patterns in the case of self-administered questionnaires (Gribble, Miller, Rogers, & Turner, 1999). However, employing the Internet to deliver surveys has the potential to circumvent many of these limitations (Hewson, Laurent, & Vogel, 1996). For example, demand characteristics and response biases should be attenuated in Internet studies compared with face-to-face and telephone interviews (see Joinson, 1999, for a demonstration of how anonymity reduced social desirability factors online). To protect the research program against unwanted multiple responses, the program could be made to detect identical responses or multiple responses from the same location and time period (Cooper et al., 1997). Potential checks on honesty of responses include the use of repeated questions, internal consistency checks of the data, and comparison of client responses to normative data sets. The respondent can also be given individualized feedback that is personally relevant in exchange for participating in the study. This factor has the potential to increase honesty and thoughtfulness of responses since the feedback will be seen as directly dependent on the participant's own responses (Schmidt, 1997).

Validity of data collected is also an important issue. If subjects are required to e-mail materials back to the researcher, there is a risk of errors as well as the need to integrate the returned data into the relevant database (Hewson et al., 1996). Depending on the sophistication of the software program controlling data collection, interactive surveying may provide a good solution to both problems. Automated survey programs can manage the complexities of contingent data collection. For example, automated range checking of respondent inputs can ensure collection of valid data from a Web page-based survey. A well-planned Web page can also minimize the requirement of high literacy through the use of help buttons and graphics that provide clarifications when needed. Gribble and colleagues (1999) described computerized auditory solutions to the literacy issue that can be applied to Web pages, as the Internet can support audio and video transmissions as well as text. However, if visually oriented materials are included (e.g., to poll subjects' responses to erotic visual stimuli), it could be difficult to control the exact presentation of the stimulus materials on the subjects' computer monitor (cf. McGraw, Tew, & Williams, 2000).

Participant's Online Experience

Many of the features discussed above will also impact on participants' experiences of study involvement in a positive way. For example, the interactive nature of the Internet can provide study participants with individualized feedback, and it makes participation convenient and private. Mutually anonymous follow-up and longer term interactions can also be conducted online through the use of technical methods such as data encryption and anonymous remailers (e.g., Binik, Mah, & Kiesler, 1999). The perceived privacy of even unsecured Internet-based communications has obvious benefits when trying to obtain data concerning highly personal issues such as sexual preferences or responding. To the extent that this increases subject comfort, it should also improve data validity. Studies that manipulate the variables of anonymity and privacy (to the extent allowed by ethical considerations) could test this hypothesis. Anonymity of responding should also ameliorate experimenter or subject response biases that are based on interpersonal-visual cues such as sex, age, and race (Hewson et al., 1996). For a useful theoretical discussion concerning reporting-bias factors in assessing human sexuality, see Catania (1999).

☐ Ethical Issues in Online Research

From the previous sections, it is obvious that the potential for the Internet as a venue for sex research is enormous. However, ethical issues have arisen that must be addressed to maintain research integrity within this venue. Research and governmental institutions are responding to the growing recognition of the ethical threats that the Internet holds. Discussions of online research ethics are available (e.g., Bier, Sherblom, & Gallo, 1996; Binik et al., 1999; Childress & Asamen, 1998; Jones, 1999; King, 1996; Libutti, 1999; Michalak & Szabo, 1998; Plaut & Donahey, 2002). In June of 1999, the Office for Protection of Research Risks and the American Association for the Advancement of Science convened a workshop to explore the ethical, legal, and technical concerns in Internet-based research and to stimulate further collaborative dialogue by professional, research, government, and online communities (Frankel & Siang, 1999). An initial report (Frankel & Siang, 1999) is available. While a detailed discussion is beyond the scope of this chapter, we will highlight some core issues. The issues are discussed under the relevant stages of the research process: recruitment, informed consent, and data collection and storage.

Recruitment

Advertisements are an essential tool in subject recruitment, and the Internet can deliver an electronic ad almost instantly to a huge number of individuals. Recruitment ads, though, should include enough detail to enable individuals to make an informed decision about further participation. Such information would include the investigator(s) and their affiliation, an overview of the study, inclusion criteria, duration, and compensation. Many institutional review boards (IRBs) require recruitment ads to be included in research proposals submitted for review.

Unsolicited advertisements are a fact of life in cyberspace. In general, though, the practice of e-mailing unsolicited material to a large number of e-mail addresses, or "spamming," is objectionable by "Netiquette" standards. Researchers should understand the potential and often embarrassing consequences that this practice can incur (e.g., Frankel & Siang, 1999; Mehta & Sivadas, 1995). For example, many read their e-mail at work, the contents of which may be legally monitored by employers. E-mail read at public terminals, or through shared home e-mail accounts, may also be viewed by those other than the targeted individual. Recruiting through listservs is also popular, because they are viewed as large, readily available sources of potential subjects. However, as members typically view the listserv as private, posting a recruitment ad without prior consultation with and approval from the listserv owner would be akin to spamming.

Informed Consent

Upholding people's rights and well-being is integral to professional ethics codes like the APA's (1992). This means providing detailed information for individuals to make an informed decision about participating in a study. Ads should not include deceptive statements or inappropriate or excessive inducements that may coerce participation (APA, 1992). Local IRBs and professional ethical codes thoroughly outline the kinds of information to be given to potential subjects, and they should be consulted.

However, the lack of face-to-face dialogue between researcher and subjects makes obtaining valid informed consent for Internet studies difficult. Researchers cannot directly assess either individuals' comprehension of study demands and risks or the impact of participation (Binik et al., 1999; Frankel & Siang, 1999).

The adoption of pseudonyms and pseudoidentities is also a salient part of many Internet services that makes authentication of personal information difficult. The issue becomes even more complicated when considering that children routinely access the Internet without supervision. The issue of the open availability of pornographic materials on the Internet has led to discussions of censorship and attempts to block children's access through warnings, online age-verification services, and policing software. These have met with little success. Minors may try, probably successfully at times, to enroll in studies inappropriate for their age. Binik and colleagues (1999) have suggested verifying personal data with follow-up phone calls and cross-validating with information from other sources.

Informed consent is also complicated by the widely held misperception that Internet communications are completely private. In fact, the sense of privacy is often more a perception than reality. For example, e-mail is transmitted within an open network, within which unauthorized individuals can access copies of the e-mail or at least parts of it. A copy of the e-mail may also be stored in and thereby accessed from computer caches or server logs. Private logs and e-mails can be traced to the IP address of the computer of origin. Furthermore, whether the Internet is a uniformly public forum or whether private domains exist where informed consent would be required is controversial (Frankel & Siang, 1999; King, 1996). Many online groups are public to attract membership, but within the groups themselves, communications may be regarded to be as private as those within real-world support groups. Monitoring group exchanges without informed consent may thus violate expectations of privacy in particular groups and would be prohibited by the APA (1992) ethics codes. A conservative strategy may be adopted where targeted individuals or groups are always made aware of threats to privacy and the steps taken to minimize them.

Data Collection and Storage

The perceived anonymity and confidentiality of Internet communications may facilitate more honest disclosure of highly personal behaviors, as well as socially undesirable or illegal behaviors (Richman, Kiesler, Weisband, & Drasgow, 1999). Ensuring objective anonymity and confidentiality during data collection, though, is another issue. The Electronic Communications Privacy Act, an American federal law enacted in 1986, prohibits unauthorized access to private electronic exchanges, including e-mail interception and hacking. However, these illegal acts still occur, and so steps should always be implemented to minimize such intrusions. Several approaches are available for this purpose. First, anonymous remailers employ different methods to maintain anonymity, such as removing e-mail headers to prevent the origin of a message from being traced. "Anonymity on the Internet," a Web site located at http://www.sendfakemail.com/~raph/remailer-list.html, provides an extensive list of remailers as well as some discussion of their legal and ethical use. Second, encryption prevents feasible retrieval of subjects' identities by converting personal information into a cryptographic representation (see Binik et al., 1999). Finally, interactive forms enhanced through secure-transmission technology are now routinely employed by online businesses to transmit sensitive data to secure servers. Such forms can be easily generalized to Internet data collection.

Because the Internet is an open-network system, data stored on network servers or in e-mail files are vulnerable to unauthorized access. Even when e-mail files are deleted, backup copies of e-mail files are routinely stored within the server; erased files can also be restored. Data files should be transferred to secure databases and then deleted. Researchers should also consult with system operators to find out about file backups and how to maintain their confidentiality.

☐ Further Recommendations

One of the best strategies for developing a viable Internet-based project and minimizing harm is to thoroughly inform oneself of the technology and limitations of the Internet. In fact, we see this as a prime responsibility for prospective online researchers, just as researchers must ensure that real-world studies will not harm subjects' well-being. The references cited throughout this section offer other recommendations on conducting sex-related and other research online as well as more extensive discussion of issues presented. Finally, some other basic recommendations are offered:

1. Develop the project in extensive collaboration with an Internet system operator. Most institutional networks or Web site development and security services are managed by system operators knowledgeable in the procedures for secure data transmission.
2. If there are limitations to confidentiality even with safeguard measures installed, individuals should be notified of these risks. Provide more rather than less information in all phases of the research process.
3. Test and refine all Internet data collection and security tools before starting the study. Researchers should complete and submit interactive forms themselves to ensure that routed form information is intact and sent only to them. Safeguard measures and data integrity should be evaluated, for example, by asking a knowledgeable person to hack into the research server.

☐ Discussion of Future Online Research Possibilities

Access to Research Participants

The potential for access to extremely large populations is of particular benefit. The rapid growth of the Internet-connected population makes truly large-scale surveys of sexual behavior possible with different societal hierarchies. These can range from focusing on a single country's population (e.g., North American) to accessing a worldwide population. Furthermore, geographically and culturally delineated subgroups (e.g., residents of small towns, recent immigrants) and subcultures (e.g., homosexuals) could also be identified and targeted. Currently invisible and dispersed populations could be identified via their participation in online groups that researchers could contact for research purposes (Cooper et al., 2000).

The development of more sophisticated automated data validation strategies will dramatically expand both the quantity and quality of information for research purposes. As the Internet becomes the social venue for more sexual expression, basic data about this variation of sexual expression could be investigated and used to contrast with data obtained from traditional sources of sexual behavior data (e.g., laboratory-based questionnaires and interviews). The use of visual images (including video) will allow investigators to conduct sex research that relies less on textual presentations of information. This opens up the possibility of comparing textual and visual modalities in basic research, as well as allowing for a reduction in user literacy requirements for obtaining information or treatments online.

Development of Innovative Techniques

In the domain of applied psychology, online intervention studies suggest the possibility of a vastly expanded range of clinical tools in treating far greater numbers of patients than ever before. Special attention should be given to the expanded use of automated health promotion systems online (Hawkins, Gustafson, Chewning, Bosworth, & Day, 1987; Ochs & Binik, 2000). The use of virtual reality techniques (Biocca, 1992; Jerome et al., 2000) and an expanded capacity for the exchange of information online could also be incorporated into unique therapeutic approaches. The evolution and development of e-mail-based therapeutic approaches has already shown promise. In conjunction with the new generation of handheld Internet access devices, the potential for increased ease of data gathering and for the provision of more flexible interventions is enormous. For example, a patient struggling to overcome a pornography addiction could have instant access, via a handheld Internet-enabled device, to an automated cognitive–behavioral intervention program.

Treatments for sexual dysfunctions involving phobic responses to sexual behaviors could employ systematic desensitization remotely supervised by a qualified sex therapist (or an automated expert system) via e-mail. Internet information resources can also be incorporated into ongoing sex therapy. Discussion groups on specific topics could be encouraged and then used as adjuncts for sex therapy patients.

☐ Concluding Remarks

Our review of the online study literature reveals that much promising research has already been published, but as yet, very little research has been directed to the uses of the Internet to collect data concerning normative sexual behavior or to test treatments for sexual dysfunctions. Methodological and ethical issues specific to the Internet as a research venue also exist that require attention. Given the tremendous potential that the Internet represents for both basic and applied research, we hope that this chapter will stimulate further online research activity in the area of human sexuality. Careful attention to the methodological advantages and limitations of online research and clinical intervention, in conjunction with a well-informed respect for the ethical issues such activities engender, has the potential to advance the scientific study of sexuality and bring relief to those suffering from sexual dysfunction.

☐ References

American Psychological Association. (1992). *Ethical principles of psychologists and code of conduct.* Retrieved from http://www.apa.org/ethics/code.html

Aradi, N. S. (1985). The application of computer technology to behavioral marital therapy. *Journal of Psychotherapy and the Family, 1,* 167–177.

Baer, L., & Greist, J. H. (1997). An interactive computer-administered self-assessment and self-help program for behavior therapy. *Journal of Clinical Psychiatry, 58,* 23–28.

Baer, L., Minicheillo, W. E., Jenike, M. A., & Holland, A. (1988). Use of a portable computer program to assist behavioral treatment in a case of obsessive compulsive disorder. *Journal of Behavior Therapy and Psychiatry, 19,* 237–240.

Bier, M. C., Sherblom, S. A., & Gallo, M. A. (1996). Ethical issues in a study of internet use: Uncertainty, responsibility, and the spirit of research relationships. *Ethics & Behavior, 6*(2), 141–151.

Binik Y. M., Mah, K. M., & Kiesler, S. (1999). Ethical issues in conducting sex research on the Internet. *The Journal of Sex Research, 36,* 82–90.

Binik, Y. M., Meana, M., & Sand, N. (1994). Interaction with a sex-expert system changes attitudes and may modify sexual behavior. *Computers in Human Behavior, 10,* 395–410.

Binik, Y. M., Servan-Schreiber, D., Freiwald, S., & Hall, K. S. (1988). Intelligent computer-based assessment and psychotherapy: An expert system for sexual dysfunction. *Journal of Nervous and Mental Disease, 178,* 387–400.

Binik, Y. M., Ochs, E. P., & Meana, M. (1996). Sexpert: An expert system for sexual assessment, counseling, and treatment. In M. J. Miller, K. W. Hammond, & M. G. Hile, (Eds.), *Computers and medicine: Mental health computing* (pp. 17–33). New York: Springer-Verlag.

Binik, Y. M., Servan-Schreiber, D., Freiwald, S., & Hall, K. S. (1988). Intelligent computer-based assessment and psycho-therapy: An expert system for sexual dysfunction. *Journal of Nervous and Mental Disease, 178,* 387–400.

Binik, Y. M., Westbury, C. F., & Servan-Schreiber, D. (1989). Interaction with a "sex-expert" system enhances attitudes towards computerized sex therapy. *Behavior Research and Therapy, 27,* 303–306.

Biocca, F. (1992). Communication within virtual reality: Creating a space for research. *Journal of Communication, 42*(4), 5–22.

Birnbaum, M. H. (2000). SurveyWiz and FactorWiz: JavaScript Web pages that make HTML forms for research on the Internet. *Behavior Research Methods, Instruments, & Computers, 32*(2), 339–346.

Buchanan, T., & Smith, J. L. (1999). Research on the Internet: Validation of a World-Wide Web mediated personality scale. *Behavior Research Methods, Instruments, & Computers, 31* (4), 565–571.

Carnes, P. J. (Ed). (2000). Cybersex: The dark side of the force. *Sexual Addiction & Compulsivity, 7* [Special Issue].

Catania, J. A. (1999). A framework for conceptualizing reporting bias and its antecedents in interviews assessing human sexuality. *The Journal of Sex Research, 36,* 25–38.

Childress, C. A., & Asamen, J. K. (1998). The emerging relationship of psychology and the Internet: Proposed guidelines for conducting Internet intervention research. *Ethics & Behavior, 8*(1), 19–35.

Clark, A., Kirkby, K. C,. Daniels, B. A., & Marks, I. M. (1998). A pilot study of computer-aided vicarious exposure for obsessive-compulsive disorder. *Australian & New Zealand Journal of Psychiatry, 32,* 268–275.

Coldwell, S. E., Getz, T., Milgrom, P., Prall, C. W., Spadafora, A., & Ramsay, D. S. (1998). CARL: A LabView 3 computer program for conducting exposure therapy for the treatment of dental injection fear. *Behavior Research & Therapy, 36,* 429–441.

Cooper, A. L., Boies, S., Maheu, M., & Greenfield, D. (2000). Sexuality and the Internet: The next sexual revolution. In L. T. Szuchman & F. Muscarella, et al. (Eds.), *Psychological perspectives on human sexuality* (pp. 519–545). New York: Wiley.

Cooper, A., Griffin-Shelley, E., Delmonico, D. L., & Mathy, R. M. (2002). Online sexual problems: Assessment and predictive variables. *Sexual Addiction and Compulsivity, 8,* 267–285.

Cooper A., Scherer, C. R., Gordon, B. L., & Boies, S. C. (1999). Sexuality on the Internet: From sexual exploration to pathological expression. *Professional Psychology, 30,* 154–164.

Curry, S. J., McBride, C., Grothaus, L. C., Louie, D., & Wagner, E. (1995). A randomized trial of self-help materials, personalized feedback, and telephone counseling with nonvolunteer smokers. *Journal of Consulting and Clinical Psychology, 63,* 1005–1014.

Erdman, H. P., Klein, M. H., & Greist J. H. (1985). Direct patient computer interviewing. *Journal of Consulting and Clinical Psychology, 53,* 760–773.

Frankel, M. S., & Siang, S. (1999, June). Ethical and legal aspects of human subjects research on the Internet: A report of a workshop, Washington, DC. Retrieved from http://www.aaas.org/spp/dspp/sfrl/projects/intres/main.htm

Ghosh, A., Marks, I. M., & Carr, A. C. (1984). Controlled study of self-exposure treatment for phobics: preliminary communication. *Journal of the Royal Society of Medicine, 77,* 483–487.

Goodson, P., McCormick, D., & Evans, A. (2000). Sex and the Internet: A Survey instrument to assess college students' behavior and attitudes. *Cyberpsychology & Behavior, 3*(2), 129–149.

Gribble, J. N., Miller, H. G., Rogers, S. M., & Turner, C. F. (1999). Interview mode and measurement of sexual behaviors: Methodological issues. *The Journal of Sex Research, 36*(1), 16–24.

Harcourt, L., Kirkby, K., Daniels, B. & Montgomery, I. (1998). The differential effect of personality on computer-based treatment of agoraphobia. *Comprehensive Psychiatry, 39,* 303–307.

Hawkins, R. P., Gustafson, D. H., Chewning, B., Bosworth, K., and Day, P. M. (1987). Reaching hard-to-reach populations: interactive computer programs as public information campaigns for adolescents. *Journal of Communication, 37,* 8–28.

Hewson, C. M., Laurent, D., & Vogel, C. M. (1996). Proper methodologies for psychological and sociological studies conducted via the Internet. *Behavior Research Methods, Instruments, & Computers, 28*(2), 186–191.

Jerome, L. W., DeLeon, P. H., James, L. C., Folen, R., Earles, J., & Gedney, J. J. (2000). The coming of age of telecommunications in psychological research and practice. *American Psychologist, 55*(4), 407–421.

Joinson, A. (1999). Social desirability, anonymity, and Internet-based questionnaires. *Behavior Research Methods, Instruments, & Computers, 31*(3), 433–438.

Jones, S. G. (1999). *Doing Internet research: Critical issues and methods for examining the Net.* Thousand Oaks, CA: Sage Publications.

Kann, L. K. (1987). Effects of computer-assisted instruction on selected interaction skills related to responsible sexuality. *Journal of School Health, 57,* 282–287.

King, S. A. (1996). Researching Internet communities: Proposed ethical guidelines for the reporting of results. *The Information Society, 12,* 119–127.

Krantz, J. H., Ballard, J., & Scher, J. (1997). Comparing the results of laboratory and World-Wide Web samples on the determinants of female attractiveness. *Behavior Research Methods, Instruments, & Computers, 29*(2), 264–269.

Libutti, P. O. (1999). The Internet and qualitative research: Opportunities and constraints on analysis of cyberspace discourse. In M. Kopala & L. A. Suzuki (Eds.), *Using qualitative methods in psychology* (pp. 77–88). Thousand Oaks, CA: Sage Publications.

Lieff, J. D. (1987). *Computer applications in psychiatry.* Washington, DC: American Psychiatric Press.

Marks, I. M., Baer, L., Greist, J. H., Park, J. M., Bachofen, M., Nakagawa, A., Wenzel, K. W., Parkin, J. R. Manzo, P. A., Dottl, S. L. Mantle, J. M. (1998). Home self-assessment of obsessive-compulsive disorder. Use of a manual and a computer-conducted telephone interview: Two UK–US studies. *British Journal of Psychiatry, 172,* 406–412.

McGraw, K. O., Tew, M. D., &Williams, J. E. (2000). The integrity of Web delivered experiments: Can you trust the data? *Psychological Science,* 11(6), 502–506.

McKenna, K. Y. A., & Bargh, J. A. (1998). Coming out in the age of the Internet: Identity "demarginalization" through virtual group participation. *Journal of Personality and Social Psychology, 75,* 681–694.

Mehta, R., & Sivadas, E. (1995). Comparing response rates and response content in mail versus electronic mail surveys. *Journal of the Market Research Society, 37,* 429–439.

Michalak, E. E., & Szabo, A. (1998). Guidelines for Internet research: An update. *European Psychologist, 3*(1), 70–75.

Miller, M. J., Hammond, K. W., & Hile, M. G. (Eds.). (1996). *Mental health computing.* New York: Springer.

Neigigh, L., & Kinder, B. N. (1987). The use of audiovisual materials in sex therapy. *Journal of Sex and Marital Therapy, 13,* 64–72.

Newman, B. (1997). The use of online services to encourage exploration of ego-dystonic sexual interests. *Journal of Sex Education and Therapy, 22*(1), 25–48.

Newman, M. G., Consoli, A., & Taylor, C. B. (1997). Computers in assessment and cognitive behavioral treatment of clinical disorders: Anxiety as a case in point. *Behavior Therapy, 28,* 211–235.

Noell, J., Biglan, A., Hood, D., & Britz, B. (1994). An interactive videodisc-based smoking cessation program: Prototype development and pilot test. *Computers in Human Behavior, 10,* 347–358.

North, M. M., North, S. M., & Coble, J. R. (1997). Virtual reality therapy: An effective treatment for psychological disorders. In G. Riva (Ed.), *Virtual reality in neuro-psychophysiology: Cognitive, clinical and methodological issues in assessment and rehabilitation. Studies in health technology and informatics* (pp. 59–70). Amsterdam, Netherlands Antilles: IOS Press.

Ochs, E. P., & Binik, Y. M. (1998). A sex-expert computer system helps couples learn more about their sexual relationship. *Journal of Sex Education and Therapy, 23*(2), 145–156.

Ochs, E. P., & Binik, Y. M. (2000). A sex-expert system on the Internet: Fact or fantasy. *CyberPsychology & Behavior, 3*(4), 617–629.

Ochs, E. P., Meana, M., Mah, K., and Binik, Y. M. (1993). The effects of exposure to different sources of sexual information on sexual behavior: Comparing a "sex-expert system" to other educational material. *Behavior Research Methods, Instruments, & Computers, 25*(2), 189–194.

Ochs, E. P., Meana, M., Pare, L., Mah, K., & Binik, Y. (1994). Learning about sex outside the gutter: Attitudes toward a computer sex-expert system. *Journal of Sex & Marital Therapy, 20*(2), 86–102.

Pettit, F. A. (1999). Exploring the use of the World Wide Web as a psychology data collection tool. *Computers in Human Behavior, 15,* 67–71.

Plaut, S.M., & Donahey, K. M. (2002). Sexuality and the Internet: Ethics and Regulation. In A. Cooper (Ed.), *Sex and the Internet: A guidebook for clinicians*. Philadelphia: Brunner-Routledge.

Reitman, R. (1984). The use of small computers in self-help sex therapy. In M. D. Schwartz. (Ed.), *Using computers in clinical practice*, 363–380, New York: Haworth.

Richman, W. L., Kiesler, S., Weisband, S., & Drasgow, F. (1999). A meta-analytic study of social desirability distortion in computer-administered questionnaires, traditional questionnaires, and interviews. *Journal of Applied Psychology, 84*, 754–775.

Riva, G. (Ed). (1997). *Virtual reality in neuro-psycho-physiology: Cognitive, clinical and methodological issues in assessment and rehabilitation. Studies in health technology and informatics.* Amsterdam, Netherlands Antilles: IOS Press.

Rothbaum, B. O., Hodges, L. F., Kooper, R., Opdyke, D., Williford, J. S., & North, M. (1995). Effectiveness of computer-generated (virtual reality) graded exposure in the treatment of acrophobia. *American Journal of Psychiatry, 152*, 626–628.

Schmidt, W. C. (1997). World-Wide Web survey research: Benefits, potential problems, and solutions. *Behavior Research Methods, Instruments, & Computers, 29*(2), 274–279.

Schneider, S. J. (1986). Trail of an Online Behavioral Smoking Cessation Program. *Computers in Human Behavior, 2*, 277–286.

Schneider, S. J., Walter, R., & O'Donnell, R. O. (1990). Computerized communication as a medium for behavioral smoking cessation treatment: Controlled evaluation. *Computers in Human Behavior, 6*, 141–151.

Schwartz, M. D. (Ed.). (1984). *Using computers in clinical practice: Psychotherapy and mental health applications.* New York: Haworth Press.

Selmi, P. M., Klein, M. H., Greist, J. H., Sorrell, S. P., & Erdman, H. P. (1990). Computer-administered cognitive-behavioral therapy for depression. *American Journal of Psychiatry, 147*, 51–56.

Sidowski, J. B., Johnson, J. H., & Williams, T. A. (Eds.). (1980). *Technology in mental health care delivery systems.* Norwood, NJ: Ablex.

Smith, J. J. (1987). The effectiveness of a computerized self-help stress coping program with adult males. *Computers in Human Services, 2*, 37–49.

Stern, S. E., & Faber, J. E. (1997). The lost e-mail method: Milgrams's lost-letter techniques in the age of the Internet. *Behavior Research Methods, Instruments, & Computers, 29*(2), 260–263.

Szuchman, L. T., & Muscarella, F. (Eds.). (2000). *Psychological perspectives on human sexuality.* New York: Wiley.

Wagman, M. (1988). *Computer psychotherapy systems: Theory and research foundations.* Gordon and Breach.

White, R. J., & Hammer, C. A. (2000). Quiz-o-matic: A free Web-based tool for construction of self-scoring online quizzes. *Behavior Research Methods, Instruments, & Computers, 32*(2), 250–253.

White, H., McConnell, E., Clipp, E., Bynum, L., Teague, C., Navas, L., Craven, S., & Halbrecht. H. (1999). Surfing the net in later life: A review of the literature and pilot study of computer use and quality of life. *The Journal of Applied Gerontology, 18*, 358–378.

Whiteley, J. M. (Ed.). (1983). Special section on computers in counseling psychology. *Counseling Psychologist, 11*(4), pp. 9–74.

Wilson, F. R., Omeltschenko, L., & Yager, G. G. (1991). Coping with test stress: Microcomputer software for treatment of test anxiety. *Journal of Behavior Therapy & Experimental Psychiatry, 22*, 131–139.

Azy Barak
William A. Fisher

The Future of Internet Sexuality

Niels Bohr, the Danish physicist, was known to remark, "Prediction is very difficult, especially about the future." Indeed, the business of fore casting future developments—known as futurism—is far from an exact science. Forecasting through extrapolation of historical trends, or through building of formal models based on mathematical equations, is essentially arbitrary, because most of the relevant data are lacking. Moreover, as cognitively active decision makers, we have some control over our destiny, and forecasting passive continuation of current trends seems to underestimate the powerful impact of human agency and imagination. At best, one can illustrate a few possible future scenarios, each using one or another set of assumptions (Rice, 1997). Such forecasts themselves may become a basis for reflection and alteration of current trends, based upon the application of human imagination and agency.

Unlike futurists, psychologists see prediction as an integral part of their scientific business, and efforts to predict outcomes—and to verify the prediction of outcomes—an essential part of the psychological scientists' activities. This can be illustrated, for example, in the fields of artificial intelligence (Johnson & Erneling, 1998), employee and organizational behavior (Sparrow, 2000), and clinical health and forensic psychology (Belar, 1997). Miller (1998), in fact, has offered a visionary perspective for the future. Based on specific predictions—such as cancer advances prolonging life; psychological testing as we know it being replaced by a complex analytic system which integrates effects of genetic factors, psychological markers, thoughts and behavior—he portrayed "a psychologist with 20/20 vision."

Modern technology and the Internet are fast-growing ventures. There are differences as to what is considered to be the length of "an era" in the computer age. Most scientists agree, however, that changes in technologies and applications are extremely rapid, a fact that requires quick a pace of personal and social adaptations, more rapid than ever before (Jones & Jones, 1998). Moreover, we now know that emerging technology and scientific breakthroughs will change most what we currently know and even what we used to know. Wireless networks, revolutionary cyber-optic-based communications, artificial intelligence, advanced expert systems, and biologically based chips will propel demands for human adjustment and mastery of conditions and challenges not yet dreamed of. The recent discovery that metabolic networks—identical in many organisms—closely resemble the communication systems of the Internet (Jeong, Tombor, Albert, Oltvai, & Barabási, 2000) may be a signal that human–computer interactions are destined to be wed evermore closely to one another in a system of reciprocal influence.

In this concluding chapter of *Sex and the Internet: A Guidebook for Clinicians*, we have been asked to forecast future developments in Internet sexuality that have special relevance to clinical concerns. In assembling this forecast, and in line with the above premises, we must assume that future developments in Internet sexuality will reflect core characteristics of Internet sexuality that exist at the present time. Also, we must assume unanticipated technological breakthroughs in Internet capabilities and societal and individual adaptations and reactions to them. We will consider first the factors known as "the triple-A engine" (Cooper, 1998; Cooper, McLoughlin, & Campbell, 2000; Cooper & Sportolari, 1997): accessibility, affordability, and anonymity of Internet sexuality. In addition to these factors, we propose that two other important engines, acceptability (King, 1999) and aloneness (Barak & Fisher, 2002), make a powerful *penta-A engine*. However, a rational analysis of existing trends and projection to the future suggests the significance of additional factors that we consider essential, including attempts to regulate Internet sexuality and generational disparities in Internet sophistication.

☐ Accessibility

Spectacular growth in Internet accessibility, with movement toward universal connectedness, is anticipated in future years. Growth in Internet accessibility will include growth in *ease of access*, with PC-independent, wireless handheld, or cable television-based Internet access becoming the easy-to-use norm. Growth in *age-inclusive access* across both younger and older segments of society not now connected is also anticipated: A recent survey reports that the number of Internet users worldwide will nearly triple to close to 1.2 billion by 2005 (see http://www.etforecasts.com/pr/pr201.htm). With growth in *cross-national access*, as a part of the globalization process, the Internet will penetrate presently closed societies and economically deprived third world countries.

Growth in ease of access is expected to facilitate future developments in Internet sexuality in multiple ways. For example, while current PC-based wired access to the Internet acts to restrict Internet use to work and study at a computer desk in relatively asocial settings, easy access to cable-television-based Internet portals is likely to promote Internet use solely for entertainment purposes in the social environment of the living room, den, or bedroom. Given the nearly unlimited amount of sexual content already on the Internet, growth in easy accessibility will likely translate into expanded contact with Internet sexuality in social and sexual as opposed to vocational settings. Moreover, this expansion is expected to be a two-way proposition, with Internet users both accessing sexual content and originating such content via Webcams and other modalities. This may result in Internet-mediated "flashing" and individual, couple-, and group-based visually explicit sexual exchanges. Similarly, growth in wireless handheld Internet portals may make it easier for compulsive or situationally inappropriate Internet sexuality consumption.

Increases in age inclusiveness will bring with them the likelihood of increased contact with Internet sexuality for both younger and older cohorts of society than is presently the case. Whether the ultimate impact is positive or negative depends upon the degree to which the Internet provides adaptive and age-appropriate sexual information, motivational messages, and behavioral models or the opposite. Increases in cross-national access to the Internet can be expected to have a significant impact on the sexual values and expression of members of formerly closed, religiously fundamentalist, and impoverished third-world societies that may later provoke responses ranging from individual dissatisfaction and behavior change to government backlash and draconian punishment. Internet-based sexuality education could also act to focus local and international attention on culturally specific sexual patterns.

Increased accessibility across ages and cultures is also related to two other factors that lie close to the core of the experience of internet sexuality: convenience and escape (Young, Griffin-Shelley, Cooper, O'Mara, & Buchanan, 2000). Convenience refers to the ease, comfort, and perceived safety of virtual environments, while at the same time offering stimulation. It seems obvious that with the advancement of technology these characteristics of computer use will become more prominent and may well result in greater attractiveness of virtual sexual experiences and consequent personal pleasure. The escape factor refers to the envisioned harmless flirting, or the tendency to flee from boring or threatening reality into a convenient other world—sexual cyberspace—impossible to match in "the real world." Growing globalization of the Net, on the one hand, and improved communication networks, on the other, will facilitate the sense of escape and the individual's ability to flee reality into a rich, rewarding, and personally constructed optimum alternative. These might contribute to either growing possibilities for innocuous pleasure or to growing difficulties with cybersex addiction (Griffiths, 2000; Young, 1998). Convenience and escape characteristics of the Internet underscore the human factor involved in exploiting new technologies and emphasize that it is people's use and understanding of technology that is the agent of change, rather than technology itself (Grint & Woolgar, 1997).

☐ Affordability

At present, Internet access and Internet content are relatively affordable. However, technological advances and growth in competition are expected to make Internet access ever more inexpensive. Even at present (Cooper, Delmonico, & Burg, 2000; Cooper, Scherer, Boies, & Gordon, 1999; W. A. Fisher & Barak, 2000; King, 1999), there is a vast amount of cost-free explicit sexual content available at the click of a mouse. With easier access, more users, and increased competition, along with expected quantum improvements in Internet technology, the Internet's ability to deliver exceedingly high-quality products for dramatically lower costs will be vastly enhanced. An increase in no-cost sexual "teaser" material of high quality and low-cost or no-cost sexual and relationship chatrooms, which capitalize on augmented Internet technology, will add audio and video channels for sexual communication on a routine basis. The high end of the market will offer broadcast-quality sexual videos, perhaps interactive, with paid performers in real time—virtual prostitution. Equivalently, high-quality interactive sexual counseling will become available.

☐ Anonymity

At present, one of the central and most attractive characteristics of the Internet experience is its anonymity (McKenna & Bargh, 1999, 2000). Individuals can surf sexually explicit Web sites devoted to female–female sex, bondage and discipline, and bestiality in complete privacy and with a feeling of complete anonymity. This despite the reality that many employers, parents, and others utilize surveillance software that makes anonymity more of an illusion than a reality (see, e.g., http://www.enfiltrator.

com or http://www.remote-spy.com). Perceptions of compromised anonymity may act to limit important positive sex-related Internet developments including use of online sexual counseling and education sites and involvement with online sexual addition intervention sites. Sophisticated Web-based software will soon be provided on a commercial basis to regain anonymous surfing, and perhaps even advanced false online personas, for interested users.

☐ Regulation

Another characteristic of the Internet that is especially relevant to sexuality is the fact that it has proven all but impossible to regulate the content of the Internet (e.g., Lessig, 1999; Lipschultz, 2000). These attempts have and will stimulate complicated constitutional issues in regard to free speech. Inability to regulate the content of Internet sexuality communicated by widely distributed providers including corporate, "cottage industry," and individual users, may well be related in paradoxical fashion to expected increases in ability to penetrate anonymity of Internet users. Future Internet sexuality developments may thus create the problem of individuals who have increasing access to completely unregulated Internet sexuality content but whose anonymity is regularly compromised, bringing unwanted attention from parents, spouses, teachers, employers, and criminal justice authorities.

☐ Generational Disparities in Internet Sophistication

Despite the fact that Internet accessibility is expected to extend to both increasingly younger and older segments of society, it is anticipated that relatively younger individuals as a group will continue to be the most facile adopters of Internet technology (Calvert, 1998; Freeman-Longo, 2000; Williams, 1999). This will provide an opportunity to impact concerns of society and clients such as early sexual behavior and coital debut and unsafe sexual practices. It may also prove to be the case that the younger individual involved with Internet sexuality may experience sexual compulsiveness problems (Putnam, 2000), relationship problems (Levine, 2000), employment problems (Furnham, 2000), and criminal justice problems in relatively greater numbers. At the same time, a generational clinician–patient disparity in Internet sophistication may represent an important clinical skill deficit that will need to be remedied in order to provide meaningful assistance to clients with Internet-related sexuality concerns.

For better and for worse, the future development of Internet sexuality will have individual, relationship, and societal impacts that clinicians must anticipate and acquire the insight and skill to manage. In anticipating this trend and the challenges it will pose, it would be inaccurate and unhelpful to convey a doomsday vision that is uniformly negative. While the future developments in Internet sexuality we have anticipated will certainly exploit sex, they will also cultivate sex, in relation to desire, function, diversity, tolerance, and assertive and self-enhancing sexuality (Barak & King, 2000). While these developments may exploit and objectify women—and men—we also expect that there will be educational elements supportive of sexual tolerance, sexual diversity, and assertive and self-enhancing sexuality for both women and men (Döring, 2000; Podlas, 2000). At present, Internet sexuality includes access to online relationships, sexual merchandise, sexual stimulation, accurate and erroneous sex-related information, and formal sexual education for the lay public and for professionals.

The following sections of this chapter address a number of specific aspects of the future of Internet sexuality, the clinical concerns that each may pose, and possible roles and strategies for the clinician in addressing challenges posed by these developments.

☐ Sexually Explicit Materials on the Internet

At present, anyone can acquire Internet materials that portray and endorse the full range of sexual activities, from the consensual to the coercive, from the enriching to the degrading. Psychological theory and research suggest that individual differences will influence the nature of the materials acquired and the consequences of exposure to them (Barak, Fisher, Belfry, & Lashambe, 1999; Bogaert, 1993; W. A. Fisher & Barak, 2002).

The future of Internet sexually explicit materials will be influenced heavily by a number of underlying factors. First, we note that unprecedented access to vast amounts of sexually explicit material was arguably *the* primary engine that drove adoption, growth, and utilization of the Internet during its first decade of development. By extension, we expect that the creation and consumption of these types of materials will continue to be a primary factor. Moreover, that will drive the development of new Internet technologies that will be utilized to deliver ever richer experiences. Where Internet sexually explicit materials are now more or less restricted to the relatively passive selection and consumption of "prefabricated" sexually explicit text, images, and sounds, soon individuals will be able to interactively construct and obtain virtual sexual stimulation that represents their optimally arousing "fit" (Mosher, 1980). We also expect to see the development of a range of Internet sexual peripherals, including Internet-driven vibrators embedded within rich and individually reactive sexual stimulus arrays, and other technosexual advances. Increasingly important to the dissemination of this material will be the findings of psychological research and expert opinion in this area. As we have asserted on a number of occasions (W. A. Fisher & Barak, 1989, 1991, 2002), psychological research has had a poor and politicized track record when it comes to providing empirically strong and compelling accounts of the prevalence and effects of pornography.

Individual, couple, and societal reactions to developments of Internet sexually explicit materials will determine future clinical concerns. On an individual level they may act then as they do now, as an adjunct to sexual fantasy (Mah<?>u & Subotnik, 2001). Like other types of sexual fantasy, experience with augmented Internet sexually explicit materials may have positive as well as negative outcomes. Individuals may use enriched Internet sexual explicitness to play safely at sexual activities they have no intention of ever enacting and offer the possibility of adaptive outcomes (e.g., "safe place to play"). Couples may draw sexual information, motivation, and behavioral skills that will enrich their sexual and emotional relationship. Alternatively, participants may retreat from reality into the fantasy world of augmented Internet sexuality and fail to discern the difference between it and reality (Civin, 2000). This might be accompanied by the possibility of seriously maladaptive behavior and amplify existing concerns about the Internet and sexual compulsivity and deviance (e.g., Barak & King, 2000; Cooper, 2000; Schwartz & Southern, 2000).

☐ Cybersex and Intimate Relations on the Internet

Cyberspace has become an ideal place to meet people and to develop interpersonal relationships (Parks & Floyd, 1996). This is true for any type of social relationship, including intimate relationships. Some of these contacts remain online while others are transformed into face-to-face relationships, especially when they seem to be attractive and gratifying (McKenna & Bargh, 1999; Parks & Floyd, 1996; Parks & Roberts, 1998). Numerous couples have met online (Baker, 2000; Gwinnell, 1998) as the Net provides a safe and legitimate acquaintance space, allowing an "inside-out" process of familiarization with one another (Merkle & Richardson, 2000). Moreover, there is a clear trend to look for online partners, perhaps because of the combination of the need for relatedness, feelings of alienation, and the perceived safety of online contacts (Civin, 2000; Cooper & Sportolari, 1997). Web pages designated for self-presentation have become legitimate and widespread (Chan, 2000), as have matchmaking sites (see, for example, http://www.matchmaker.com). While men's and women's Net behavior still differs (Sussman & Tyson, 2000; Wolf, 2000), there are speculations (still to be empirically examined) that women experience more activism, freedom, and equality than off the Net (Harcourt, 1999; Morahan-Martin, 2000). Similarly, field observations show that women, just as men, engage heavily in cybersex, that is, virtual sexual relations that involve manual masturbation (Levine, 1998, 2000).

In the future this trend will continue, as growing numbers of people find cyberspace a fascinating environment in which to enjoy intimate relations. Certain minorities—physically disadvantaged, sick, older, younger, shy, the unattractive (and those who think they are)—will crowd the Net's social meeting points in greater numbers. Many people will find the Net an easy, convenient, inexpensive, efficient place to find a partner; thus, formal and informal matchmaking will flourish. Based on the borderless nature of the Internet, this last phenomenon will inevitably increase the number of international, intercultural, and interreligious marriages, ultimately affecting global social patterns.

On the negative side, it seems that the current trend of "online infidelity" (Maheu & Subotnik, 2001; Shaw, 1997; Young et al., 2000) will increase in tandem with growth in the communications capabilities of the Net, negatively affecting couple relationships and families (Schneider, 2000). If the current trend does continue, cybersex relations, often transformed into in-person sexual relations (Gwinnell, 1998), will become a major factor in deteriorating marital relations and, therefore, a cause of relationship distress and divorce. Also, the potential false nature of Internet-based relationship makes impersonating and emotional manipulating of online partners a reality, to be abused by growing numbers of malicious users. In addition, the addictive nature of Internet-based intimate relations in general, and cybersex in particular (Cooper, Delmonico, & Burg, 2000; Griffiths, 2000), will increase the number of people engaged in this activity at work or school, hence affecting productivity, work relations, personal achievements, and the like. Sophisticated electronic surveillance and new regulations may help in controlling this development, but their effectiveness may well be only partial.

☐ The Internet and Homosexuality

It is our view that the Internet's penta-A engine makes it an exceptionally suitable channel for addressing same-sex concerns and an extremely likely area for future development of Internet sexually related capabilities. Same-sex issues are sensitive, personal, and stigmatized, and—even more than is the case in other areas of sexual information seeking—comprise an area in which the very seeking of information is itself a highly stigmatizing activity (Weinrich, 1997). Similarly, cyberspace has and will become more of a common environment for transsexuals and intersexuals and other highly stigmatized and disenfranchised populations.

With its unique characteristics, the Internet will increasingly be used as an unusually safe venue for individuals with same-sex interests to meet one another, to explore same-sex attraction; to seek same-sex stimulation from sexually explicit materials, to be involved in same-sex political activity, and to explore the coming-out process (Burke, 2000; Lax, 2000; Sampson, 1998; Tikkanen & Ross, 2000). The Internet will also serve increasingly as a particularly useful venue for self-help activities, ranging from counseling about sexual orientation to online support groups, to distribution of information about safer sex issues, to dissemination of referral networks of gay-friendly service providers in psychology, medicine, or travel.

☐ Internet Sexuality and Children

As has been mentioned earlier, the factors projected to expand Internet use will affect children as well as adults. Children's ever greater exposure to the Internet means that their exposure to sexual content will grow as well, with both the benefits and the risks this implies (Bremer & Rauch, 1998). In addition to organizations and Web sites that emphasize creating rules and teaching cautious surfing (see, for example, http://www.state.nv.us/ag/agpub/internet.htm), and in addition to software packages designed to limit children's exposure to Internet sexuality (e.g., CyberSitter; see http://www.cybersitter.com), the future will likely bring with it educational attempts to equip children with the skills of "smart surfing" (Dorman, 1997; Teicher, 1999).

One can expect several positive processes to result. First, age-appropriate and nontraumatic exposure to sexuality can help in developing more positive attitudes and a greater acceptance of sex as a normal part of human existence. This advantage may serve as an effective vehicle in counterbalancing culturally common erotophobic messages and facilitating more erotophilic tolerance of sexuality, thus contributing to the promotion of physical and mental health (W. A. Fisher, Byrne, Kelley, & White, 1988; W. A. Fisher & Fisher, 1999). Second, exposure to quality sexuality education materials may contribute to a better assimilating of sex information, promoting the knowledge factor that is necessary for healthier sexual conduct (e.g., W. A. Fisher & Fisher, 1999). Third, the growing use of chatrooms and forums as a venue for children's interpersonal communication will probably result in more conversations about sex and more intimate relations between youngsters. Although this might sometimes be considered detrimental, positive aspects of developing social skills related to intimacy should not be ignored (such as age-appropriate courting or negotiating a face-to-face meeting). Fourth, improving Internet capabilities will allow more sophisticated and effective sexuality education (Barak & Fisher, 2002). In contrast to using the Net as a resource that is basically text- and graphics-based, as presently done, dynamic and highly interactive Internet-driven sexuality education sites will be developed to enhance active and effective learning.

On the negative side, it is apparent that the growing use of the Net may be linked with withdrawal from face-to-face social interactions (Sanders, Field, Diego, & Kaplan, 2000) and with the substitutions of virtual for in-vivo relations. Second, as kids have relatively little countervailing normative sexual information, they are likely to develop distorted perceptions and norms about sexuality from exposure to age-inappropriate, extreme, and sometimes entirely erroneous sexual images on the Internet.

☐ Compulsive Sexual Behavior on the Net

The compulsive use of Internet sexuality—also known as cybersex addiction—is a well-documented phenomenon (Cooper, Delmonico, & Burg, 2000; Cooper, Putnam, Planchon, & Boies, 1999; Cooper, Scherer, Boies, & Gordon, 1999; Griffiths, 2000; Greenfield, 1999; Putnam, 2000; Putnam & Maheu, 2000; Schwartz & Southern, 2000; Young, 1998). Future developments in Internet technology will contribute to enriched, more attractive sex sites, and consequently to increases in this problem in dramatic and nonlinear ways. Instead of a 1% problematic use of Internet sexuality at present time (Cooper, Delmonico, & Burg, 2000), we may, in a few years, observe a figure of 2% or 5%, or tens of millions of Internet users worldwide who compulsively use the Net for sex. Needless to say, this number of people may significantly influence social norms and behaviors ranging from work habits and job performance to sex crimes.

At the same time it is possible that virtual engagements could substitute for real encounters (Waskul, Douglass, & Edgley, 2000) and thus prevent, or reduce, a variety of negative sex-related behaviors (e.g., stalking, voyeurism, exhibitionism).

☐ The Internet and Atypical Sexual Behavior

Clinicians are aware that many individuals engage in what might be considered atypical sexual behaviors: sexual acts that are rare, novel, and unexpected, that are shocking or antisocial in nature, and that may have disadvantageous consequences for the individual and others. Future strengthening of the Internet's already prodigious capacity to deliver an extraordinary range of sexual stimulation poses the possibility of provoking atypical sexual behavior (see Palandri & Green, 2000, on a sadomasochist chatroom).

Consider, for example, the possible effects of the range of paraphilic sexual stimuli now available on the Internet, including beastiality, coprophilia, sadomasochism, and sexually aggressive portrayals (Kim & Bailey, 1997), when combined with preexisting limited capacity, diminished capacity, or serious mental illness. While we would emphasize that individuals who have little internal restraint or who cannot differentiate between fantasy and reality do not need Internet sexuality to provoke problem sexual behaviors (see W. A. Fisher & Barak, 1991, 2002; Waskul, Douglass, & Edgley, 2000), the future development of Internet sexuality will pose at least three challenges to the clinician. First, when working with individuals with diminished capacity or serious psychopathology, it may be incumbent on the future clinician to work out practical approaches to avoiding contact with Internet sexual stimuli that could provoke problems. Second, the clinician will assist individuals to modify patterns of atypical sexual behavior and to redirect sexual interests in the context of an Internet environment that supplies considerable stimuli that model and reinforce the behavior in question. Third, clinicians will encounter more couples in which one individual has imported what the other regards as atypical sexual desires from Internet sources. Thus, their task will be to help couples negotiate different preferences. Finally, in keeping with our assertion that nearly all future developments of Internet sexuality have therapeutic as well as pathogenic possibilities, we remind the clinician that there is an entire class of atypical sexual behavior that would not apriori be judged harmful

☐ Illegal Sexual Behaviors on the Internet

Illegal online sexual behaviors are already concerns, from the distribution of and trade in child pornography (McCabe, 2000) to stalking and sexual harassment (Deirmenjian, 1999) to illegal paraphilic activity (Kim

& Baily, 1997) and pedophilia (Durkin, 1997; Durkin & Bryant, 1999). Increasing accessibility and affordability of the Internet will likely enlarge the number of sex offenders and the range and reach of sexual offenses, with cyberspace becoming a relatively congenial environment for wrongdoing. The inherent difficulty in tracking and exposing the identity of Net users undermines legislative attempts to apply criminal law to cyberspace even as sex offenders creatively develop and deploy forms of virtual sexual assault and other online sex offenses. It seems reasonable to believe, however, that governments and public organizations will attempt to implement various solutions, from "Internet police" (e.g., http://www.web-police.org; http://www.internet-police.co.uk) to making laws more strict in order to reduce Internet sex crimes. In this connection, legislation will have to develop to consider virtual sex crimes in ways that will raise a host of practical and moral issues.

There is a positive aspect to the growing use and exposure of the Internet in this regard as authorities advertise and distribute information concerning sex crimes and sex offenders (e.g., http://www.sexualpredators.org). In the end, this educational use of the Net may ultimately contribute to the reduction of offline sex crimes.

☐ Internet-Assisted Sex Therapy and Consultation

As is the case with all psychological applications on the Internet (Barak, 1999), online counseling and psychotherapy are relatively new ventures (e.g., Maheu & Gordon, 2000; Smith & Senior, 2001). Such services currently flourish and are expected to expand greatly as a joint function of improvements in Internet technology and improvements in counseling and therapeutic applications (Maheu, in press; Suler, 2000). (For a comprehensive portal, see http://www.metanoia.org/imhs)

Internet-based or Internet-supported sex therapy is in its infancy. Although more than a few Web sites offer sex advice (see, for example, Dr. Ruth's online advice at http://webcenter.drruth.aol.com/DrRuth/?pg=qatopics&partner=AOW), not many offer actual online therapy (see, for example, Sex Therapy Online at http://www.sexology.org) as there are a host of current, ethical, legal, and technical concerns to be overcome (see Plaut and Donahey, chapter 12). Predictions as to the future of online sex therapy opportunities are generally supportive but urge caution (Leiblum, 1997; Noonan, 1998; Ochs & Binik, 2000). Similarly, support has been provided for therapy for compulsive users of online sex (Putnam, 2000).

There is good reason to believe that with the growth of online psychotherapy and online health care in general (Maheu, in press; Maheu &

Gordon, 2000; Maheu, Whitten, & Allen, 2001), online sex therapy will flourish as well. Following the penta-A engines, anonymous interaction promotes consultations (Graugaard & Winther, 1998) while face-to-face interaction may impede those interested in sexual counseling. The Internet will allow access to qualified sex therapists and make them available essentially everywhere. And, finally, in terms of cost-effectiveness, components of the therapeutic process are expected to be increasingly automated and thereby decline in price. In addition to reducing costs, Internet-driven, diagnostic software, such as Sexpert (Ochs & Binik, 2000), and Web-based survey instruments (Goodson, McCormick, & Evans, 2000) will make Internet-assisted sex counseling more practical and effective (see Cooper, Scherer, and Marcus, this volume). Advanced video-conferencing technology will enable synchronous therapy together with the visual components specifically necessary for sex therapy. Moreover, online instructions to and feedback from clients will bring virtual therapists closer to actual sexual behaviors, allowing the therapist to become almost an in-vivo observer of problematic behaviors and a behavior change facilitator.

At the same time there may also be a growing number of both professional service providers who have not been appropriately trained and outright impostors. More emphasis on appropriate training and ethical guidelines (e.g., http://www.ismho.org/suggestions.html) will inevitably develop.

☐ Internet-Assisted Sex Education

We have emphasized elsewhere (Barak & Fisher, in press) that the Internet's core characteristics are exceedingly well suited to the delivery of expert, multimedia-rich, interactive, and individually targeted sexual and reproductive health education interventions. Internet-assisted sex education has been proposed (e.g., Barak & Safir, 1997; Flowers-Coulson, Kushner, & Bankowski, 2000; Roffman, Shannon, & Dwyer, 1997) for its strengths and suitability in this area. Such procedures will be exploited more fully to provide educational opportunities aimed at improving sexual and reproductive health.

As a two-way expert system, Internet-based sexuality education interventions, guided by theory, can be used both to assess individuals' sexual and reproductive health strengths and weaknesses and to create individually tailored intervention elements designed to address these issues. For example, a sexuality education intervention aimed at reducing risk (e.g., unsafe sexual behavior) could be structured in accord with sophisticated behavior change models (J. D. Fisher & Fisher, 1992). Future deployment of Internet-based sexual and reproductive health education will be mainstreamed as an integral component of formal sexual and reproductive health education in school settings and as an integral element in the clinical care of special populations.

☐ Conclusions

The Internet sexuality of the future will be different: It will be more engaging, more impactful, more beneficial, and potentially more dangerous, than any communications technology advance in history. For all these reasons, future sexual expression on the Internet will require very active involvement of clinicians—as clinicians per se, and as scientists, educators, and opinion leaders. Their role will be to assist and inform the public as it struggles to accommodate quantum changes in a fashion that is individually and socially beneficial and that avoids the serious pitfalls that await the unwary.

The future of sex on the Internet is ours to engage, and in many ways it is ours to create. As clinicians, we can look forward to a challenging range of clinical assessment and intervention, using tools that currently exist and those we will have to invent. As clinician-scientists, we will be uniquely positioned to identify critical applied research topics, to provide pivotal insights concerning psychological processes, and to conduct cutting edge research. As clinician-educators, we are uniquely informed about the general concerns about sexuality that we all experience and about the special opportunities and challenges. Finally, as clinician–opinion leaders, we will need to remain calm and dispassionate, and we will need to avoid precipitous and potentially unfounded declaration of yet another sexuality-related crisis. Above all, as clinician–opinion leaders address the Internet sexuality of the future, we must never forget our scientific roots, and we must always ask, "Where's the science?"

☐ References

Baker, A. (2000). Two by two in cyberspace: Getting together and connecting online. *CyberPsychology & Behavior, 3,* 237–242.

Barak, A. (1999). Psychological applications on the Internet: A discipline on the threshold of a new millennium. *Applied and Preventive Psychology , 8,* 231–246.

Barak, A., & Fisher, W. A. (2002). Towards an Internet-based, theoretically-driven, innovative approach to sexuality education. *Journal of Sex Research,* 39.

Barak, A., Fisher, W. A., Belfry, S., & Lashambe, D. R. (1999). Sex, guys, and cyberspace: Effects of Internet pornography and individual differences on men's attitudes toward women. *Journal of Psychology and Human Sexuality, 11,* 63–92.

Barak, A., & King, S. A. (2000). The two faces of the Internet: Introduction to the special issue on the Internet and sexuality. *CyberPsychology and Behavior, 3*, 517–520.

Barak, A., & Safir, M. P. (1997). Sex and the Internet: An Israeli perspective. *Journal of Sex Education and Therapy, 22*, 67–73.

Belar, C. D. (1997). Clinical health psychology: A specialty for the 21st century. *Health Psychology, 16*, 411–416.

Bogaert, A. F. (1993) *The sexual media: The role of individual differences.* Unpublished doctoral dissertation, Department of Psychology, University of Western Ontario, London, ON, Canada.

Bremer, J., & Rauch, P. K. (1998). Children and computers: Risks and benefits. *Journal for American Academy of Child & Adolescent Psychiatry, 37*, 559–560.

Burke, S. K. (2000). In search of lesbian community in an electronic world. *CyberPsychology & Behavior, 3*, 591–604.

Calvert, S. L. (1999) *Children's journeys through the information age.* New York: McGraw-Hill.

Chan, S. Y. M. (2000) Wired_Selves: From article to performance. *CyberPsychology & Behavior, 3*, 271–285.

Civin, M. A. (2000). *Male, female, e-mail. The struggle for relatedness in a paranoid society.* New York: Other Press.

Cooper, A. (1998). Sexuality and the Internet: Surfing into the new millennium. *CyberPsychology & Behavior, 1*, 187–193.

Cooper, A. (2000). Cybersex and sexual compulsivity: The dark side of the force. *Sexual Addiction and Compulsivity, 7*, 1–3.

Cooper, A., Delmonico, D. L., & Burg, R. (2000). Cybersex users, abusers, and compulsives: New findings and implications. *Sexual Addiction & Compulsivity, 7*, 5–29.

Cooper, A., McLoughlin, I. P., & Campbell, K. M. (2000). Sexuality in cyberspace: Update for the 21st century. *CyberPsychology & Behavior, 3*, 521–536.

Cooper, A., Putnam, D. E., Planchon, L. A., & Boies, S. C. (1999). Online sexual compulsivity: Getting tangled in the net. *Sexual Addiction and Compulsivity, 6*, 79-104.

Cooper, A., Scherer, C. R., Boies, S. C., & Gordon, B. L. (1999). Sexuality on the Internet: From sexual exploration to pathological expression. *Professional Psychology: Research and Practice, 30*, 154–164.

Cooper, A., & Sportolari, L. (1997). Romance and cyberspace: Understanding online attraction. *Journal of Sex Education and Therapy, 22*, 7–14.

Deirmenjian, J. M. (1999). Stalking in cyberspace. *Journal American Academic Psychiatry Law, 27*, 407–413.

Döring, N. (2000). Feminist views of cybersex: Victimization, liberation and empowerment. *CyberPsychology & Behavior, 3*, 863–884.

Dorman, S. M. (1997). Internet safety for schools, teachers, and parents. *Journal of School Health, 67*, 355.

Durkin, K. F. (1997). Misuse of the Internet by pedophiles: Implications for law enforcement and probation practice. *Federal Probation, 61*(3), 14–18.

Durkin, K. F., & Bryant, C. D. (1999). Propagandizing pederasty: A thematic analysis of the on-line exculpatory accounts of unrepentant pedophiles. *Deviant Behavior, 20*, 103–127.

Fisher, J. D., & Fisher, W. A. (1992). Changing AIDS-risk behavior. *Psychological Bulletin, 111*, 455–474.

Fisher, W. A., & Barak, A. (1989). Sex education as a corrective: Immunizing against possible effects of pornography. In D. Zillman & J. Bryant (Eds.), *Pornography: Recent research, interpretations, and policy considerations* (pp. 289–320). Hillsdale, NJ: Erlbaum.

Fisher, W. A., & Barak, A. (1991). Pornography, erotica, and behavior: More questions than answers. *International Journal of Law and Psychiatry, 14*, 65–83.

Fisher, W. A., & Barak, A. (2000). Online sex shops: Phenomenological, psychological, and ideological perspectives on Internet sexuality. *CyberPsychology & Behavior, 3,* 575-589.

Fisher, W. A., & Barak, A. (2002). Internet pornography: Psychological perspectives on Internet sexuality. *Journal of Sex Research, 39.*

Fisher, W. A., Byrne, D., Kelley, K., & White, L. A. (1988). Erotophobia—Erotophilia as a dimension of personality. *Journal of Sex Research, 25,* 123-151.

Fisher, W. A., & Fisher, J. D. (1999). Understanding and promoting sexual and reproductive health behavior: Theory and method. In R. Rosen, C. M. Davis, & H. J. Ruppel, Jr. (Eds.), *Annual review of sex research. Vol IX* (pp. 39–76). Mason City, IA: Society for the Scientific Study of Sex.

Flowers-Coulson, P. A., Kushner, M. A., & Bankowski, S. (2000). The information is out there, but is anyone getting it? Adolescent misconceptions about sexuality education and reproductive health and the use of the Internet to get answers. *Journal of Sex Education & Therapy, 25,* 178–188.

Freeman-Longo, R. E. (2000). Children, teens, and sex on the Internet. *Sexual Addiction and Compulsivity, 7,* 75–90.

Furnham, A. (2000). Work in 2020: Prognostications about the world of work 20 years into the millennium. *Journal of Managerial Psychology, 15,* 242–254.

Goodson, P., McCormick, D., & Evans, A. (2000). Sex and the Internet: A survey instrument to assess college students behavior and attitudes. *CyberPsychology & Behavior, 3,* 129–149.

Graugaard, C., & Winther, G. (1998). Sex counselling on the Internet—A year with www.lyst.dk. *Scandinavian Journal of Sexology, 1,* 201–204.

Greenfield, D. N. (1999). *Virtual addiction.* Oakland, CA: New Harbinger Publications.

Griffiths, M. (2000). Excessive Internet use: Implications for sexual behavior. *CyberPsychology & Behavior, 3,* 537–552.

Grint, K., & Woolgar, S. (1997). *The machine at work: Technology, work and organization.* Cambridge, UK: Polity.

Gwinnell, E. (1998). *Online seductions: Falling in love with strangers on the Internet.* New York: Kodansha International.

Harcourt, W. (Ed.). (1999). *Women@Internet: Creating new cultures in cyberspace.* London, UK: Zed Books.

Jeong, H., Tombor, B., Albert, R., Oltvai, Z. N., & Barabási, A. L. (2000). The large-scale organization of metabolic networks. *Nature, 407,* 651–654.

Johnson, D. M., & Erneling, C. E. (Eds.). (1998). *The future of the cognitive revolution.* New York: Oxford University Press.

Jones, S., & Jones, S. G. (Eds.). (1998). *Cybersociety 2.0: Revisiting computer-mediated communication and community.* Thousand Oaks, CA: Sage.

Kim, P. Y., & Bailey, M. (1997). Sidestreets on the information highway: Paraphilias and sexual variations on the Internet. *Journal of Sex Education & Therapy, 22,* 35–43.

King, S. A. (1999). Internet gambling and pornography: Illustrative examples of the psychological consequences of communication anarchy. *CyberPsychology & Behavior, 2,* 175–193.

Lax, S. (2000). The Internet and democracy. In D. Gauntlett (Ed.), *Web.studies: Rewiring media studies for the digital age* (pp. 159–169). New York: Oxford University Press.

Leiblum, S. R. (1997). Sex and the Net: Clinical implications. *Journal of Sex Education and Therapy, 22,* 21–28.

Lessig, L. (1999). *Code and other laws of cyberspace.* New York: Basic Books.

Levine, D. (1998). *The joy of cybersex.* New York: Ballentine Books.

Levine, D. (2000). Virtual attraction: What rocks your boat. *CyberPsychology & Behavior, 3,* 565–573.

Lipschultz, J. H. (2000). *Free expression in the age of the Internet*. Boulder, CO: Westview.

Maheu, M. (in press). *Practicing psychotherapy online: Clinical, ethical and legal perspectives.* Mahwah, NJ: Erlbaum.

Maheu, M. M., & Gordon, B. L. (2000). Counseling and therapy on the Internet. *Professional Psychology: Research and Practice, 31,* 484–489.

Maheu, M. M., & Subotnik, R. (2001). *Infidelity on the Internet.* Naperville, IL: Sourcebooks.

Maheu, M., Whitten, P., & Allen, A. (2001). *E-health, telehealth & telemedicine: A guide to program startup and success.* San Francisco, CA: Jossey-Bass.

McCabe, K. (2000). Child pornography and the Internet. *Social Science Computer Review, 18,* 73–76.

McKenna, K. Y. A., & Bargh, J. A. (1999). Causes and Consequences of social interaction on the Internet: A conceptual framework. *Media Psychology, 1,* 249–269.

McKenna, K. Y. A., & Bargh, J. A. (2000). Plan 9 from cyberspace: The implication of the Internet for personality and social psychology. *Personality and Social Psychology Review, 4,* 57–75.

Merkle, E. R., & Richardson, R. A. (2000). Digital dating and virtual relating: Conceptualizing computer mediated romantic relationships. *Family Relations: Interdisciplinary Journal of Applied Family Studies, 49,* 187–192.

Miller, T. W. (1998). The psychologist with 20/20 vision. *Consulting Psychology Journal: Practice and Research, 50,* 25–35.

Morahan-Martin, J. (2000). Women and the Internet: Promise and perils. *CyberPsychology & Behavior, 3,* 683–691.

Mosher, D. L. (1980). Three dimensions of depth of involvement in human sexual response. *Journal of Sex Research, 16,* 1–42.

Noonan. R. J. (1998). The psychotherapy of sex: A mirror from the Internet. In J. Gackenbach (Ed.), *Psychology and the Internet, intrapersonal, interpersonal, and transpersonal implications* (pp. 143–167). San Diego: Academic Press.

Ochs, E. P. P., & Binik, Y. M. (2000). A sex-expert system on the Internet: Fact or fantasy. *CyberPsychology & Behavior, 3,* 617–629.

Palandri, M., & Green, L. (2000). Image management in a bondage, discipline, sadomasochist subculture: A cyber-ethnographic study. *CyberPsychology & Behavior, 3,* 631–641.

Parks, M. R., & Floyd, K. (1996). Making friends in cyberspace. *Journal of Communication, 46,* 80–97.

Parks, M. R., & Roberts, L. D. (1998). "Making Moosic": The development of personal relationships on line and a comparison to their off-line counterparts. *Journal of Social and Personal Relationships, 15,* 517–537.

Podlas, K. (2000). Mistresses of their domain: How female entrepreneurs in cyberporn are initiating a gender power shift. *CyberPsychology & Behavior, 3,* 847–854.

Putnam, D. E. (2000). Initiation and maintenance of online sexual compulsivity: Implication for assessment and treatment. *CyberPsychology & Behavior, 3,* 553–564.

Putnam, D. E., & Maheu, M. M. (2000). Online sexual addiction and compulsivity: Integrating Web resources and behavioral telehealth in treatment. *Sexual Addiction & Compulsivity, 7,* 91–112.

Rice, C. E. (1997). Scenarios: The scientist-practitioner split and the future of psychology. *American Psychologist, 52,* 1173–1181.

Roffman, D. M., Shannon, D., & Dwyer, C. (1997). Adolescents, sexual health, and the Internet: Possibilities, prospects, and the challenges for educators. *Journal of Sex Education and Therapy, 22,* 49–55.

Sampson, J. P. (1998). The Internet as a potential force for social change. In C. L. Courtland, & R. W. Walz, (Eds.), *Social action: A mandate for counselors* (pp. 213–225). Alexandria, VA: American Counseling Association.

Sanders, C. E., Field, T. M., Diego, M., & Kaplan, M. (2000). The relationship of Internet use to depression and social isolation among adolescents. *Adolescence, 35*(138), 237–242.

Schneider, J. P. (2000). A qualitative study of cybersex participants: Gender differences, recovery issues, and implications for therapists. *Sexual Addiction & Compulsivity, 7,* 249–278.

Schwartz, M. F., & Southern, F. (2000). Compulsive cybersex: The new tea room. *Sexual Addiction & Compulsivity, 7,* 127–144.

Shaw, J. (1997). Treatment rationale for Internet infidelity. *Journal of Sex Education and Therapy, 22,* 29–34.

Smith, M. A., & Senior, C. (2001). The Internet and clinical psychology: A general review of the implications. *Clinical Psychology Review, 21,* 129–136.

Sparrow, P. R. (2000). New employee behaviours, work designs and forms of work organization: What is in store for the future of work? *Journal of Managerial Psychology, 15,* 202–218.

Suler, J. (2000). Psychotherapy in cyberspace: A 5-dimensional model of online and computer-mediated psychotherapy. *CyberPsychology & Behavior, 3,* 151–159.

Sussman, N. M., & Tyson, D. H. (2000). Sex and power: Gender differences in computer-mediated interactions. *Computers in Human Behavior, 16,* 381–394.

Teicher, J. (1999). An action plan for smart Internet use. *Educational Leadership, 56,* 70–74.

Tikkanen, R., & Ross, M. W. (2000). Looking for sexual compatibility: Experiences among Swedish men in visiting Internet gay chat rooms. *CyberPsychology & Behavior, 3,* 605–616.

Waskul, D., Douglass, M., & Edgley, C. (2000). Cybersex: Outercourse and the enselfment of the body. *Symbolic Interaction, 23,* 375–397.

Weinrich, J. D. (1997). Storage bedfellows: Homosexuality, gay liberation, and the Internet. *Journal of Sex Education and Therapy, 22,* 58–66.

Williams, P. (1999). The net generation: The experiences, attitudes and behavior of children using the Internet for their own purposes. *Aslib Proceedings, 51,* 315–322.

Wolf, A. (2000). Emotional expression online: Gender differences in emoticon use. *CyberPsychology & Behavior, 3,* 827–833.

Young, K. (1998). *Caught in the net.* New York: Wiley.

Young, K. S., Griffin-Shelley, E., Cooper, A., O'Mara, J., & Buchanan, J. (2000). Online infidelity: A new dimension in couple relationships with implications for evaluation and treatment. *Sexual Addiction & Compulsivity, 7,* 59–74.

INDEX

281